Teach Yourself
►DOS◄

Herbert Schildt

Osborne McGraw-Hill

Berkeley   New York   St. Louis   San Francisco
Auckland   Bogotá   Hamburg   London   Madrid
Mexico City   Milan   Montreal   New Delhi   Panama City
Paris   São Paulo   Singapore   Sydney
Tokyo   Toronto

Osborne **McGraw-Hill**
2600 Tenth Street
Berkeley, California 94710
U.S.A.

For information on translations and book distributors outside of the U.S.A.,
write to Osborne **McGraw-Hill** at the above address.

IBM®, ProPrinter®, and PS/2® are registered trademarks of International
Business Machines Corporation.

Teach Yourself DOS

567890 DOC 9987654321

ISBN 0-07-881630-0

▶ Contents ◀

B Quick Command Reference   331

▶ Introduction ◀

DOS is the program that is in charge of your computer, and it is, by some accounts, the most widely used program in the world. DOS is involved with everything your computer does. It helps you run other programs, manages the components of your system, and organizes your information. Knowing how to run DOS opens a new world of computing because it gives you full control of your system.

DOS is a complex program that contains many commands and features. This book emphasizes the parts of DOS that you will use on a day-to-day basis. The material is presented in a way that lets you begin using DOS as soon as possible. In fact, by the end of Chapter 2, you will already be performing simple DOS operations, and by the end of Chapter 3, you will be ready to start using your own application programs.

ABOUT THIS BOOK

This book is unique because it teaches you to use DOS by applying *Mastery Learning Theory.* Mastery Learning Theory presents one idea at a time. It uses numerous examples and exercises to help you master each topic before you move on. Because learning is best accomplished by doing, each example and exercise is designed so that you can perform it on your own computer as you read along.

The material in this book is presented sequentially, with each section using and building upon those that came before. By working through each section, you ensure that your knowledge and understanding are sufficient to advance to the next topic.

DOS is a very rich system, and some of its many features are rarely used by nonprogrammers. This book focuses on the features that you will need and use, so that you can be "up and running" with DOS as soon as possible.

HOW THIS BOOK IS ORGANIZED

This book comprises 11 chapters and 4 appendixes. Each chapter begins with a Skills Check, which consists of questions that cover material presented in preceding chapters. Each Skills Check emphasizes the immediately preceding chapter, but material in all preceding chapters is fair game. Every chapter contains several sections. Each section covers a topic, shows examples, and presents exercises to test your understanding. At the end of each chapter is a Mastery Skills Check, which tests your knowledge of the material presented in the chapter, and an Integrating Skills Check, which tests how well you are applying new information to concepts presented earlier.

ADDITIONAL HELP FROM OSBORNE/MCGRAW-HILL

Osborne/McGraw-Hill provides top-quality books for computer users at every level of computing experience. To help you build your skills, we suggest that you look for the books in the following Osborne/McGraw-Hill series that best address your needs.

The "Teach Yourself" series is perfect for people who have never used a computer before or who want to gain confidence in using program basics. These books provide a simple, slow-paced introduction to the fundamentals of popular software packages and programming languages. The Mastery Skills Check format ensures that you understand concepts thoroughly before you progress to new material. Plenty of examples and exercises are used throughout the text, and answers are provided at the back of the book.

The "Made Easy" series is also for beginners or users who may need a refresher on the new features of an upgraded product. These in-depth introductions guide users step-by-step from program basics to intermediate use. Every chapter includes plenty of hands-on exercises and examples.

The "Using" series presents fast-paced guides that quickly cover beginning concepts and move on to intermediate techniques and some advanced topics. These books are written for users already familiar with computers and software who want to get up to speed fast with a certain product.

The "Advanced" series assumes that the reader is a user who has reached at least an intermediate skill level and is ready to learn more sophisticated techniques and refinements.

The "Complete Reference" series provides handy desktop references for popular software and programming languages that list every command, feature, and function of a product along with brief but detailed descriptions of their use. These books are fully indexed and often include tear-out command cards. The "Complete Reference" series is ideal for both beginners and pros.

The "Pocket Reference" series is a pocket-sized, shorter version of the "Complete Reference" series. It provides the essential commands, features, and functions of software and programming languages for users of every level who need a quick reminder.

The "Secrets, Solutions, Shortcuts" series is for beginning users who are already somewhat familiar with the software and for experienced users at intermediate and advanced levels. This series provides clever tips, points out shortcuts for using the software to greater advantage, and indicates traps to avoid.

Osborne/McGraw-Hill also publishes many fine books that are not included in the series described here. If you have questions about which Osborne books are right for you, ask the salesperson at your local book or computer store, or call us toll-free at 1-800-262-4729.

LEARN MORE ABOUT DOS

Here is an excellent selection of other books on DOS by Osborne/McGraw-Hill that will help you build your skills and maximize the power of this widely used operating system.

For a more detailed introduction to DOS, look for *DOS Made Easy,* by Herbert Schildt, a step-by-step, in-depth introduction to PC-DOS and MS-DOS through version 3.3. Or, see *DOS 4 Made Easy,* also by Herbert Schildt, if you use PC-DOS or MS-DOS version 4.0.

If you're looking for an intermediate-level book, see *Using MS-DOS,* by Kris Jamsa, which covers all DOS versions through 3.3. This fast-paced, hands-on guide is organized into 15-minute sessions that quickly cover basics, before going on to intermediate techniques and even some advanced topics. If you have DOS version 4, see *Using DOS 4,* by Kris Jamsa.

For DOS users at every skill level, *DOS: The Complete Reference, Second Edition,* by Kris Jamsa, is a handy encyclopedia of every MS-DOS and PC-DOS command, feature, and function through version 3.3.

For all PC-DOS and MS-DOS users with versions up to 3.3 — from beginners who are somewhat familiar with the program to veteran users — *DOS: Secrets, Solutions, Shortcuts*, by Kris Jamsa, provides clever tips, points out shortcuts for using DOS to greater advantage, and indicates traps to avoid.

►Why This Book Is for You ◄

If you want to learn to run DOS, this book is for you. This book is designed to help you start running DOS as soon as possible. In fact, you will be able to begin using your application programs after just the first few chapters. By the time you have worked your way through the entire book, you will definitely be running DOS like a pro.

This book assumes no previous computer experience. So, even if you have never used a computer before, this book is for you. (However, if you already know how to use some kind of computer, this knowledge will be helpful and will allow you to move more quickly.)

There are many versions of DOS, and this book covers all versions, including 3.3 and 4. No matter what version of DOS you have, you can learn to use it from this book. This book applies *Mastery Learning Theory* to help you learn DOS as fast and as easily as possible. The Mastery Learning approach presents one topic at a time, thoroughly discusses that topic, and presents examples and exercises before moving on to the next topic. The consistent combination of information, examples, and exercises makes it easy for you to advance at your own pace, confident in your knowledge and understanding of each topic.

One final point: This is a practical book that emphasizes hands-on learning. Toward that end, the examples and exercises are designed so that you can actually perform them on your own computer.

Learn Computer Basics

▶1◀

Before you begin your study of DOS, it is important that you know some things about your computer and how it works. It is also important that you learn the meaning of some common computer terms. This chapter concentrates on these topics.

1.1 KNOW THE BASIC COMPONENTS OF A COMPUTER

Instead of being a single unit, a microcomputer is comprised of several different, but interconnected, components. It is important to understand that all computers are not the same. To some extent, exactly what comprises a computer depends on the task it is used to perform. However, all computer systems contain at least three parts: a system unit, a keyboard, and a monitor. Many systems also include additional devices, such as a printer. Figure 1-1 shows a representation of a typical computer.

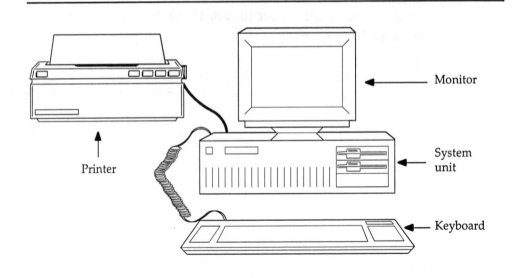

Monitor

Printer

System unit

Keyboard

FIGURE 1-1.   The main components of a microcomputer

It is important to be aware that microcomputers have different appearances, depending on their intended use. People who work on the go need the small size of a laptop computer, but a full-sized computer is more useful for office work. And people who do their work in several locations must have a portable computer. Although these three types of computers look very different, they work more or less the same. So, no matter what your computer looks like, if it can run DOS, this book will teach you how to use it.

Let's examine the parts of your computer in greater detail.

EXPLORE THE SYSTEM UNIT

1.2

The system unit is the core of your computer. It is inside the system unit that data is processed and stored. The system unit consists of four primary elements: a CPU (Central Processing Unit), memory, disk drives, and various optional equipment. Let's look closely at these items now.

The heart of the system unit is the CPU. The fact that your computer can run DOS means that the CPU in your computer belongs to the 8086 family of processors. This family includes the original 8086 as well as the 8088, the 80186, the 80286, the 80386, and the 80486. Although each of these processors has different capabilities, they can all run DOS. The CPU is the part of your computer that actually does the computing.

Although the CPU performs manipulations on data, it can only hold data that it is currently working on. Most of the information in a computer is stored in the computer's main memory until it is needed by the CPU. Memory is often called *RAM*, an acronym for Random Access Memory. The smallest unit of memory is a *byte*. A byte is just large enough to store a single character. Each byte contains 8 bits. A bit can be either on or off. Information is stored in the computer as a series of on and off bits.

References to amounts of RAM are often followed by a K. As you may know, in the metric system a K stands for *kilo*, which means units of 1000. However, for rather technical reasons, when K is used in reference to RAM, it means 1024 units! Nonetheless, if someone tells you that you have 256K of memory, you can loosely assume that you have approximately enough memory to store 256,000 characters.

Basically, two things are stored in RAM: data and programs. When a program is executing, it resides in RAM, along with the data needed by the program.

RAM is used to store information and programs temporarily, as long as your computer is running. If you turn your computer off, anything stored in RAM will be lost. For this reason, your computer contains at least one disk drive. A disk drive is used to store information and programs permanently and does not lose its information when the computer is turned off.

A disk drive stores data by recording the information on a circular magnetic disk. To retrieve the data, the information is read from the disk. To accomplish these operations, the disk is rotated and the *read-write* head is positioned over the part of the disk that contains the desired information. When a disk is in use, you will hear the noise made by the read-write head positioning itself.

There are two types of disk drives: floppy and fixed. A floppy disk drive uses a *diskette*—a thin, flexible sheet of magnetic medium, encased in plastic—to store information. Diskettes can be removed from the floppy disk drive. A fixed disk drive stores information on an immovable, rigid magnetic disk. While floppy disk drives offer the advantange of removable diskettes, they can store far less information than a fixed disk can. Also, a fixed disk is much faster than a floppy disk. Most likely, your computer contains one fixed disk and one floppy disk, but wide variations in system configuration are possible.

Your system unit also contains one or more additional devices called *adapters,* which are used to operate the video display, the printer, or other external units.

LEARN MORE ABOUT FLOPPY DRIVES

1.3

There are two basic "flavors" of floppy drives: the 5 1/4-inch minifloppy and the 3 1/2-inch microfloppy. The minifloppy was introduced with the original IBM PC and was also used by the IBM AT line of computers. The microfloppy was introduced with IBM's PS/2 line of computers. These floppies are illustrated in Figure 1-2.

As you can see in Figure 1-2, both types of floppy disks have a *write-protect notch.* For the 5 1/4-inch floppy, when the write-protect notch is uncovered,

(a)

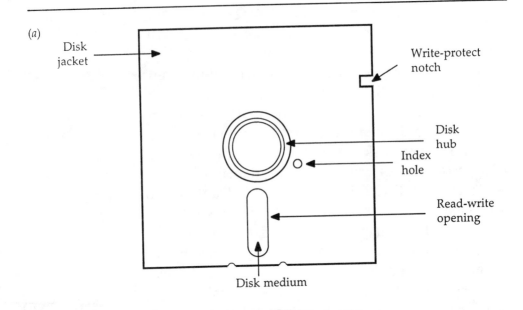

Disk jacket

Write-protect notch

Disk hub

Index hole

Read-write opening

Disk medium

Shutter

(b)

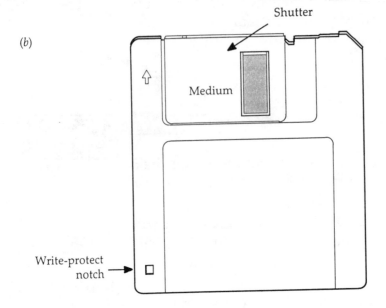

Medium

Write-protect notch

FIGURE 1-2.   Elements of (a) 5 1/4-inch minifloppy and (b) 3 1/2-inch microfloppy diskettes

the disk drive can write data to the disk. When the notch is covered (using an adhesive strip usually supplied with the diskette), the drive can read from the disk but not write to it. For the 3 1/2-inch floppies, the mechanics are reversed. When the write-protect notch of a 3 1/2-inch diskette is covered, the disk can be written to. When the notch is uncovered, the disk cannot be written to. Unlike the minifloppy, to write-protect a microfloppy, you simply move a built-in slider; no adhesive strip is required. In either case, when a disk cannot be written to, it is *write-protected.*

The magnetic medium that actually holds the information should be considered quite fragile. In the case of a minifloppy, a small portion of the medium is always exposed because the read-write opening is uncovered. In the case of a microfloppy, the *shutter* protects the medium when the diskette is not in use. When a microfloppy is inserted into the disk drive, the shutter is opened automatically when the diskette is accessed. Because the magnetic medium is fragile and susceptible to contamination by dust or smoke and erasure by magnetic fields, you should always follow the rules shown in Figure 1-3. Above all else, remember this basic rule about diskettes: If the medium is damaged, it will be impossible to retrieve any information stored on that diskette.

When you insert a minifloppy into a disk drive, you must latch the door by either turning or pushing down the drive latch. When you insert a microfloppy, you simply insert it into the drive until it drops into place. In either case, the drive cannot access the diskette until it is properly inserted and, in the case of a minifloppy, latched.

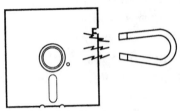

Never place diskettes near magnetic devices.

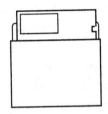

Always place diskettes back into a disk envelope when you are not using them.

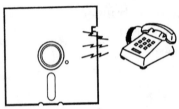

Keep diskettes away from your telephone.

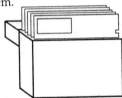

Store your diskettes in a safe location.

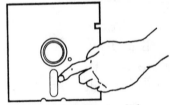

Never touch your floppy disk medium.

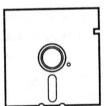

Always make backup copies of your floppy disks.

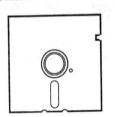

Never smoke near floppy disks.

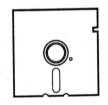

Keep room temperature in the range of 50° F to 110° F.

Never bend floppy disks.

FIGURE 1-3.   Protecting your diskettes

If your computer has only one floppy disk drive, it is drive A. If your computer has two floppy drives, one is drive A and the other is drive B. Usually, the drive that is either on top or on the left is drive A and the other is drive B. You will see why this is important a little later on.

The storage capacity of floppies varies from approximately 360,000 to 1,400,000 bytes of information. However, you run DOS in the same way no matter what type of floppy disk drive your system has.

UNDERSTAND THE FIXED DISK

1.4

Most likely, your computer contains at least one fixed disk. If it does, this disk is drive C. Fixed disks are also referred to as *hard disks* because their magnetic medium is rigid. As stated, the magnetic medium of a fixed disk is not removable. Your computer probably contains a fixed disk for two reasons: It is much faster at reading and writing information than a floppy drive and it can hold far more information. Fixed disks can hold anywhere from 10 million to 300 million bytes of information. In computerese, the prefix *mega* (sometimes abbreviated M) denotes 1 million. Therefore, if someone says that you have a 40 megabyte drive, this means it can hold about 40 million bytes of information.

One thing to remember about the fixed disk is that it is the most fragile component in your system. A severe shock can damage it. Therefore, make sure your system is located in a place that is free from excessive vibration.

1.5 LEARN ABOUT THE MONITOR

The monitor, often called the *video display* or sometimes just the *display*, is the TV-like screen on which the computer outputs data. The display also *echoes* what you type at the keyboard. In essence, the monitor is your portal to the computer.

There are two broad classifications of monitors: monochrome and color. A monochrome monitor displays information in black and white, while a color monitor is capable of displaying color. Essentially, DOS makes no use of color, so for the purposes of this book, it is irrelevant which type of monitor you have.

One term you need to know is *cursor*. The cursor is a small, possibly blinking, square or underscore, which appears on your monitor at the point where the next output will occur. It pinpoints the "current position" on the screen.

1.6 KNOW YOUR KEYBOARD

The keyboard is the main input device for your system. It is the way you will most commonly communicate with DOS. Since the first IBM PC came out in 1981, there have been two basic styles of keyboards. The first, called the PC-style keyboard, was used by the original IBM PCs and XTs. The second, called the AT style, was used by IBM's second-generation computer, the AT. The AT style is also used by IBM's PS/2 line. The PC and AT keyboard styles are shown in Figure 1-4.

(a)

(b)

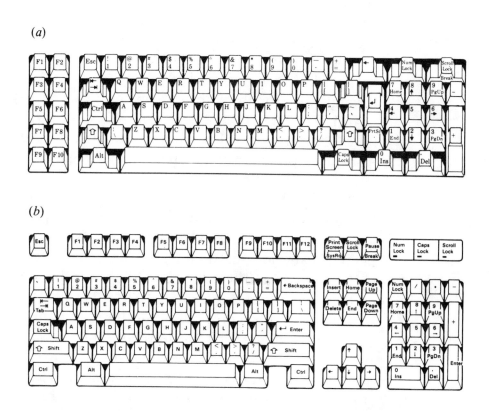

FIGURE 1-4. The two most common keyboard styles: (a) the PC/XT style and (b) the AT style

In addition to the two basic keyboard styles supported by IBM, several independent manufacturers have created replacement keyboards for users who want a different layout. Even if your keyboard looks different from those depicted in the figure, it still contains all the necessary keys.

Aside from the letters of the alphabet, the digits, and the punctuation keys found on any typewriter keyboard, your computer's keyboard also contains several other types of keys. Let's take a quick look at some of these special keys. Along the top of the AT-style keyboard and on the left side of a PC-style keyboard are the *function keys*. They are labeled [F1] through [F12] (or through [F10] on the PC-style keyboard). DOS uses some of these keys for special functions that you will learn about in later chapters. Also, other programs that you use may assign various tasks to the function keys.

[Num Lock] is used to alter the purpose of the numeric keypad. When [Num Lock] is on, you can use this keypad to enter numbers rapidly. When [Num Lock] is off, the numeric keypad takes on a second purpose, which is indicated by the arrows and words printed beneath the digits on the keys. When [Num Lock] is off, the arrow keys are used to maneuver the cursor around the screen in the directions indicated by the arrows. You *toggle* between the two uses of the numeric keypad each time you press [Num Lock]. Although DOS provides only limited support for the arrow keys, other programs that you run on your computer might use them.

Also on the numeric keypad are [Home], [PgUp] (Page Up), [End], [PgDn] (Page Down), [Ins] (Insert), and [Del] (Delete). While not used by DOS, these are special keys that might be used by your other programs.

On the AT-style keyboard, an additional set of arrow and special keys is supplied. If you use this second set of keys to move the cursor, you can simply leave [Num Lock] on and reserve the numeric keypad for entering numbers.

[Esc] (Escape) is used to terminate certain operations. Also, BREAK is sometimes used to cancel an operation.

[Alt] (Alternate) and [Ctrl] (Control) are used to alter the meaning of another key in somewhat the same way [Shift] changes the case of a letter when it is held down. You will learn more about these keys later.

The [PrtSc] (Print Screen) key causes what is on the screen to be printed on the printer.

[Scroll Lock] is not used by DOS, but may be used by other programs that you run.

EXAMINE OTHER DEVICES

1.7

The most common additional device that may be attached to your computer is a printer. Printers come in a wide variety, each with substantially different capabilities. The most common type of printer is the *dot-matrix* printer. This printer creates the poorest quality (but still quite good) output. Another common printer is the *letter-quality* printer, which produces output resembling that of a high-quality electric typewriter. Typeset-quality output requires a *laser* printer. As far as DOS is concerned, however, it doesn't matter what kind of printer you have, as long as it is connected to your system properly.

Another common device is the *mouse.* A typical mouse is illustrated in Figure 1-5. While most versions of DOS do not use a mouse, many application programs do. You operate the mouse by moving it

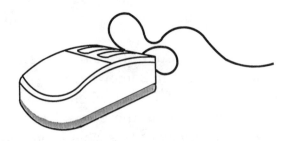

FIGURE 1-5.   A typical mouse

around the surface of your desk. As you move it, a special cursor called the *mouse pointer* moves around the screen in the same direction as you move the mouse. Programs that support a mouse use the buttons on the mouse to select various options.

To communicate with another computer over a telephone line you need a *modem*. Years ago, most modems were external devices. However, today many modems are simply another adapter installed inside the computer, so you might not be sure whether your computer has a modem or not. In any case, DOS cannot directly use a modem, but you may have other programs that can.

Another device that is becoming fairly common is a tape backup unit. Even though fixed disks are very reliable, they do, from time to time, fail. Quite often, when a fixed disk fails the data on that disk is lost permanently. Although DOS does allow you to copy the contents of your fixed disk to several floppies (as you will learn), some people prefer to copy the contents of the fixed disk to tape because it is more convenient. The process of copying the contents of the fixed disk is called *backing up* the disk. Also, the copy created in the process is often referred to as a *backup*.

LEARN ABOUT SOFTWARE
1.8

Software is the general term applied to the programs your computer runs. Programs consist of instructions that are executed by the CPU. Several types of programs may be run by your computer. The most common types are word processors, databases, and spreadsheets. Without software, your computer, quite literally, could do nothing. Basically, the computer is simply the engine that carries out instructions it receives from a program. Without a program, the engine simply idles.

You have probably heard about "bugs" in programs. A *bug* is simply a malfunction in the way a program works. Although computer programmers work very hard to eliminate errors in the programs they write, due to the complexity of contemporary software, it is safe to assume that you will run across a bug one day. If you do, it is a good idea to report it to the person in charge of maintaining your system, so the problem can be corrected. Remember, bugs can only be fixed if the people who wrote the programs are told about the problem.

1.9 UNDERSTAND THE ROLE OF DOS

First and foremost, DOS is a program. However, DOS is a very special program because it is the program that is in charge of your computer. Programs that are in charge of a computer are called *operating systems*, and DOS is one. In fact, DOS is an acronym for Disk Operating System. With very few exceptions, any other program that runs on your computer does so with the help of DOS. In fact, it is DOS that loads other programs from your disk drive into memory so they can execute.

You communicate with DOS via the keyboard and the screen. DOS is said to be *command driven*. This means that when you use DOS, you give it commands and it follows them to the best of its ability. Fortunately, most commands are, or resemble, English words, such as COPY or BACKUP. In a very real sense, as it relates to your computer, DOS is your personal servant.

Like most things in life, DOS has changed frequently since it was first released in 1981. Most of the changes have been made to improve and enhance the program. DOS, like most programs, has a specific version number assigned to it. The first version of DOS had the version number 1.00. Each time DOS is changed, a new version number is assigned to it. The most popular version of DOS at the time of this writing is version 3.30. No matter what version of DOS you have, this book will teach you how to use it. However, if the DOS you are using has a version number smaller than 3.30, some of the features discussed in this book may not be available in your version. (You will see how to find the DOS version number in the next chapter.)

Special note for users of DOS 4.00: If you are using DOS with a version number of 4.00 or greater, read Appendix C before proceeding to Chapter 2.

Software version numbers have two parts: the *major revision number* and the *minor revision number*. The major revision number, on the left side of the decimal point, is changed only when a major alteration or enhancement is made. The minor revision number, on the right side, is changed when small updates or bug fixes are made.

EXERCISES

At this point, you should be able to answer these questions and perform these exercises:

MASTERY
SKILLS CHECK

1. What three parts do all computers have in common?

2. A computer can have two types of disk drives. Name the two kinds and briefly explain how they differ.

3. Is it a good idea to smoke around your floppy disks?

4. What does the term *byte* mean?

5. On your own, examine your computer and determine what types of devices are attached to it.

Run DOS for
the First Time

►2◄

In this chapter you will run DOS for the first time. You will also learn a few simple DOS commands and find out how to back up your DOS master disk.

For this and all subsequent chapters you will need one or more blank diskettes and access to the original DOS master diskette, or to a copy of the master. (Usually, the DOS master diskette is kept in the DOS user's manual.)

EXERCISES

Before proceeding you should be able to answer these questions and perform these exercises:

1. What type of drive uses a diskette?

2. Identify the major parts of your system.

3. Locate the master copy of DOS.

2.1   START THE COMPUTER

When you turn on the computer, it automatically tries to load and execute DOS. If your computer has a fixed disk, DOS has probably been installed on it. If this is the case, simply turning on the computer will cause DOS to load and execute from the fixed disk. If your computer does not have a fixed disk, DOS will load from a floppy disk. Exactly how this is accomplished varies among versions of DOS and also depends on the storage capacity of your diskette drives.

If you have version 3.30 of DOS, the program is either split between two minifloppies labeled *Startup* and *Operating* or it is all on a single diskette labeled *Startup/Operating*. As you know from Chapter 1, different kinds of diskettes have different storage capacities. For some types of disks, DOS is too big to fit on a single floppy, so two are used. Other types of floppies have sufficient room to hold all of DOS on one disk. To start DOS from a floppy disk, insert the diskette called Startup (or Startup/Operating) into drive A and turn on the computer. DOS will automatically load from the diskette in drive A. If DOS is on two floppies, you must remove the Startup diskette from drive A once DOS is running and insert the Operating diskette in its place.

If you have a version of DOS that is earlier than 3.30, you probably have two diskettes labeled *DOS* and *Supplemental Programs*. The only diskette you need to learn DOS is the one called DOS. Insert this diskette into drive A and turn on the computer.

Even though your copy of DOS may require two diskettes, for the sake of simplicity, the diskette or diskettes that you use to start DOS will often be referred to as your *DOS diskette* in this book.

If your computer has a fixed disk and has been used by other people, what you see on the screen when DOS begins may bear little resemblance to the examples presented in this chapter. The reason for this is that DOS can be customized in many different ways, which you will learn about later in this book. If your screen looks much different than the examples, you may want to load DOS from your original DOS diskette. This is possible because your computer tries to load DOS from drive A first. If no diskette is present, it then tries the fixed disk. Therefore, if you put the DOS diskette into drive A, DOS will load from that drive. If you've loaded DOS from the master DOS diskette, your screens should match the examples presented in this chapter. (The examples in this book are based on DOS 3.30. If you have another version, you may see minor differences.) The examples in this book assume DOS has been loaded from a diskette.

Examples

1. Insert the DOS diskette into drive A (unless you want to load DOS from your fixed disk) and turn on your computer. When DOS begins execution, it determines what type of devices are present in the system and then asks you two questions. The first question is about the current system date. All computers can keep track of the date and time while they are running and many can do so even while they are turned off. As you will learn later, it is important that DOS know the correct date and time. Therefore, one of the first things DOS does is ask you to verify that the current system date is correct. It prompts you as shown here (of course, the date will be different on your screen):

```
Current date is Mon 01-01-90
Enter new date (mm-dd-yy):
```

When this prompt appears, the cursor will be located at the end of the second line. If the date is incorrect, you may enter the correct date, but you must use the exact form indicated in the prompt. For example, if the actual date were Tuesday, January 2, 1990, you would type this:

```
01-02-90
```

You must always press ⏎Enter after you have typed the date. Although we will come back to this point later, it is important to understand that DOS does *not* know what you have typed until you press ⏎Enter. If you accidentally press an incorrect key, you can use ⏎Backspace to back up and correct your mistake, as long as you have not yet pressed ⏎Enter.

If you try to enter the date using an invalid format, DOS will not understand what you mean and will repeat the date prompt. For example, if you responded to the date prompt like this:

```
Jan 1, 1990
```

DOS would display this message:

```
Invalid date
Enter new date (mm-dd-yy):
```

Then it would wait for you to try again. DOS also repeats the prompt if you enter an out-of-range date such as 023090, which can't be correct because February does not have 30 days.

If the date shown on the screen when DOS begins executing is correct, you can simply press Enter .

At this time, either enter the correct date or press Enter to accept the date shown on your screen.

2. The next thing you see is the current system time. It looks something like this:

```
Current time is 12:43:23.40
Enter new time:
```

Again, the cursor is located at the end of the second line. As you may have guessed, the time is displayed in this format:

hours:minutes:seconds.hundredths of seconds

If the time is incorrect, you can enter the correct time. Although you must use the same time format that DOS uses, you don't have to enter the entire format. For example, to tell DOS that it is 10:20, you can simply enter **10:20**; any field that you do not specify is automatically set to zero.

One very important point to remember about setting or interpreting the system time is that DOS uses a 24-hour (military-style) clock. This means that you would enter 00:00 to specify midnight, and 23:45 to specify 11:45 P.M.. If you format the time incorrectly, DOS will prompt you again for correct input.

If the time is correct as DOS shows it, simply press ⌊Enter⌉ to accept it.

Many computers have built-in battery powered clocks that automatically maintain the time and date. If you have such a system, the time and date will usually be correct. However, if this is not the case for your computer, you should always be sure to enter the correct time and date when you start work. The reasons for this will become clear as you learn more about DOS.

Now go ahead and either set the time or accept it as shown by pressing ⌊Enter⌉.

3. When you have set the date and time, you will see DOS's sign-on message, shown in Figure 2-1. The sign-on message contains DOS's version number. You should make a note of it before you go on.

Below the sign-on message is the symbol pair A>. This is the *DOS prompt*. Put simply, DOS displays this prompt whenever it is ready to accept a command. For this reason, the line the prompt appears on is often referred to as the *command line*.

As stated earlier, it is possible to customize DOS. One customization is to change the way the DOS

```
Current date is Tue    7-17-1990
Enter new date (mm-dd-yy):
Current time is  3:51:46.14
Enter new time:

The IBM Personal Computer DOS
Version 3.30 (C) Copyright International Business Machines Corp 1981, 1987
            (C) Copyright Microsoft Corp 1981, 1986

A>
```

FIGURE 2-1.   The DOS sign-on screen on the IBM PC

prompt looks, so if you loaded DOS from a fixed disk, someone may have customized the DOS prompt, and it may not look anything like what is shown here.

The A in the prompt is not arbitrary. It tells you which drive is currently the focus of DOS. If you loaded DOS from a floppy, then the prompt will be the A> shown in the example. If you loaded DOS from a fixed disk, then most likely the prompt will be C>.

Exercise

1. If you have not yet done so, work through the previous examples at this time.

LEARN TO ENTER COMMANDS

2.2

As stated before, you use DOS by giving it commands. All DOS commands are entered at the DOS prompt.

You may enter a command using upper- or lowercase letters. DOS doesn't care which case you use; however, the examples in this book will show all DOS commands in uppercase so you can recognize them easily.

Again, keep one very important point in mind: DOS does not know what you have typed until you press ⌷Enter⌷. Thus, if you make a typing mistake, you can simply use ⌷Backspace⌷ to back up and make corrections as long as you have not yet pressed ⌷Enter⌷.

Examples

1. For a very simple first command, enter **VER** and then press ⌷Enter⌷. The VER command, which is short for *version*, tells DOS to display its version number. As you will see, many DOS commands are abbreviations of words that reflect the function of the command. DOS responds like this:

```
IBM Personal Computer DOS Version  3.30
A>
```

Notice that after the version is reported, the DOS prompt is again displayed. This means that DOS has finished what you asked it to do and is ready for your next command.

2. Perhaps the most commonly used DOS command is DIR, which is short for *directory*. This command tells DOS to display a list of all the files that are on the disk in the current drive. In computer terms, this list is called a directory. Although you will learn more about files and disks in the next chapter, a brief explanation is in order here. A file is a collection of

related information that is stored on a disk. For
example, one file might contain the text to a letter,
another file might hold a customer database, and
still another might be a program. In DOS, every file
has a name. The DIR command causes the names of
the files on a disk to be displayed on the screen. If
you think of a disk file as the electronic equivalent
of a paper file, the disk is analogous to the file
cabinet.

Enter the DIR command now. You will notice
that there are more files on the disk than will fit on
the screen and that many lines *scroll* off the top.
Don't worry about this now. Scrolling is a normal
process that DOS performs automatically; you do
not lose information when it scrolls off the screen.
After you've tried the DIR command, your screen
will resemble Figure 2-2.

Again, after DOS has completed your last command, it redisplays its prompt.

3. If you accidentally enter something that is not a
   valid DOS command, DOS responds with this message:

   `Bad command or file name`

   For example, if you accidentally entered DOR instead of DIR, you would see that message. If this
   happens, simply reenter the command correctly.

Exercise

1. If you have not already done so, complete the
   previous examples on your own computer.

```
Output from the DIR command.

    MORE      COM       313    3-17-87  12:00p
    NLSFUNC   EXE      3060    3-17-87  12:00p
    PRINT     COM      9026    3-17-87  12:00p
    PRINTER   SYS     13590    3-17-87  12:00p
    RECOVER   COM      4299    3-18-87  12:00p
    REPLACE   EXE     11775    3-17-87  12:00p
    RESTORE   COM     34643    3-17-87  12:00p
    SELECT    COM      4163    3-17-87  12:00p
    SHARE     EXE      8608    3-17-87  12:00p
    SORT      EXE      1977    3-17-87  12:00p
    SUBST     EXE      9909    3-17-87  12:00p
    SYS       COM      4766    3-17-87  12:00p
    TREE      COM      3571    3-17-87  12:00p
    VDISK     SYS      3455    3-17-87  12:00p
    XCOPY     EXE     11247    3-17-87  12:00p
    EGA       CPI     49065    3-18-87  12:00p
    LCD       CPI     10752    3-17-87  12:00p
    4201      CPI     17089    3-18-87  12:00p
    5202      CPI       459    3-17-87  12:00p
    BASIC     PIF       369    3-17-87  12:00p
    BASICA    PIF       369    3-17-87  12:00p
    MORTGAGE  BAS      6251    3-17-87  12:00p
         50 File(s)     128512 bytes free

A>
```

FIGURE 2-2.   Output from the DIR command

2.3   MAKE A COPY OF YOUR DOS MASTER DISKETTE

Before you proceed any further, it is important that you make a copy of the DOS diskette or diskettes. Once you have made a copy, you can use it as your *work disk* and store the master disk in a safe place. The reason for this strategy is that diskettes do, in fact, malfunction from time to time. Also, floppy diskettes deteriorate with prolonged use, and a diskette that is in constant use may be damaged—spilled coffee has destroyed countless floppies. The point is that you must keep your DOS master diskette safe and free from harm, so that it is always available if needed. Then, if your work disk is ever destroyed or malfunctions, you can simply make a new copy using the DOS master.

Be sure to label the copies you make of your DOS master disk. The label should contain the name of the diskette and the date it was made. It is also a good idea to put your name on the disk if you work in an environment in which many people use the computer. If you make more than one copy of the disk, you might consider adding a copy number as well.

The exact backup procedure varies among systems with two diskette drives and those with either one diskette drive or a diskette drive and a fixed disk. Follow the example that applies to the configuration of your computer. Once you have made the copy, be sure to put your DOS master diskette or diskettes in a safe place.

To copy a disk, you will use DOS's DISKCOPY command. This command tells DOS to copy the entire contents of one diskette to another diskette. Be careful—if that other disk already contains information, that information will be overwritten and thus lost. For this reason, be sure to use a blank diskette for making your DOS work disks.

As DISKCOPY executes, it displays some information about what it is doing that probably won't make any sense at this time. Don't worry. This information will be explained when you learn more about DISKCOPY later in this book. The copy process will take a few minutes on most computers, so be prepared for a short wait.

IMPORTANT: Whenever DOS makes a copy of a diskette, there is always the possibility that an error will occur. The most likely cause of an error is that the target diskette (the new copy) is physically damaged in a way that prevents the copy from being made. If you see an error message while attempting to copy your DOS master diskette, try a new target diskette. If, after repeated attempts, you cannot make a copy of your DOS master, you should seek out someone who is knowledgeable about DOS and your computer to see if they can remedy the problem. After you have learned more about DOS and how it works, we'll discuss some of the most common errors.

Examples

1. If your computer contains two diskette drives, follow this example.

   NOTE: Some computers may have two diskette drives that are not the same size or that have different storage capacities. If you suspect that this is the case with your computer, follow the procedure described in example 2.

   To begin the backup procedure, type the command DISKCOPY A: B: and press (Enter). Just before you press (Enter), the command line should look exactly like this:

   ```
   A>DISKCOPY A: B:
   ```

After you press (Enter), you will see the following messages:

```
Insert SOURCE diskette in drive A:
Insert TARGET diskette in drive B:
Press any key when ready . . .
```

Since the DOS diskette is already in drive A, you can just put a blank diskette in drive B and close the drive door. After that, press any key, and DOS will copy the contents of the DOS diskette onto the blank diskette.

   After the copy is complete you will see the message

```
Copy another diskette (Y/N)?
```

If you wish to make another copy of the DOS diskette, type **Y** and the copy process will be repeated. Otherwise, type **N**. As you will see, many DOS commands require yes/no responses. The (Y/N)? prompt tells you when this kind of response is required.

2. If your computer has only one diskette drive, follow this example.

   To begin the backup process in a system with only one diskette drive, type **DISKCOPY A: A:** at the prompt and press (Enter). Before you press (Enter), the command line should look like this:

```
A>DISKCOPY A: A:
```

After you press (Enter), you will see the following messages:

```
Insert SOURCE diskette in drive A:
Press any key when ready . . .
```

If the DOS diskette is not already in drive A, put it there now and close the drive door. After that, press any key. DOS first reads the contents of the DOS diskette into the computer's memory and then displays these messages:

```
Insert TARGET diskette in drive A:
Press any key when ready . . .
```

At this time, remove the DOS diskette from the computer, put the blank diskette into drive A, and press a key. DOS will then copy the information it read from the DOS diskette onto the blank diskette.

After the copy is complete you will see the message

```
Copy another diskette (Y/N)?
```

If you wish to make another copy of the DOS diskette, type **Y** and the copy process will be repeated. Otherwise, type **N**. As you will see, many DOS commands require yes/no responses. The (Y/N)? prompt tells you when this kind of response is required.

Exercise

1. Make two backup copies of your DOS master diskette or diskettes.

2.4 LEARN TO RESTART DOS

You can cause your computer to restart DOS at any time by pressing these three keys at the same time:

Ctrl, Alt, and Del. Restarting DOS can be helpful in many situations, but it may be particularly beneficial for you, as a beginner, because it can act as an emergency stop if the computer begins to do something unexpected. As a beginner, if you think you have done something that you shouldn't have, restarting DOS may be the best course of action.

When DOS is restarted, it again prompts you for the date and time. This is because DOS has no way of knowing that it was just previously running; as far as DOS knows, you just turned the computer on.

Examples

1. To see the effect of restarting DOS, press the Ctrl, Alt, and Del keys. The screen will clear, DOS will reload from disk, and you will be prompted for the date and time.

2. One thing that might cause you to restart DOS is a bug in an application program that damages the copy of DOS in memory. If the damage is severe enough, DOS will not be able to run, and you will have to restart the program.

   Although rare, it is possible for a program to fail so severely that even pressing Ctrl, Alt, and Del does not work. In a case like this, you must turn the computer off and then on again.

Exercise

1. Try restarting DOS at this time.

EXERCISES

MASTERY SKILLS CHECK

You should now be able to answer these questions:

1. How do you start DOS on your computer?

2. How do you give DOS a command?

3. What command do you use to view the directory of a diskette?

4. What command do you use to make a backup copy of DOS?

5. How do you restart DOS?

Learn Some Essential DOS Commands

►3◄

This chapter introduces some of the most commonly used DOS commands. It also discusses several important concepts that are central to DOS, such as files and directories.

Before you go on, make sure your DOS diskette is in drive A, and turn on the computer.

EXERCISES

SKILLS CHECK

Before proceeding you should be able to answer these questions and perform these exercises:

1. What command lists the contents of the directory?

2. If you have typed a command incorrectly but have not yet pressed ⟨Enter⟩, how can you correct the error?

3. When DOS prompts you for the date and time, what formats must you use to enter this information? What does DOS do if you enter an incorrect date or time?

4. Give one reason why you might restart DOS.

3.1 | UNDERSTAND FILES AND THE DIRECTORY

Before you continue your study of DOS, you need to understand some things about files and the directory.

As stated in the preceding chapter, a file is a collection of information that is stored on a disk. All files have a *file name* associated with them. Every file on a disk has its file name stored in the disk directory along with several other pieces of information about the file. Let's take a closer look at the directory now.

List the directory by entering the DIR command. As you can see, five pieces of information are provided for each entry. Moving from left to right, the first two columns contain the complete file name. A complete file name has two parts; the first part is the name itself, or the *filename,* and the second part is the *extension.* We will come back to file names in a moment. The next column contains the length of the file in bytes. (Remember, a byte can hold one character.) Finally, the last two columns show the date and time of the file's creation or last modification.

Notice that there are two additional pieces of information at the end of the directory listing. After listing the files, the DIR command reports how many files are in the directory and how many bytes of storage are left on the disk. The parts of the directory are labeled in Figure 3-1.

Aside from telling you what files are on a disk, the directory's function is to help DOS locate specific files. Although this information does not appear in the directory listing, the directory keeps a record of where each file on a disk resides. When you reference a file, DOS looks it up in the directory and uses its starting location on the disk to access the file. As you can see, the directory serves both you and DOS; it is an important part of the information stored on a disk.

As stated previously, a complete file name consists of two parts: the filename and the extension. In many ways file names are similar to people's names. The filename is like a person's first name and the extension is analogous to a person's last name. Basically, the extension broadly defines the type of a file. Within that classification, the filename uniquely identifies a specific file.

The filename may be from one to eight characters long and the extension may be up to three characters

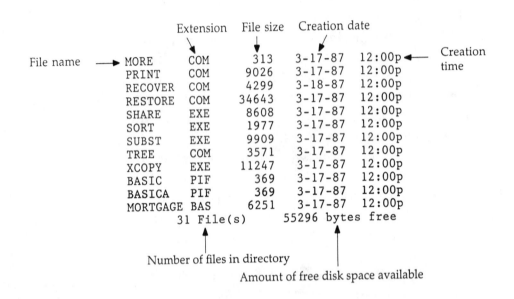

FIGURE 3-1.   The elements of a directory

long. Although the extension is technically optional, in actual practice it will be present for most files. Most file names are comprised of letters, but they may also consist of digits and several other characters. The only characters you cannot use in a file name are these:

. " / \ [ ] : | < > + = ; ,

When you need to tell DOS about a file, use this form:

filename.ext

The two parts of a file name are joined by the period. To tell DOS about a file called TREE.COM, for example, you would type **TREE.COM**. There can be no spaces between the two parts of the name and the period.

Within a single directory no two files can have exactly the same name. (If they did, DOS would not be able to distinguish one from the other.) Two files can have the same filename or the same extension, but never both. However, two files may contain the same information, even if they don't have the same name.

You will encounter three general categories of files: program files, data files, and text files. A *program* file contains a program that the computer can execute. All program files have either a .COM or an .EXE extension. Although there is a slight technical difference between .COM and .EXE files, you can think of them as the same. It is very important to realize that DOS only knows a file is a program that can be loaded and executed when it has one of these two extensions. This means that if you rename a program and give it a different extension, DOS will no longer recognize it as a program. In effect, DOS has reserved these two extensions and you should not use them for any other type of file. (You will learn how to change a file's name in the next chapter.)

A *data* file is a file that holds information created and maintained by a program. Most often, the information in a data file is meaningful only to the program that uses it. The contents of most data files cannot be read by people. Although it is not required, many data files use the .DAT extension.

A *text* file is actually a special type of data file that contains information you *can* read. Text files are generally created by word processors. Because text files are so diverse, no single extension is consistently applied to them. However, many people use .TXT to indicate a text file.

Examples

1. In addition to the .COM and .EXE extensions, which are reserved for program files, DOS reserves several other extensions for its own purposes. As you know, DOS assumes any file with a .COM or .EXE extension is a program file. In addition, DOS reserves .BAT, .SYS, .CPI, and .PIF as extensions. A .BAT extension is used for *batch files,* which are essentially lists of commands for DOS to execute. (You will learn more about batch files later.) A .SYS extension indicates a file that contains system information used only by DOS. Files with extensions of .CPI and .PIF contain hardware-related information used by DOS.

   It is important to understand one point: Although DOS reserves several extensions and gives them special meanings, you are not technically prohibited from using them. However, doing so will confuse DOS. For example, if you create a text file called TEXT.EXE, DOS will attempt to treat it as a program file, so it is important that you never use any of DOS's reserved extensions for your own files.

   In addition to the extensions reserved by DOS, and depending upon how your system is being used, there may be additional extensions you should avoid when naming your own files. For example, if your computer is used to running BASIC programs (which are different from .EXE or .COM programs), those programs will use the .BAS extension.

2. When you create your own files, you will need to think of names for them. The best names are descriptive ones that provide a clue to the content of the file. For example, you might call a file that holds general ledger information used by your accounting software GENLED.DAT.

   It is also important to use file name extensions to help you manage your files. For example, if you are creating several form letters using a word processor, you might give them all an .FML extension. Using this extension, the following file names would tell you both the subject of the letter and that it is, indeed, a form letter:

```
PASTDUE.FML   OUTSTOCK.FML   BACKORD.FML
```

Exercises

1. Which of these are valid file names and which are not? For those that are not, state the reason.

   a. MYFILE.WP
   b. ACCOUNTS.DAT
   c. MYPROGRAM.EXE
   d. LETTER.FORMLET
   e. ONE+TWO.DAT
   f. [MYFILE].INF
   g. MYFILE

2. What extensions does DOS reserve for program files?

3. What are the three basic types of files?

4. What information about each file does the DIR command display?

3.2 | LEARN TWO DIR OPTIONS

Although you have been introduced to the DIR command, you have only seen its simplest form. Because DIR is probably the most commonly used DOS command, it is the first one we will examine in detail. The effect of DIR, like that of many other DOS commands, can be altered slightly by following the command with an option. In DOS, an option begins with a slash (/), which is directly followed by the option itself. DIR supports two options, which we will explore now.

One of the most useful DIR options is /W. This option eliminates everything but the file names from the directory listing. Because the file names are displayed across five columns, this kind of listing is sometimes called a *wide listing*, which makes it easy to remember that the option is specified using /W. By using the /W option you get many more file names on the screen than you do when all the other information is displayed.

A second option to the DIR command is /P, which is sometimes referred to as the *pause* option. It tells DIR to display full directory information for 23 files and then stop, display the following message, and wait until you press a key:

```
Strike a key when ready . . .
```

```
Volume in drive A has no label
Directory of  A:\
APPEND    EXE    ASSIGN   COM    ATTRIB   EXE    BACKUP   COM    BASIC    COM
BASICA    COM    CHKDSK   COM    COMMAND  COM    COMP     COM    DEBUG    COM
DISKCOMP COM     DISKCOPY COM    EDLIN    COM    FIND     EXE    FORMAT   COM
GRAFTABL COM     GRAPHICS COM    JOIN     EXE    LABEL    COM    MORE     COM
PRINT    COM     RECOVER  COM    RESTORE  COM    SHARE    EXE    SORT     EXE
SUBST    EXE     TREE     COM    XCOPY    EXE    BASIC    PIF    BASICA   PIF
MORTGAGE BAS
        31 File(s)      55296 bytes free
```

FIGURE 3-2.   A directory listing of the DOS diskette using DIR's /W option

Each time you press a key, information about the next 23 files is displayed. The advantage of the /P option is that it prevents the directory listing from scrolling off the top of the screen before you have a chance to examine it.

Examples

1. To obtain a wide listing of the file names that are in the directory of your DOS work disk, be sure your command line looks like this before you press Enter :

```
A>DIR /W
```

Although there need not be a space between the DIR command and its option, one or more spaces are permitted, and they improve readability. After DIR executes, your screen will look like Figure 3-2.

   The main advantage of the /W option is that many more file names are displayed before some scroll off the top of the screen.

Assuming they have not scrolled off the screen, you will see these two lines at the start of the listing:

```
Volume in drive A has no label
Directory of  A:\
```

The first line tells you that the disk has no volume label. This does not refer to the paper label you attach to a diskette. A volume label is essentially a name that you give the disk, which is stored magnetically on the disk. You will learn how to give a disk a volume label later on in this book. Since volume labels are optional, you don't have to worry about them now.

The second line simply tells you what disk directory is being displayed. When you have learned more about DOS, the meaning of the rather cryptic A:\ will be clear.

2. Try the /P option by using this form of DIR:

```
DIR /P
```

Your screen will look similar to that in Figure 3-3. When you press any key, the rest of the directory will be displayed.

3. You might be surprised to know that you can use both the /P and the /W options at the same time. For example, if you had a disk that contained several hundred files, this command would be useful:

```
DIR /P /W
```

It would cause file names alone to be displayed, using the wide listing format and pausing every 23 lines. In general, as long as two options are not mutually exclusive, they can be combined.

```
APPEND   EXE    5825    3-17-87   12:00p
ASSIGN   COM    1561    3-17-87   12:00p
ATTRIB   EXE    9529    3-17-87   12:00p
BACKUP   COM   31913    3-18-87   12:00p
BASIC    COM    1063    3-17-87   12:00p
BASICA   COM   36403    3-17-87   12:00p
CHKDSK   COM    9850    3-18-87   12:00p
COMMAND  COM   25307    3-17-87   12:00p
COMP     COM    4214    3-17-87   12:00p
DEBUG    COM   15897    3-17-87   12:00p
DISKCOMP COM    5879    3-17-87   12:00p
DISKCOPY COM    6295    3-17-87   12:00p
EDLIN    COM    7526    3-17-87   12:00p
FIND     EXE    6434    3-17-87   12:00p
FORMAT   COM   11616    3-18-87   12:00p
GRAFTABL COM    6128    3-17-87   12:00p
GRAPHICS COM    3300    3-17-87   12:00p
JOIN     EXE    8969    3-17-87   12:00p
LABEL    COM    2377    3-17-87   12:00p
MORE     COM     313    3-17-87   12:00p
PRINT    COM    9026    3-17-87   12:00p
RECOVER  COM    4299    3-18-87   12:00p
RESTORE  COM   34643    3-17-87   12:00p
Strike a key when ready...
```

FIGURE 3-3.   Output from the DIR command using the /P option

Exercises

1. If you haven't done so, try the examples at this time.

2. What is wrong with this command?

   ```
   DIR \P
   ```

LEARN TO DISPLAY GROUPS OF FILES

3.3

In its simplest form, the DIR command lists all the files in a directory. However, there will be times when you want only a specific group of files to be displayed. This is often the case when there are a great many files in a directory. Since the simplest group is a single file, this is a good place to start.

To display information about a specific file, simply specify that file's name after the DIR command. (Be sure to leave a space between DIR and the file's name, however.) When you specify a file name after the DIR command, DIR searches the directory, looking for any name that matches the one you specified. If it finds a match, DIR displays information about the file. For example, this command would display information about a file called MORE.COM:

```
DIR MORE.COM
```

You might list information about a specific file for a number of reasons, but the most common one is simply to determine whether the file is on the current disk. If the file name you specify is not on the current disk, DOS responds with this message:

```
File not found
```

Once you begin to use DOS for daily work, you will often want to list information about related groups of files. To accomplish this task, DOS supports two special *wildcard* characters, which can be substituted for parts of a file name. These special characters allow DIR to match a wide range of files. The two wildcard characters are the asterisk, or star (*), and the question mark (?). The * is the more commonly used of the two.

The * wildcard character matches any sequence of letters starting from its own position and continuing to the end of the filename or the extension, depending on where the * is relative to the period. For example, if you entered this command,

```
DIR TEXT*.TXT
```

DIR would display all files that have a name that begins with TEXT and is followed by any other characters, and that also have the extension .TXT. For example, if these files existed in the directory, they would be displayed:

```
TEXT.TXT        TEXT1.TXT        TEXT23.TXT
TEXTURE.TXT
```

However, a file with a name like MYTEXT.TXT would not be matched because the * only matches characters at or beyond the point at which it occurs.

As the preceding example illustrates, the * will also match a zero-length sequence. That is why TEXT.TXT was matched—it has no characters after TEXT.

The second wildcard character, the ?, will match any single character. This differs from the *, which matches a sequence of characters. For example, given this command,

```
DIR TEXT?.TXT
```

information about the following files would be displayed (assuming, of course, these files were on the disk):

```
TEXT.TXT        TEXT1.TXT        TEXT2.TXT
```

However, the previous command would not match a file called TEXT23.TXT because the ? can only match a single character. As this example shows, the ? will also match the absence of a character. Thus, TEXT.TXT is considered a match.

Examples

1. Enter the following command:

```
DIR FIND.EXE
```

This command causes DOS to look for the file FIND.EXE. Since this file exists, DOS displays information about it, as shown here (the output you obtain may vary slightly):

```
Volume in drive A has no label
Directory of  A:\

FIND      EXE     6434   3-17-87  12:00p
          1 File(s)   55296 bytes free
```

Notice that this time, DIR tells you it found one file that matched the file name you specified.

2. To see the effect of the * wildcard character, try this command:

```
DIR *.EXE
```

The resulting output will be similar to that shown here:

```
Volume in drive A has no label
Directory of  A:\
APPEND    EXE      5825   3-17-87  12:00p
ATTRIB    EXE      9529   3-17-87  12:00p
FIND      EXE      6434   3-17-87  12:00p
JOIN      EXE      8969   3-17-87  12:00p
SHARE     EXE      8608   3-17-87  12:00p
SORT      EXE      1977   3-17-87  12:00p
SUBST     EXE      9909   3-17-87  12:00p
XCOPY     EXE     11247   3-17-87  12:00p
          8 File(s)    54272 bytes free
```

Notice that this time, DIR reports eight files match the specified file name. In general, DIR always reports how many files match the specified name.

3. For another example of the * wildcard, try the following command:

```
DIR S*.*
```

The output will be similar to this:

```
Volume in drive A has no label
Directory of  A:\

SHARE    EXE     8608   3-17-87  12:00p
SORT     EXE     1977   3-17-87  12:00p
SUBST    EXE     9909   3-17-87  12:00p
         3 File(s)      54272 bytes free
```

This example illustrates the fact that you can use the * in both the filename and the extension. As you can see in this example, only files that begin with an S are matched.

4. To see the effect of the ? wildcard, try this command:

```
DIR RE?????.COM
```

You will see output similar to this:

```
Volume in drive A has no label
Directory of  A:\

RECOVER  COM     4299   3-18-87  12:00p
RESTORE  COM    34643   3-17-87  12:00p
         2 File(s)      55296 bytes free
```

5. The following three commands are identical in their affect:

```
DIR
```

```
DIR *.*
```

```
DIR ????????.???
```

They each cause the entire contents of the directory to be listed.

6. You can also use the /P and /W options when specifying a file name with the DIR command. For example, this command

```
DIR *.EXE /W
```

produces output similar to this:

```
Volume in drive A has no label
Directory of  A:\

APPEND EXE   ATTRIB EXE   FIND   EXE   JOIN   EXE   SHARE  EXE
SORT   EXE   SUBST  EXE   XCOPY  EXE
        8 File(s)     55296 bytes free
```

7. If you specify only the filename portion of a file name after DIR, then the extension automatically defaults to .*. Thus, if the following files were on your disk,

```
TEST.DAT
TEST.COM
TEST.WP
```

this command

```
DIR TEST
```

would cause all three files to be displayed.

If you specifically want to display only files that have no extension, you must follow the filename with a period, but nothing else. This causes DIR to find only files that match the filename and have no extension. For example, if you had these files on your disk,

```
TEST
TEST.COM
TEST.EXE
```

this command

DIR TEST.

would only display information about TEST.

Exercises

1. What command would you use to find out whether a file called MORE.COM was on your disk?

2. What command lists all files that start with a D and use the .COM extension?

3. What command lists all the files on a disk that have no extensions?

4. What is the difference between the * and the ? wildcard characters?

LEARN ABOUT INTERNAL AND EXTERNAL COMMANDS

3.4

DOS has two types of commands: internal and external. *Internal* commands are included in the part of DOS that remains resident in memory. Both DIR and VER are internal commands. *External* commands reside on your DOS disk and are only loaded into memory when you use them. When you made a backup copy of your DOS diskette, you used the external command DISKCOPY. The internal and external DOS commands are shown in Table 3-1.

| TABLE 3-1. | Internal and External DOS Commands |

Internal Commands

BREAK	MKDIR
CHCP	PATH
CHDIR (CD)	PROMPT
CLS	RENAME (REN)
COPY	RMDIR (RD)
CTTY	SET
DATE	TIME
DEL (ERASE)	TYPE
DIR	VERIFY
ERASE (DEL)	VOL

External Commands

APPEND	KEYB
ASSIGN	LABEL
ATTRIB	MODE
BACKUP	MORE
CHKDSK	NLSFUNC
COMMAND	PRINT
COMP	RECOVER
DISKCOMP	REPLACE
DISKCOPY	RESTORE
FASTOPEN	SELECT
FDISK	SHARE
FIND	SORT
FORMAT	SUBST
GRAFTABL	SYS
GRAPHICS	TREE
JOIN	XCOPY

Because internal commands are already in memory, an internal command executes the instant you enter it. For example, as soon as you enter **VER**, DOS responds with its version number. However, because external commands must be loaded from disk, there is a slight delay between the moment you enter an external command and the moment it actually begins executing.

The reason DOS uses internal and external commands is to conserve memory. The resident portion of DOS uses memory, and there is a finite amount of memory in your computer. The more memory DOS uses, the less there is available for your application programs. Therefore, internal commands are limited to those that are commonly used in the day-to-day operation of your system. Less frequently used commands are stored on disk until they are needed.

One very important point to remember is that external commands reside on the DOS diskette, so you must have a copy of it available in order to use an external command.

List the directory of your DOS disk at this time. Notice that all the external commands have either an .EXE or a .COM extension. As you know, DOS reserves these extensions for files that contain programs, so the DOS external commands are actually programs. In fact, the only difference between one of your application programs and a DOS external command is that the external commands are part of DOS! Even though the external commands have extensions, you do not use these extensions when you give DOS an external command.

With very few exceptions, once an external command has completed, DOS effectively "forgets" that it was loaded. Therefore, even if you execute the same external command twice in a row, it will be loaded from disk each time; that is, most external commands are transient—they are not *installed* in memory when they are executed.

Examples

1. Another of DOS's internal commands is CLS, which clears your computer's screen. Try this command now. As you can see, the screen instantly clears and the DOS prompt is displayed in the upper-left corner.

    There are two main reasons why you might want to clear the screen. First, you may be dealing with private information that you do not want to remain on the screen. Second, when you won't be using the computer for a while, clearing the screen protects the *phosphors* in the picture tube from excessive wear. (The phosphors, which light up when a character is displayed, slowly burn out with use.)

2. A very helpful external command is CHKDSK, which is an abbreviation for *check disk*. This command checks the condition of your disk and reports various information about it. It also reports the total amount of memory in your computer and how

much memory is free for your applications to use. Try CHKDSK now by entering the command as shown here:

```
CHKDSK
```

Notice that no extension is given. DOS automatically searches for CHKDSK.COM. Specifying the extension is not an error, but it is completely unnecessary. As soon as you enter the command, the disk drive starts; DOS is loading CHKDSK into memory. After a while, CHKDSK displays information about the disk. Here is some sample output from the CHKDSK command:

```
362496  bytes total disk space
     0  bytes in 1 hidden files
307200  bytes in 31 user files
 55296  bytes available on disk

655360  bytes total memory
600496  bytes free
```

As you can see, CHKDSK reports the total amount of space on the disk, the number of bytes used by hidden files and user files, and the total amount of unused storage available. A *hidden file* is a file that is used only by DOS and does not show in the directory. Since hidden files are not for your use, you can simply ignore them. A *user file* is any file that displays in the directory. This includes DOS external commands, application programs, and data files.

The CHKDSK command also displays the total amount of memory available in your system and the amount available for your application programs. The difference between the two is the amount of memory used by the resident portion of DOS (plus any other memory-resident software that is running on your system). It is important to understand that the maximum amount of memory DOS can manage is 655,360 bytes. However, your computer may contain additional memory, which can be used by special programs. Even if this is the case, CHKDSK does not report the extra memory; it erroneously displays 655,360 instead. So, if this situation arises, don't worry. There is nothing wrong with your computer. DOS is simply unaware of the extra memory.

CHKDSK has several options, which we will examine later in this book.

Exercises

1. Try the previous examples now, if you haven't already done so.

2. Which of these commands are internal and which are external?

   a. FIND   d. RESTORE
   b. BACKUP   e. COMP
   c. RENAME   f. TYPE

3. Why does the DOS diskette have to be available for you to use an external command?

LEARN ABOUT DRIVE SPECIFIERS

3.5

Up to this point, you have been working with the current drive, which is drive A if you have been loading DOS from a diskette, or drive C if you have been loading DOS from a fixed disk. For the most part, DOS commands operate relative to the current drive by default. The current drive is often called the *logged-in* drive. (Remember, the letter of the logged-in drive is the first character of the DOS prompt.) For example, in the previous section both DIR and CHKDSK operated on the current drive. However, since most computers have at least two disk drives, DOS provides a means of switching between drives. When you switch to a new drive, that drive becomes the current drive and the focus of DOS.

To switch to another drive, simply specify the letter of the drive followed by a colon at the DOS prompt and press (Enter). For example, if you had just switched to drive B, your screen would look like this:

```
A>B:

B>
```

The letter followed by the colon is called a *drive specifier*. You may use either upper- or lowercase for the letter—DOS is not sensitive to case. If you entered the DIR command at this point, the directory of the disk in drive B would be displayed.

Many DOS commands allow a drive specifier to be used as an option, which causes the focus of the command to be temporarily shifted to a different drive. You saw an example of this when you used DISKCOPY to make backups of the DOS master. If you have two diskette drives, you used this form of DISKCOPY to make the backup:

```
DISKCOPY A: B:
```

This command causes the contents of the disk in drive A to be copied to the disk in drive B.

You can also use a drive specifier to make DOS look for an external command on a disk other than the one that is currently logged in. For example, if a copy of the DOS diskette is in drive B, but the current disk is drive A, the following command will cause DOS to load CHKDSK from drive B:

```
B:CHKDSK
```

No space is allowed between the specifier and the command. When the drive specifier precedes an external command, it causes DOS to look for that command on the specified drive. However, the focus of the specified command is still the currently logged-in disk, not the disk from which the command is loaded.

Examples

NOTE: The following examples are written for a system that contains two diskette drives. If your system has one diskette drive and a fixed disk, substitute drive C for drive B. The examples also assume that you have loaded DOS from a floppy disk in drive A. If your system does have two diskette drives, insert a second copy of your DOS master into drive B at this time.

1. When you use a drive specifier as an option to a command, the specifier must always follow the command. For example, to view the directory of drive B, you would use this command:

    DIR B:

    After the directory had been listed, the current disk would still be drive A. As this example demonstrates, the change in focus is temporary.

2. The CHKDSK command can also be directed at another drive. For example, this command checks the condition of the disk in drive B:

    CHKDSK B:

3. You can load an external command from a disk that is different from the one in the currently logged-in drive. For example, log in to drive A and enter this command:

    B:CHKDSK

    As you can see, the CHKDSK command loads from drive B, but the disk that is checked is the one in drive A.

Exercises

1. What would you enter to make drive C the current drive?

2. If you wanted to execute the CHKDSK command from drive C, what command would you give DOS?

3. What command would you use to list the directory of drive C?

EXERCISES

MASTERY SKILLS CHECK

At this point, you should be able to answer these questions and perform these exercises:

1. What is the disk directory and what function does it perform?

2. What are the two parts of a file name called? How long can each part be? Name two characters that cannot be used in a file name.

3. What command would you use to list the directory and pause every 23 lines?

4. What are DOS's two wildcard characters and what do they do?

5. What command would you use to list all files that share the .COM extension?

6. What is the difference between an internal and an external command?

7. How do you log in to a different disk drive? How do you execute an external DOS command which is located on a disk that is not the currently logged-in drive?

Master More DOS Commands

►4◄

In this chapter, you will increase your repertoire of common DOS commands by learning how to format a disk and how to copy, rename, and erase a file. You will also learn about some common DOS error messages and keyboard techniques.

EXERCISES

SKILLS CHECK

Before you proceed with this chapter, you should be able to answer these questions and perform these exercises:

1. What command do you use to display the contents of a directory using the wide format?

2. What command clears the screen?

3. What command displays all the files in a directory that have a .DAT extension?

4. What is a drive specifier? Assume that the current disk is A. What command would cause DOS to display the directory of the C drive?

5. Is the following statement true or false? Once an external command has been loaded into memory for execution, it remains resident and does not have to be reloaded to be used a second time.

6. What command reports information about the status of your disk?

4.1 LEARN TO FORMAT A DISKETTE

Before DOS can use a diskette, the diskette must first be *formatted*. Formatting prepares a disk for use by organizing the magnetic medium into the form that

DOS expects. It also creates the directory. You did not have to format the diskettes that you used to make your DOS work disks because the DISKCOPY command automatically formats the target diskette. The DOS command that formats a diskette is called FORMAT. Several of the examples in this and later chapters require a blank, formatted diskette, so this is a good time to learn about FORMAT.

Before you actually try to format a disk, you need to know how DOS stores information on disks. Also, you need to learn a few new terms so you can interpret certain DOS prompts and messages. It is not important that you understand the technical details, but you will feel more confident running DOS if you've been introduced to some of the program's more cryptic terms and concepts.

When you purchase a blank diskette, its magnetic medium has no organization. Formatting organizes the disk into two related elements: tracks and sectors. A *track* is a narrow band that forms a complete circle on the disk. Each disk contains several concentric tracks. A *sector* is a portion of a track, as you can see in Figure 4-1. The number of tracks on a disk and the number of sectors per track varies and does not affect your ability to use DOS.

A sector is the smallest unit of disk space DOS can access. In virtually all situations, a sector is 512 bytes long. This does not mean that you can't have files that are shorter than 512 bytes; in fact, a file can be 0 bytes long. It means that DOS will use a complete sector for a file, even if that sector is not completely filled with information. While this scheme may seem wasteful, it is necessary to provide fast disk accesses.

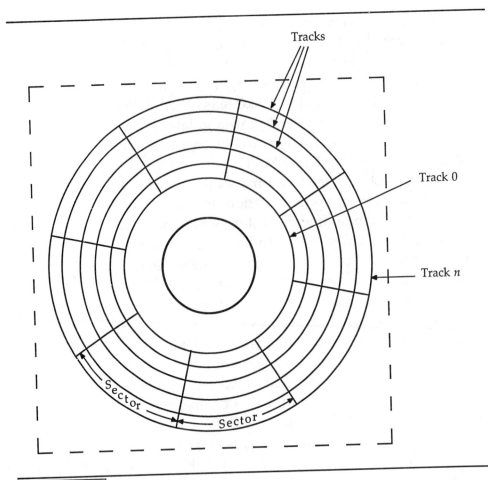

FIGURE 4-1.   Sectors and tracks of a diskette

Although DOS can access an individual sector of disk space, the smallest amount of disk space DOS can allocate to a file is a *cluster*, which is a group of adjacent sectors. The actual number of sectors in a cluster varies for different types of disks, but it is generally two to four.

When DOS stores information on a disk, it does not necessarily use adjacent clusters and tracks. In fact, it is very common for parts of a single file to be scattered around the disk (the directory keeps track of where the parts are located). Because individual files are often scattered, even a small amount of damage to a disk can destroy several files.

When you load a file, you can hear the disk drive's read-write head moving across the disk, jumping from track to track. The fact that clusters typically include two to four sectors prevents excessive head motion while still providing reasonable storage efficiency.

REMEMBER: The physical organization of tracks and sectors is not built into the disk. Instead, this organization is created when the disk is formatted. DOS cannot use an unformatted diskette.

Most floppy disk drives are double sided. This means that they have two read-write heads, one for each side of the diskette. Collectively, the two corresponding tracks on each side of a disk are referred to as a cylinder (see Figure 4-2).

Now that you understand how DOS stores information on a disk and know the meaning of a few more terms, it's time you learned how to format a diskette.

IMPORTANT: Formatting destroys all preexisting information on a disk, so be very careful that you don't accidentally format the wrong diskette by mistake. (Write-protecting a diskette prevents accidental

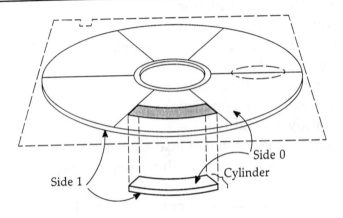

Side 0

Cylinder

Side 1

| FIGURE 4-2. | A double-sided floppy disk |

formatting, in case you have concerns about formatting the wrong disk.) Also, in general, never format a
fixed disk yourself. Usually, the person who sells you
a computer will format the fixed disk for you.

The simplest form of the FORMAT command is
shown here:

FORMAT *drive specifier*

Although some DOS commands operate on the current drive if no drive specifier is provided, this is not
the case with FORMAT; you must explicitly specify
the drive when using the FORMAT command. The
drive specifier determines which drive will be used to
format the diskette. For example, this command
causes the diskette in drive B to be formatted:

```
FORMAT B:
```

Note that FORMAT is an external command, so have your DOS disk available when you use it.

Because the formatting process takes a few minutes, it is a good idea to keep several formatted diskettes on hand so you will have one ready when needed.

Examples

1. Although the general procedure is the same, precisely what you do to format a diskette depends on how many and what kind of disk drives you have. If you have two diskette drives, you can use drive B to do the actual formatting (unless A and B are of different types, in which case you must format the diskette in the appropriate drive). If you have only one diskette drive, you will use drive A to format the disk.

   If you are using drive B to format, give DOS this command:

   FORMAT B:

   If you are using drive A, give DOS this command:

   FORMAT A:

   After FORMAT has loaded and started executing, you will see this message if you are using drive B for formatting:

   ```
   Insert new diskette for B:
   and strike ENTER when ready
   ```

   You will see this message if you are using drive A:

   ```
   Insert new diskette for A:
   and strike ENTER when ready
   ```

Now put a blank diskette into the appropriate drive. If you have only one disk drive and you executed FORMAT using a DOS diskette in drive A, you must first remove your DOS diskette and insert the diskette that you want formatted in drive A. Once you have inserted the diskette, press [Enter].

The formatting process takes several seconds, during which time you will hear the disk drive working. While the formatting is taking place, FORMAT displays information that tells you which read-write head is being used to format which cylinder (DOS version 4 displays the percentage of the disk that has been formatted).

Once the diskette is formatted, you will see something like this on your screen:

```
Format complete

     362496 bytes total disk space
     362496 bytes available on disk

Format another (Y/N)?
```

Remember, there are several types of disk drives, each capable of storing different amounts of data, so the total amount of disk space that DOS reports may vary.

As you can see, FORMAT asks whether you want to format another disk. If you do, simply remove the formatted disk from the drive, insert another blank disk, and type **Y** followed by [Enter].

Aside from formatting a diskette, FORMAT also checks for any parts of the disk that are incapable of storing information accurately. Sometimes, in the manufacturing process, the magnetic component of the disk is not evenly applied and a portion of the diskette cannot be used to store information. If FORMAT encounters such an error, it marks all unusable sectors of the disk in the directory. DOS refers to unusable sectors as *bad sectors*. If a disk does have some bad sectors, FORMAT will also report the number of bytes that are unusable. As long as the amount of unusable storage is small— less than ten percent of the disk's total capacity is a good rule of thumb—it is all right to use a disk that has some bad sectors. However, if the damaged area is greater than ten percent, other parts of the diskette will probably be prone to failure after a little use, and it should be discarded.

2. Basically, there are two types of diskettes: those that can hold programs and/or data but cannot be used to load DOS and those that can be used to load DOS as well as to hold programs and data. You can store more information on the first type of disk than on the second type, because the resident part of DOS, which is initially loaded, takes several thousand bytes of disk space. If a disk does not contain the files required to load DOS, this space is available for other uses.

   Simply formatting a disk only prepares it to store data and programs. If you want to be able to load DOS from the disk you are formatting, you must specify the /S FORMAT option. The /S option causes the part of DOS that is initially loaded and that remains resident in memory to be copied onto the diskette. This part of DOS is referred to as the *system.* A diskette that contains the system can be used to start DOS running.

As you know, DOS includes two types of commands, internal and external commands. The /S option does not cause the external commands to be copied to the disk. Only the internal commands are included in the part of DOS that resides in memory. Therefore, if you want to make a complete copy of your DOS disk, do so using DISKCOPY, as explained in Chapter 2.

You might need to put the system on a diskette for some application programs to execute correctly. If you need to have the system on the disk for this reason, the instructions that accompany the application program will tell you so.

Let's put the system on a disk now. Insert your DOS diskette in drive A and enter this command:

```
FORMAT A: /S
```

The program will display this message:

```
Insert DOS disk in drive A:
and strike ENTER when ready
```

To install the system on the target disk, FORMAT must first read it from an existing DOS diskette. Therefore, it asks you to put a DOS disk in drive A. Since your DOS work disk is already in A, just press [Enter]. After FORMAT reads the system, you will see this prompt:

```
Insert new diskette for A:
and strike ENTER when ready
```

Remove the DOS diskette, insert a blank diskette and press [Enter]. (You can use the disk you formatted in Example 1, if you like. Formatting a diskette a second time does it no harm, although any preexisting information on the disk is lost.) After formatting the diskette, DOS copies the system and displays a message similar to the one shown here (remember, disk sizes vary):

```
Format complete
System transferred


     362496 bytes total disk space
      78848 bytes used by system
     283648 bytes available on disk


Format another (Y/N)?
```

You can reserve space for the DOS system but not actually install it by specifying the /B option to FORMAT. You will learn more about this option later.

Exercises

1. What command would cause the diskette in drive B to be formatted?

2. If you format a diskette that already contains information, what happens to that information?

3. How do you cause the DOS system to be copied to a diskette during the formatting process?

4. If you haven't already done so, format a diskette now.

5. Define *track, sector,* and *cylinder.*

6. What does formatting a diskette accomplish?

4.2 BECOME FAMILIAR WITH COPY

Second only to DIR, COPY is one of the most frequently used DOS commands. It copies the contents of one file into another file. COPY is very versatile and flexible. In this section, we will only look at its most common form.

The general form of the COPY command is

COPY *source destination*

For example, to copy a file called LETTER.WP to a file called LETTER.BAK, you would use this command:

```
COPY LETTER.WP LETTER.BAK
```

A good way to remember which file name comes first is to think of "COPY" as "COPY from to."

When a file is copied, an exact duplicate is made that is just as good as the original. As you may know, when an audio tape is copied to a second tape, the second tape is of lower quality. If the second tape is copied to a third, the third is of even lower quality than the second. With audio tape, each generation is of lower quality than the one that precedes it. However, when you copy a file, each generation is exactly like the original—the quality remains consistent no matter how many times you copy a file.

There are two important things you must remember about copying files. First—although the practice has fallen out of favor for most commercial programs—some files may still be *copy-protected*, which means you won't be able to copy them using DOS.

Copy protection was invented to prevent the unauthorized distribution of copyrighted programs. Copy
protection prevents DOS from copying a file. Second,
even if a program is not copy-protected most programs are copyrighted and protected by federal law.
This means that while you have the right to copy a
program for the purpose of backing it up, you probably don't have the right to make a copy for someone
else to use. If you use a computer at work and also
have one at home, you may be violating copyright law
if you copy programs at work and use them at home.

Examples

From this point on, you will be issuing some commands that will alter the contents of your DOS work
disk. For this reason, make sure you are using a copy
of your DOS master disk, *not* the master itself.

1. As a first example, issue the following command:

```
COPY CHKDSK.COM TEST.COM
```

Now, list all files on the disk that have the .COM
extension, using DIR *.COM. You will see output
similar to that shown in Figure 4-3.
   Notice that the creation date of TEST.COM is the
same as that of the original CHKDSK.COM. According to the program's logic, DOS does not actually
create a file when it copies an existing one; instead,
it simply propagates all of the original file's charac-
teristics to the copy.

```
              Volume in drive A has no label
              Directory of  A:\

          ASSIGN    COM     1561   3-17-87   12:00p
          BACKUP    COM    31913   3-18-87   12:00p
          BASIC     COM     1063   3-17-87   12:00p
          BASICA    COM    36403   3-17-87   12:00p
     ┌──►  CHKDSK    COM     9850   3-18-87   12:00p
     │     COMMAND   COM    25307   3-17-87   12:00p
     │     COMP      COM     4214   3-17-87   12:00p
     │     DEBUG     COM    15897   3-17-87   12:00p
     │     DISKCOMP  COM     5879   3-17-87   12:00p
     │     DISKCOPY  COM     6295   3-17-87   12:00p
     │     EDLIN     COM     7526   3-17-87   12:00p
     │     FORMAT    COM    11616   3-18-87   12:00p
     │     GRAFTABL  COM     6128   3-17-87   12:00p
     │     GRAPHICS  COM     3300   3-17-87   12:00p
     │     LABEL     COM     2377   3-17-87   12:00p
     │     MORE      COM      313   3-17-87   12:00p
     │     PRINT     COM     9026   3-17-87   12:00p
     │     RECOVER   COM     4299   3-18-87   12:00p
     │     RESTORE   COM    34643   3-17-87   12:00p
     │     TREE      COM     3571   3-17-87   12:00p
     └──►  TEST      COM     9850   3-18-87   12:00p
                21 File(s)        45056 bytes free
```

Figure 4-3.	CHKDSK.COM and TEST.COM are the same length and show the same creation date and time

Because the contents of TEST.COM are the same as CHKDSK.COM, when you execute TEST.COM it reports the status of your disk just the way CHKDSK does. To execute TEST.COM, simply type **TEST** at the DOS prompt. (In general, to execute any program you simply enter its name at the prompt.) Try this, and you will see that TEST.COM does, in fact, check the contents of your disk.

The previous example makes another important point: What a program does is completely independent of its name. To execute a program, DOS simply loads the file that matches the name you enter at the prompt; it can't interpret program names. Nonetheless, most programs have descriptive names to help *you* remember what they do.

2. You can copy a file to another diskette by putting a drive specifier in front of the destination file name. For example, this command would copy TEST.COM to drive B and name the new file TEST2.COM:

```
COPY TEST.COM B:TEST2.COM
```

Furthermore, you can copy a file from any disk to any other disk using the appropriate drive specifiers. For example, assuming drive A were the current drive, this command would copy a file called TEST1.COM on drive B to a file called TEST2.COM on drive C:

```
COPY B:TEST1.COM C:TEST2.COM
```

3. When a copy of a file will reside in the same directory as the original, the copy must have a different name because a directory can't have two files with the same name. However, if you copy a file to another disk, you may use the same file name. For example, assuming drive A were current, this command would copy TEST.COM to the diskette in drive B:

```
COPY TEST.COM B:TEST.COM
```

Actually, the COPY command allows a shorthand version of this command. If you are copying a file from one disk to another and you want the destination file name to be the same as that of the source, you don't have to specify the destination file name. You still must use the drive specifier, however. For example, here is the way you would normally copy TEST.COM from drive A to drive B:

```
COPY TEST.COM B:
```

As another example, this command copies the file called TEST.EXE from drive B onto the current drive:

```
COPY B:TEST.EXE
```

COPY automatically uses the current disk and the source file name.

Exercises

1. What command would copy a file called FIND.EXE from drive A to drive C if A were the current drive? How would the command change if B were the current drive?

2. What is wrong with this command?

```
COPY CHKDSK.COM CHKDSK.COM
```

3. What command would you use to copy a file called FIND.EXE into one called MYFIND.EXE?

4.3 LEARN MORE ABOUT COPY

COPY is very versatile. This section examines several more aspects of the COPY command.

Although it is common to copy a single file, you will sometimes want to copy groups of related files. You can accomplish this by using the wildcard characters in the source file names. The wildcard specifiers work the same with COPY as they do with DIR. For example, if you wanted to copy all files from drive A that began with S and had the extension .EXE to drive B, you would use this command:

```
COPY A:S*.EXE B:
```

Since wildcards cause a group of files to be copied, it is often a good idea to first issue a DIR command using the same wildcards so you know that DOS will actually copy only the files you want. As the number of files on a disk grows, it becomes difficult to remember exactly which files a specific wildcard combination will match.

If you have only one diskette drive and you want to copy a file from one diskette to another, you can still do so using COPY. For example, assume the source diskette contains a file called TEST.TST and you want to copy that file to a second diskette. You would use this command:

```
COPY A:TEST.TST B:TEST.TST
```

Notice that the command tells DOS to copy TEST.TST from disk A to disk B. How can this work when a computer doesn't have a B drive? It works because when no B drive is present, DOS automatically makes the single disk drive in the system serve as both A and B! Furthermore, the program prompts you to insert the appropriate disks as needed. This process is much like using DISKCOPY to make a backup DOS disk using only one disk drive.

Examples

As you just learned, if you have only one diskette drive you can still use COPY commands like COPY A:TEST B: because DOS allows you to swap diskettes as needed. Therefore, the examples that follow use drives A and B. To perform these examples on your computer, put your DOS disk in A and a blank, formatted diskette in B or be prepared to swap diskettes in drive A if you don't have a B drive. Be sure to log in to drive A if it is not already the current drive. If you have a fixed disk, you can substitute appropriate drive specifiers if you like.

1. To see how wildcards can help you copy groups of related files, try this command:

```
COPY A*.EXE B:
```

When using a wildcard file name, COPY automatically displays the name of each file it copies. When the process is finished, COPY also tells you how many files were copied. After the previous command has been completed, the following lines will appear on your screen:

```
A>COPY A*.EXE B:
APPEND.EXE
ATTRIB.EXE
        2 File(s) copied
```

As you can see, only files that begin with A and have the extension .EXE were copied.

2. When copying groups of files that share a common extension, you can change that extension on the target disk by specifying a new extension for the

destination file name. For example, this command causes all files with the extension .EXE to be copied to the target disk and given the .BAK extension:

```
COPY *.EXE B:*.BAK
```

Try this command now. As it runs, the files will display with .EXE extensions. However, once it completes, if you list the directory on the target disk it will look similar to that shown here, assuming you started this section with a blank, formatted target diskette and performed the first example (you may also see some additional files).

```
Volume in drive B has no label
Directory of B:\

APPEND    EXE    5825   3-17-87   12:00p
ATTRIB    EXE    9529   3-17-87   12:00p
APPEND    BAK    5825   3-17-87   12:00p
ATTRIB    BAK    9529   3-17-87   12:00p
FASTOPEN  BAK    3919   3-17-87   12:00p
FIND      BAK    6434   3-17-87   12:00p
JOIN      BAK    8969   3-17-87   12:00p
NLSFUNC   BAK    3060   3-17-87   12:00p
REPLACE   BAK   11775   3-17-87   12:00p
SHARE     BAK    8608   3-17-87   12:00p
SORT      BAK    1977   3-17-87   12:00p
SUBST     BAK    9909   3-17-87   12:00p
XCOPY     BAK   11247   3-17-87   12:00p
       13 File(s)   261120 bytes free
```

A command like the previous one might be useful when you want to quickly distinguish between backup copies of your files and the files you are currently using. In general, you should not change the extension of a file that has one of DOS's reserved extensions because you will confuse DOS. This example is only intended to demonstrate how you can change the extension of the target files when you are copying groups of related files.

3. You can copy every file from the current drive to another disk in drive B using this form of COPY:

```
COPY *.* B:
```

Keep one point firmly in mind: Although COPY *.* B: will copy all user files found in the directory of drive A to the disk in drive B, it does not copy any hidden files used by DOS. Therefore, you still must use the DISKCOPY command if you wish to make a new DOS master diskette.

Exercises

1. What COPY command would you use to copy all files that started with DISK and had the extension .COM from drive A to drive B?

2. What does DOS do if you try to copy a file from drive A to drive B on a system that has only one disk drive?

3. What command copies all the files displayed in the directory of the disk in drive A to the disk in drive B? Extra challenge: Show a second way to accomplish the same task.

4.4 KNOW SOME DOS ERROR MESSAGES

Before you continue exploring DOS, you'll need to know how to interpret a few DOS error messages. Whenever DOS cannot complete a command, it displays an error message on the screen. From this point on, because you'll be using DOS much more rigorously, you'll be more likely to encounter error messages. Therefore, it is important that you understand the most common errors.

There are various reasons a DOS command can fail. For example, a hardware error, such as a disk drive not working, can make it impossible for DOS to complete a command. Even when the hardware is functioning correctly, a command can fail because a disk is not properly inserted, or because a disk has insufficient free space to hold a file that is being copied to it.

You have already been introduced to the most common error message:

```
Bad command or file name
```

DOS issues this message whenever you enter something at the prompt that is not an internal command, an external command, or the name of an application program. To resolve this problem you simply reenter the command correctly. The examples that follow explain a few more serious error messages.

Examples

1. Let's begin by actually generating an error message. If it is not already there, insert your work copy of the DOS diskette in drive A and log in to that drive. Next, remove the DOS diskette and leave the drive empty. Now, issue the CHKDSK command. After a

few seconds you will see this error message:

```
Not ready error reading drive A
Abort, Retry, Fail?
```

Let's look closely at this message. First, it tells you that drive A cannot be read because the drive is not ready (loading an external command involves *reading* it from a disk). In this case, the drive is not ready because there is no diskette in it. However, this error message could also be generated if the drive were broken.

A variation on the previous error message is

```
Not ready error writing drive A
```

This message would be issued if there were something wrong with the disk when DOS tried to write to it.

The second line of the error message is a prompt asking how you want DOS to respond to the error. Choosing the Abort option causes DOS to simply cancel the command. The Retry option makes DOS try the command again. Sometimes, as in this case, an error can be remedied. For example, here, you can insert your DOS diskette and then tell DOS to retry the command. Also, a device will occasionally fail momentarily because of a power surge or static discharge. For this reason, it is generally worth retrying a command at least once. Finally, choosing the Fail option tells DOS to ignore the error and continue on. This option is primarily for programmers, because its correct use requires an intimate understanding of how DOS actually performs its functions. Using the Fail option incorrectly can cause valuable data to be lost, so it is best to avoid this option completely. Some versions of DOS substitute the word *Ignore* for *Fail,* but the option is the same, and you should still avoid this choice.

Many DOS errors cause the prompt

```
Abort, Retry, Fail?
```

to be displayed. The meaning of the three options is the same for any error. As you'll see, all the error messages examined in this section issue this prompt. Also, all of these messages take the general form of the one in the previous example. That is,

error-type error reading/writing drive *drive*

where *error-type* is the nature of the error, which occurs relative to drive *drive* while either a read or a write operation is underway.

If you have not yet done so, insert the DOS diskette into drive A and retry the command at this time.

2. Here is another error message that you may see:

```
Non-DOS disk
```

DOS issues this message when it tries to access a diskette whose directory has become unreadable. If you retry your command a few times and the error persists, the only thing you can do is use a backup copy.

3. Another message a damaged disk can cause is this one:

```
Sector not found
```

As you know, a sector is the smallest unit of storage space on a disk. A long file will be stored in several sectors. DOS automatically keeps track of what sectors belong with what files. If a specific sector that DOS expects to be part of a file cannot be found, it means the disk has been damaged in some way. Should this message remain after several retries, your only recourse is to use a backup copy of the disk.

A related error message is

```
Seek
```

As you know, information on a disk is organized into concentric cicles, or tracks. If DOS attempts to position the read-write head over a track that does not exist or that is damaged, you will see this error message.

4. Another common error message is

```
General Failure
```

A general failure occurs when the disk is not formatted or its storage size does not match that of the drive.

Exercises

1. What is the difference between Abort and Retry?

2. If you have not tried the first example, do so now.

MASTER RENAMING AND ERASING A FILE

4.5

In this section you will learn two additional DOS commands that let you change the name of a file and remove a file from a disk.

To change the name of a file, use the RENAME internal command, whose general form is

RENAME *old-name new-name*

For example, to change a file called MYFILE.DAT to YOURFILE.DAT, you would use this command:

```
RENAME MYFILE.DAT YOURFILE.DAT
```

RENAME can be abbreviated REN; DOS recognizes either form. This book will use RENAME because it better expresses what the command does. Feel free to use REN if you like, however.

As you will see in some of the examples presented in this section, the file names used by the RENAME command can include wildcard characters.

To remove a file from a disk, use the ERASE internal command, which has this general form:

ERASE *file-name*

For example, to erase a file called MYFILE.DAT, you would use this command:

```
ERASE MYFILE.DAT
```

You can use wildcard characters in the file name specified after ERASE, but you must be very careful

that you don't accidentally erase something uninten-
tionally. In fact, it is usually a good idea to first issue
a DIR command using the same wildcard characters,
so you can verify that nothing unexpected is matched
by the wildcards.

It is extremely important to understand that once a
file has been erased, it is gone, so be very careful when
you use the ERASE command and always keep copies
of important files. You will learn proper backup
procedures later in this book.

DOS also recognizes the command *DEL,* which is
equivalent to ERASE. This book uses ERASE because
it is the more descriptive term; however, you may use
either ERASE or DEL.

Examples

1. If you have been following the examples in this
   chapter, your DOS work disk should contain a file
   called TEST.COM, which you made using this
   COPY command:

   ```
   COPY CHKDSK.COM TEST.COM
   ```

   If you haven't yet created TEST.COM, do so now.

   Once you have TEST.COM on your disk, try
   changing its name to MYFILE.COM using this command:

   ```
   RENAME TEST.COM MYFILE.COM
   ```

   Now list the directory of the disk; you will find that
   TEST.COM is no longer listed but MYFILE.COM
   does appear on the list.

2. By using wildcard characters you can change the extension shared by a group of files using a single RENAME command. For example, this command substitutes the .TST extension for all files that have the .EXE extension on your DOS work disk:

```
RENAME *.EXE *.TST
```

If you like, try the command and then list the directory. As you will see, all files that had the .EXE extension now use .TST. If you tried this, you should return the files to their original extension using this command:

```
RENAME *.TST *.EXE
```

3. If you have been following along, you have a file called MYFILE.COM on your DOS work disk. Since this file is redundant, erase it now, using this command:

```
ERASE MYFILE.COM
```

4. You can erase groups of files using wildcard characters. To follow along with this and the next example, make another copy of your DOS diskette following the procedure described in Chapter 2. Put this new diskette into drive A, and try this series of commands:

```
DIR A*.EXE
ERASE A*.EXE
DIR A*.EXE
```

The result will be similar to this:

```
A>DIR A*.EXE

 Volume in drive A has no label
 Directory of A:\
```

```
APPEND    EXE      5825    3-17-87   12:00p
ATTRIB    EXE      9529    3-17-87   12:00p
            2 File(s)         45056 bytes free

A>ERASE A*.EXE

A>DIR A*.EXE

 Volume in drive A has no label
 Directory of A:\

File not found
```

As you can see, the two files that matched the file name A*.EXE were erased, and if you check the directory of your disk, you will see that they were the only two files erased.

You can erase files that share a common extension by using an * for the file name. For example, this command would erase all files that have the .COM extension:

```
ERASE *.COM
```

5. To erase all user files from a disk, you would use this command:

```
ERASE *.*
```

Since this is a fairly extreme request, DOS prompts you with the following safety check:

```
Are you sure (Y/N)?
```

If you want to erase all files, type **Y**; if you do not, type **N**. You may use either upper- or lowercase letters.

6. The target files of both RENAME and ERASE can have a drive specifier applied to them. For example, the first of the following two commands renames a

file called TREE.COM on drive B to MYTREE.COM, the second command erases the SHARE.EXE file on drive B:

```
RENAME B:TREE.COM B:MYTREE.COM

ERASE B:SHARE.EXE
```

Exercises

1. Assuming there was a file called MIKE.WP on drive B, what command would erase it?

2. What command would erase all files that have the .PIF extension on the current drive?

3. What command would change the name of a file called CHKDSK.COM to DISKCHK.COM?

4. What command would change the extension of all files that have a .COM extension to a .SAV extension?

5. What are the DOS synonyms for ERASE and RENAME?

LEARN THREE SPECIAL KEYSTROKE COMMANDS

4.6

Three DOS commands differ significantly from those you have learned about so far. The main difference is that they are not English-like commands, but rather special key combinations that cause DOS to perform special functions. These three commands are sometimes called *keystroke commands*. They allow you to print to the screen, pause the display, and cancel a DOS command.

It is sometimes helpful to print the contents of your computer's screen on your printer. To do this, hold down the [Shift] key and then press the [PrtSc] key. If you have a printer properly attached to your system, whatever is on the screen will be printed. If you don't have a printer, DOS will ignore this command.

To temporarily stop output to the screen, press the Pause key. For example, you can suspend output during a directory listing by pressing Pause. To restart output, press any other key. Another way to accomplish the same thing is to hold down the [Ctrl] key and type S. This kind of pair is called a *control-key combination* and will be notated in this book using the form [Ctrl]-[S]. To restart the display after pressing [Ctrl]-[S], simply press the same combination again (or press any other key). [Ctrl]-[S] acts as a toggle, which alternates between off and on.

Sometimes you will give DOS the wrong command and want to stop it before it runs to completion. Or, you might simply want to cancel a command because you've changed your mind. A number of DOS commands can be canceled by pressing either [Ctrl]-[C] or [Ctrl]-[Break]. (Remember, to generate a control-key combination, hold down the [Ctrl] key and then type the second key.) In some situations, [Ctrl]-[Break] is a little "stronger," but in general either combination will work.

It is important to understand that some DOS commands have a "point of no return" after which the command cannot be canceled. For example, you can still cancel the FORMAT command when you see this prompt, but you must do so before you press Enter :

```
Insert new diskette for drive A:
and strike ENTER when ready
```

Once you have pressed Enter , you cannot cancel the FORMAT command. Keep one thing in mind: DOS will not let you cancel a command unless it is safe to do so, so don't be afraid to try canceling when you want to stop a command. (Remember, you can absolutely stop a command or a program by using the DOS restart keystroke command—that is, by pressing Ctrl , Alt , and Del at the same time.)

The Ctrl - C and Ctrl - Break key combinations will often work with application programs as well as with DOS commands. However, an application program may allow itself to be canceled at an inappropriate spot, which can damage the data stored on your disk, so it is best to be very careful when you attempt to stop an application program.

Examples

1. To see how the Pause key or the Ctrl - S keystroke command works, list the directory of your DOS work disk and press either Pause or Ctrl - S before it completes. Notice how the screen freezes. To restart output, press any other key.

2. If you have a printer attached to your computer, press the ⒫PrtSc⒭ key at this time. (Remember, you must hold down the ⒮Shift⒭ key while you press ⒫PrtSc⒭.) Whatever is on the screen will be sent to the printer.

   Another interesting—and potentially useful—aspect of the PRINT SCREEN command is that it also causes output to the screen to be frozen temporarily while the current screen contents are printed. Try this, for example: List the directory of your DOS work disk, but before all the files are displayed press the ⒫PrtSc⒭ key. Output to the screen will stop until the current screen contents are printed. This feature of the PRINT SCREEN command is handy, because it lets you capture the contents of the screen "on the fly."

3. To see the effect of ⒞Ctrl⒭-⒝Break⒭ or ⒞Ctrl⒭-⒞C⒭, list the directory of your DOS diskette. Before the listing completes, press either ⒞Ctrl⒭-⒞C⒭ or ⒞Ctrl⒭-⒝Break⒭. As you will see, the command is canceled and the DOS prompt is again displayed. Furthermore, notice that at the point of cancellation, a ^C displays on the screen. This is DOS's way of representing a control-key combination.

Exercises

1. How do you generate a control-key combination?

2. What are the two ways you can pause output to the screen?

3. On your own, experiment with the three keystroke commands discussed in this section. Try to make pausing the screen and canceling a command second nature, because a fast reaction time can be important when you use these two commands.

EXERCISES

At this point, you should be able to answer these questions and perform these exercises:

MASTERY SKILLS CHECK

1. What command would you use to format the disk that is in drive B?

2. Generally speaking, what function does formatting a disk serve?

3. What is the difference between a sector and a track?

4. What command would copy, from drive A to drive B, a file called BACKUP.COM?

5. What command would copy all files that begin with R and have the extension .COM from drive A to drive C?

6. What command do you use to erase a file? Show its general form.

7. What command would rename a file that is called HARRY.DAT to JERRY.INF?

8. When an error occurs, you are often confronted with the prompt

   ```
   Abort, Retry, Fail?
   ```

   What is the difference between Abort and Retry?

9. How do you pause the display?

10. How do you cancel a command? Is there any time when a command cannot be canceled?

EXERCISES

INTEGRATING SKILLS CHECK

This section checks how well you have integrated the material in this chapter with material from earlier chapters.

1. If you tried this COPY command while logged in to your DOS work disk:

   ```
   COPY CHKDSK.COM X[].COM
   ```

   you would see this error message:

   ```
   File creation error
   ```

   This message means that DOS is unable to create the file X[ ].COM. What is wrong? (Hint: Think about the target file name.)

2. When listing the directory, there are three ways to pause the display. What are they?

3. You learned in Chapter 3 that when you issue this DIR command:

```
DIR CHKDSK
```

the extension defaults to .*, causing CHKDSK.COM to be found. Would this hold true for the following COPY command—that is, would this command copy CHKDSK.COM to drive B?

```
COPY CHKDSK B:
```

(Hint: The best way to answer this question is to try the command for yourself!)

Learn More DOS
Commands

►5◄

In this chapter you will learn several additional important DOS commands. You will also learn about DOS's special editing keys and about disk volume labels.

EXERCISES

SKILLS CHECK

Before proceeding you should be able to answer these questions and perform these exercises:

1. What command copies a file called PRINT.COM from drive A to drive B?

2. What command formats and copies the system to a diskette in drive B?

3. What command changes the name of a file?

4. What command erases all files on the current disk that have the .DAT extension?

5. How do you cancel a command? Is there any time at which you cannot cancel a command?

6. What keys do you press to print the contents of the screen on the printer?

5.1   LEARN ABOUT THE TYPE COMMAND

If you use your computer for word processing, you will find the TYPE command especially useful. This command displays the contents of a text file on the screen, and since most word processing files are text files, TYPE makes it easy to see what a word processing file contains.

TYPE's general form is

TYPE *file-name*

where *file-name* is the name of the file you want displayed. TYPE is an internal command.

Actually, you can use TYPE to display the contents of any file, but only text files display in a meaningful way. Displaying program files and most data files causes unusual characters to appear on your screen, because these files contain data that is not textual in nature. Thus, using TYPE to view their contents is not very helpful. However, if you feel like experimenting with TYPE, go ahead; displaying a file won't harm the data in it.

Using the TYPE command to quickly see the contents of a text file is useful when you have several text files on a disk and you are looking for a specific one. Even if you give all your files descriptive names, at some point you probably won't remember exactly what each of them contains. Generally, you can find a file faster with TYPE than you can with your word processor.

NOTE: Some word processing programs create text files that contain special codes used only by the word processor. For this reason, some text files may display unusual characters. If you see some odd symbols interspersed with your text, don't be alarmed; there is nothing wrong with the file.

When displaying long text files, use either Pause or Ctrl-S to prevent text from scrolling off the screen before you read it. Unlike DIR, TYPE does not include an option to display 23 lines at a time.

Examples

1. Before you can use the TYPE command you will need to create a text file—your DOS work disk does not contain any text files. There are several ways to do this. If you have a word processor, you can use it to create a text file. Or, you can use EDLIN, a text editor that comes with DOS, to create one. (EDLIN is discussed in Appendix A.) However, one of the simplest ways to create a text file is to use another variation of the COPY command; COPY can be used to copy whatever you type at the keyboard into a disk file. To do this, you must specify the *from* argument as CON:. For example, to copy what you type at the keyboard into a file called MYTEXT, use this COPY command (since this command writes to disk, your diskette must *not* be write protected):

   ```
   COPY CON: MYTEXT
   ```

   This command causes COPY to read keystrokes and store them in the file called MYTEXT until you signal that you are through entering data. To stop, you press [Ctrl]-[Z] and then [Enter]. The [Ctrl]-[Z] is DOS's *end of file* marker. In some cases, when DOS reads a file, it knows that it has reached the end of the file when it encounters [Ctrl]-[Z]. In this case, when COPY receives a [Ctrl]-[Z], it knows you are finished entering information. We will come back to COPY later in this book, so don't worry if this procedure seems a little confusing now. It is necessary to "leapfrog" a bit so you can create a text file.
       Go ahead and execute this command:

```
COPY CON: MYTEXT
```

Now, enter this fragment of the Fourth Amendment
to the U.S. Constitution:

```
A>COPY CON: MYTEXT
The right of the people to be secure in their persons,
houses, papers, and effects, against unreasonable searches
and seizures, shall not be violated...
```

Once you have entered the three periods, press
[Enter]. Then press [Ctrl]-[Z] followed by [Enter]. Your
screen should look like Figure 5-1.

Now you have created a text file, and you can try
the TYPE command. To do so, issue this command:

```
TYPE MYTEXT
```

DOS will display your text file.

2. As stated earlier, it is generally not useful to display
   a program or data file using TYPE. To see why, try
   this command:

```
TYPE CHKDSK.COM
```

Since CHKDSK.COM is a program file, odd symbols
appear on screen and the computer's bell rings a

```
A>COPY CON: MYTEXT
The right of the people to be secure in their persons,
houses, papers, and effects, against unreasonable searches
and seizures, shall not be violated...
^Z
        1 File(s) copied
A>
```

FIGURE 5-1.   Text entered using COPY

few times. Remember, although it is not technically an error, using TYPE on a program file does not produce meaningful output.

Exercises

1. If you have not done so, perform the previous examples at this time.

2. If you already know how to use a word processor, go ahead and experiment with the TYPE command on your own.

5.2   PRINTING A TEXT FILE

Using DOS's PRINT command, you can print the contents of a text file on the printer. The simplest form of PRINT is

PRINT *file-name*

where *file-name* is the name of the file to be printed.

You can print more than one file by using a list of file names. If you specify a list of files, be sure to leave at least one space between the names. The files will be printed in order from left to right. PRINT is an external command.

PRINT is unique among DOS commands because it operates in *background mode.* That is, PRINT can continue printing a text file while you are using the computer to do other things, such as run an application program. Although in general DOS cannot do two things at the same time, PRINT is an exception. When PRINT is used in background mode, your computer is actually running two separate programs concurrently. When a computer is running two programs at the same time, it is *multitasking*. (Here, the term *task* is used loosely to mean "program.") When a program runs as a background task, it does not send output to the screen. Any other program you run while PRINT is printing has access to the screen and is therefore the *foreground task*. Remember, however, aside from the PRINT command, DOS can only run one program at a time.

Examples

1. As a first example, let's print the text file that you created in the previous section. To do so, enter this command:

   `PRINT MYTEXT`

   When you execute PRINT for the first time, DOS displays this prompt:

   `Name of list device [PRN]:`

   When you see this prompt, simply press (Enter). The PRINT command can route its output to devices other than the printer. However, unless you have an unusual system configuration, you will want to use the default device, a printer connected in the standard way. DOS's name for the printer is PRN and this is the default device name shown in the prompt. Later in this book you will learn about routing input and output to other devices.

After pressing [Enter], you will see this message:

```
Resident part of PRINT installed
```

PRINT is unique in many ways. Unlike other external commands, PRINT installs part of itself in memory. For example, it installs information about which device is being used for output. That is why you only see the device prompt the first time you execute PRINT.

Next, you will see the following message:

```
A:\MYTEXT is currently being printed
```

As soon as this message is displayed, the DOS prompt returns and you can enter another command, such as DIR, even though the file is still being printed. PRINT will continue to run as a background task until it has finished printing the file.

Execute PRINT MYTEXT a second time. Notice that this time you are not prompted and that printing begins immediately.

2. You can invoke PRINT with a list of files. To try this, first issue the following COPY command:

```
COPY MYTEXT MYTEXT2
```

Now, try this command:

```
PRINT MYTEXT MYTEXT2
```

DOS will display these messages:

```
A:\MYTEXT is currently being printed
A:\MYTEXT2 is in queue
```

These lines tell you that MYTEXT is being printed and that MYTEXT2 is next in line. As you can see, PRINT uses the term *queue.* Essentially, a queue is a list in which the item that enters first also exits first. To see what is currently in the print queue, enter **PRINT** by itself—that is, without a file name after it.

You can add a file to the print queue at any time. For example, try executing this series of commands in rapid succession.

```
PRINT MYTEXT MYTEXT2
PRINT
PRINT MYTEXT
```

If you are fast enough, you will see output like that in Figure 5-2.

By default, PRINT can queue up to ten files.

3. PRINT has several options. The two most important ones are /T and /C. You can terminate the printing

```
A>PRINT MYTEXT MYTEXT2

   A:\MYTEXT is currently being printed
   A:\MYTEXT2 is in queue

A>PRINT

   A:\MYTEXT is currently being printed
   A:\MYTEXT2 is in queue

A>PRINT MYTEXT

   A:\MYTEXT is currently being printed
   A:\MYTEXT2 is in queue
   A:\MYTEXT is in queue
```

FIGURE 5-2.   Sample output from the PRINT example

of all files in the print queue using the /T option. For example, try this command sequence:

```
PRINT MYTEXT MYTEXT2 MYTEXT
PRINT /T
```

As you can see, the printing is terminated. Look at the last piece of paper that has printing on it, and you will see this message:

```
All files canceled by operator
```

You can remove a file from the print queue by using the /C option. To remove a file from the queue, use this general form of PRINT:

PRINT *file-name*/C

For example, to remove the file MYTEXT2 from the queue, use this command:

```
PRINT MYTEXT/C
```

It is important to understand that the /C cancels not only the file you specify but also any others you specify after it. For example, this command would cancel the printing of MYTEXT and MYTEXT2:

```
PRINT MYTEXT/C MYTEXT2
```

To see the effect of the /C and /T options, try this series of commands:

```
PRINT MYTEXT MYTEXT2
PRINT /T
PRINT MYTEXT MYTEXT2
PRINT MYTEXT2/C
```

Exercises

1. Assume that you have three text files called LET1, LET2, and LET3. What command would print all three?

2. Assuming that LET1, LET2, and LET3 were in the print queue, what command would remove LET2?

3. What PRINT option cancels printing of all files remaining in the print queue?

4. Describe one aspect of PRINT that makes it unique.

LEARN TO COMPARE FILES AND DISKS

5.3

After you've used DOS and your application programs for a while, you may have several copies of the same file on different diskettes. In fact, you should keep several copies of any important files as backups in case the original disk fails. However, sometimes it is difficult to remember how current a backup file is. For example, you might have a database data file that is the same length as your current file, but contains slightly out-of-date information. The only way to be certain two files contain the same information is to compare their contents. For this purpose, DOS supplies the COMP command, which compares two files. Its general form is

COMP *first-file second-file*

Or, you can simply enter **COMP** and you will be prompted for the two files. If you want to compare several files, you can use wildcard characters in the file names. You can also use a drive specifier with either or both file names. This lets you compare files on disks other than the current one.

COMP will only compare files that are the same length. If the files are not the same length, COMP reports this fact and does not perform a comparison because the files obviously differ. If the files are the same length, COMP reports any differences between them; however, the way COMP reports a difference is a little odd. COMP reports the location in the file of the byte at which the difference occurs. It also reports the values of the two differing bytes. However, it does this using hexadecimal notation. In everyday life, we use decimal notation, which is based on the number 10. However, for technical reasons, computer programmers often use numbers based on 16. This system is called *hexadecimal*. In hexadecimal, the digits run from 0 to 15. Hexadecimal uses the letters A through F to represent the numbers 10 through 15. Also, each digit position to the left is 16 times greater than the position it precedes. Therefore, the number 1C is 16+12, or 28 in decimal. If you find hexadecimal confusing, don't worry! You probably don't need to understand hexadecimal numbers because most of the time all that matters is the fact that the files differ. But now you know why the output of the COMP command is so unusual.

You can also compare entire diskettes. One reason you might want to comfirm that two diskettes are the same is to verify that a backup copy of a disk is identical to the original. For example, if you use DISKCOPY to make backups of an important diskette, you might want to compare the two diskettes to verify that DISKCOPY has, in fact, copied the original accurately. In general, DISKCOPY reports an error if it cannot copy a disk successfully, but there is still a remote possibility that an error could creep in. Therefore, if only for peace of mind, you might want to compare two diskettes to verify that the backup is a faithful copy of the original. To compare two diskettes, use the DISKCOMP command, which has this general form:

DISKCOMP *first-drive-specifier second-drive-specifier*

If you have only one diskette drive in your system, specify that drive twice; you will be prompted to swap diskettes as necessary.

Just as COMP will only compare files that are the same size, DISKCOMP will only compare diskettes that have the same storage capacities. Generally, if you are comparing files that were created on the same computer, they will hold the same amount of data, so you won't have to worry about size differences. However, there are two possible exceptions: First, if you have an AT-style computer with two diskette drives, it is possible that drive A may be a 1.2-megabyte high-density floppy disk drive while drive B is a 360K medium-density diskette drive. You cannot compare a high-density diskette with a medium-density diskette. Second, on PS/2-style computers, it is possible to have a 360K external 5 1/4-inch diskette drive, and you can't compare a 3 1/2-inch diskette with a 5 1/4-inch diskette.

It is important to understand that two disks will compare as equal only if one is an identical copy of the other. The only way to guarantee that an identical copy has been made is to create the second disk using the DISKCOPY command. Simply formatting a diskette and then using COPY to copy all the files from the first disk to the second will not usually produce an identical disk, even though the informational content will be the same. The reason is that DOS allocates the first open disk space to store a file. If a disk has been in use for a while and several files have been created and erased, the information in a file will be scattered all over the disk. However, when COPY copies information to a fresh disk, it stores the data in continuous sectors, because all the disk space is free when COPY begins. Thus, even though the disks will contain the same information, COPY and DISKCOPY may arrange it differently.

One other point: You cannot use DISKCOMP to compare a fixed disk with another disk. Even if you have two identical fixed disks in your computer, you cannot compare them.

Examples

1. If you have been following along, you will have the files MYTEXT and MYTEXT2 on your DOS work disk. Try this command now:

   ```
   COMP MYTEXT MYTEXT2
   ```

   DOS will display these messages:

   ```
   Files compare ok
   Compare more files (Y/N)?
   ```

Since both files contain the same thing, it is not surprising that they compare. If you want to compare additional files, respond by typing **Y**; otherwise, type **N** and the DOS prompt will appear. This time, try typing **Y**; you will see the following prompt:

```
Enter primary file name
```

For this example, type **MYTEXT** and press [Enter]. DOS will respond with this prompt:

```
Enter 2nd file name or drive id
```

Drive id means drive specifier. If you are comparing two files with the same name on two separate disks, you only need specify the drive that the second file is on. Now, type **MYTEXT2** and press [Enter]. Again, DOS will compare the files. This time, when DOS prompts you to compare more files, type **N**.

Although the COMP command uses the phrase "primary file," you shouldn't attribute any special significance to those words. Either file can be primary or secondary; DOS does not care.

2. If you try to compare files that are not the same length, COMP responds with this message:

```
Files are different sizes
```

It also rings the computer's bell. As an example, try this command:

```
COMP MYTEXT CHKDSK.COM
```

Because these two files differ in length, COMP will not attempt to compare them.

3. To see an example comparison of two files that differ in content but not in length, you need to create a second text file with this content:

```
The right XY the people to be secure in their persons,
houses, papers, and effects, against unreasonable searches
and seizures, shall not be violated...
```

Call this file MYTEXT3. Notice that the "of" in the first line has been changed to "XY," but the length of the file is the same. To create this file, use the following command:

```
COPY CON: MYTEXT3
```

Remember, press [Enter] after the three periods and then press [Ctrl]-[Z] and then [Enter] to stop.

Once you have created MYTEXT3, try this command:

```
COMP MYTEXT MYTEXT3
```

The resulting output will be

```
Compare error at OFFSET A
File 1 = 6F

File 2 = 58

Compare error at OFFSET B
File 1 = 66

File 2 = 59
```

Remember, the information is in hexadecimal, which means that the files differed at locations 10 and 11. (In hexadecimal notation, A is 10 and B is 11.) Also, the character X is represented as 58 in hexadecimal and Y is represented as 59. However, as mentioned earlier, you probably don't need to worry about the actual differences; it is usually sufficient simply to know the files differ.

The COMP command stops comparing two files after ten mismatches have occurred.

4. The COMP command does not wait for you to insert a diskette, so if you want to compare files on a different disk than the one the COMP is on, execute COMP without any file names. This causes COMP to prompt for the file names and gives you a chance to change diskettes. Although you don't need to change diskettes, enter **COMP** at this time and specify the files MYTEXT and MYTEXT2 when prompted. The prompts will look like those shown in the first example. After the comparison is completed, type **N** to stop comparing files.

5. To see how the DISKCOMP command works, use DISKCOPY to make a copy of your DOS work disk. If you have two diskette drives, insert the copy into drive B and the DOS work disk into drive A; then, issue this command:

```
DISKCOMP A: B:
```

If you have only one diskette drive, insert your DOS work disk into drive A and issue this command:

```
DISKCOMP A: A:
```

You will be prompted to swap diskettes as necessary.

After comparing the two diskettes, you will see the following messages:

```
Compare OK
Compare another diskette (Y/N)?
```

This time, type **N** in response to the prompt.

6. To see a disk comparison fail, format another diskette and try comparing it with your DOS work disk.
   Because the diskettes differ (the newly formatted
   diskette is blank), you will see several error messages, which have this general form:

Compare error on side *X*, track *Y*

Here, *X* and *Y* specify the side and track where the
diskettes differ. This information has little significance (except to a programmer) beyond telling you
that the diskettes are not identical. Since these two
diskettes differ in virtually all locations, press [Ctrl]-
[C] to cancel the DISKCOMP command at this time.

Exercises

1. What command would compare CHKDSK.COM on
   drive A with CHKDSK.COM on drive B?

2. What command would compare a disk in drive A
   with one in drive B?

5.4   MASTER THE DOS EDITING KEYS

Along the left side or at the top of your keyboard are
several function keys. These keys are labeled [F1]
through [F10] (or [F12] for the PS/2-style keyboard). The

first five function keys, along with [Del], [Esc], and [Ins], allow you to reuse and modify the last command you gave DOS. Collectively, these are called the *DOS editing keys*.

When you give DOS a command, what you type is stored in a small region of memory called the *keyboard buffer*. Even after DOS executes your last command, what you typed remains in the keyboard buffer until you enter another command. Using the DOS editing keys, you can reuse or modify your last command without having to reenter it.

Table 5-1 summarizes the functions performed by the editing keys. The following examples illustrate the use of the individual keys.

Examples

NOTE: In these examples you will be giving DOS some commands that it does not recognize. They

TABLE 5-1.   The DOS Editing Keys

Key	Function
[F1]	Redisplays one character from the keyboard buffer each time it is pressed
[F2]	Redisplays all characters up to, but not including, the character that you enter after pressing [F2]
[F3]	Redisplays all characters in the keyboard buffer
[F4]	Deletes all characters up to, but not including, the character you enter after pressing [F4]
[F5]	Reedits the line you just typed
[Del]	Deletes a character from the keyboard buffer
[Esc]	Cancels the current line
[Ins]	Inserts the next character typed into the keyboard buffer

won't cause any harm, but DOS will repeatedly display the "Bad command or file name" message. When you see this message, simply ignore it and continue working.

1. At the DOS prompt, enter **ABCDEFG** and press [Enter]. Now, press the [F1] key three times. Your command line will look like this:

   A>ABC

   As you can see, each time you press [F1], DOS displays another character from the previous command. Continue pressing [F1] until you reach the G. At this point, pressing [F1] again has no effect because you have reached the end of the previous command.

   It is important to understand that DOS does not store the Enter character in its keyboard buffer; therefore, you must press [Enter] again at this time.

2. Pressing the [F2] key displays characters up to, but not including, the character that you enter after you press [F2]. For example, press [F2] and then type **F**. Your command line will look like this:

   A>ABCDE

   If you specify a character that is not in the previous command, no action results. Also, if the specified character occurs more than once in the command, [F2] stops after the first match; however, you can find the next match by pressing [F2] followed by the character a second time.

   Now, press [F1] until you reach the end of the line, and then press [Enter].

3. Perhaps the most used editing key is F3. Pressing F3 displays the entire previous command. This is especially useful when you want to execute the same command several times in a row. Try pressing F3 now. As you can see, the entire previous command appears. Now, press Enter.

4. You can delete characters from the previous command with the F4 key. It works much like F2, except F4 deletes all characters from the current location up to, but not including, the first character in the command that matches the one you enter after you press F4. For example, press F4 and then type **D**. Now press F1 twice. Your command line will look like this:

A>DE

The characters A, B, and C have been deleted.

You can also use the Del key to delete a letter. Press Del now. Next, press F3. The command line will look like this:

A>DEG

Pressing Del deleted the F. In general, each time you press Del, it deletes the character directly to the right of the cursor, if there is a character in that position in the keyboard buffer.

Do *not* press Enter now; go directly to the next example.

5. You can reedit a line at any time by pressing Esc. This restores the original contents of the buffer so you can start over again. Press Esc at this time. Your command line will look like the following:

```
A>DEG\
```

The \ is the way DOS indicates a command has been
canceled. Also, notice that the cursor is located
under the first character of the canceled command.
Press F3. As you can see, the entire line is restored.
Because you canceled the line in which you had
deleted A, B, C, and F, DOS automatically restores
the keyboard buffer to its original contents. Now,
press Enter.

6. You can insert one or more characters into the
   previous command by first redisplaying all characters up to the point at which you want to make the
   insertion. Then, press Ins and then type the character or characters you want to insert. For example,
   try this: Press F1 three times. Now, press Ins and
   type **HELLO**. Finally, press F3. Your command
   line will look like this:

```
A>ABCHELLODEFG
```

Press Enter before you go on.

7. Type this line, but do not press Enter:

```
SOMETIMES YOU WILL HAVE VERY LONG COMMANDS
```

As you begin to use DOS and your application
programs for real work, you will need to enter fairly
long and complex commands at times. You may
type an entire line, only to see that you've made a
mistake near the beginning. Although you can use
the Backspace key to fix your error, it is often easier to
use DOS's editing functions. For you to do so,
however, the command must be loaded into the

keyboard buffer. (Remember, until you actually press [Enter], DOS has no knowledge of what you've typed.) The way around this problem is to press the [F5] key. This key causes DOS to load the *current command* into the keyboard buffer without executing it. Press [F5] now, and then try any other editing command. As you can see, the new command can now be edited. Press [Enter].

8. One thing to keep in mind is that you can always overwrite what is in the keyboard buffer simply by entering new characters. It is perfectly valid to retrieve part of the previous command by pressing [F1], and then to type the rest manually. For example, enter this text:

THIS IS A TEST

Press [Enter]. Now, press [F1] ten times; then, add the words SECOND TEST and press [Enter]. Finally, press [F3]. As you can see, the result is

```
THIS IS A SECOND TEST
```

Exercises

For several of these exercises, you should assume that the last command entered was

```
COPY MYTEXT MYTEXT2
```

This will be referred to as the original COPY command.

1. What sequence of editing keys would transform the original COPY command into

```
COPY MYTEXT MY2TEXT
```

2. How would you transform the original COPY command into this one?

```
COPY MY* B:
```

Show the exact sequence.

3. How do you reexecute the original COPY command as is — in other words, without changing it?

4. What does the F4 key do?

5. What funtion does the Esc key perform?

5.5   LEARN THE DATE AND TIME COMMANDS

When you first start DOS, you are prompted to enter the current date and time. However, you can view or modify the system date and time whenever you wish by using DOS's DATE and TIME internal commands. In fact, DOS actually uses these commands to request date and time information when it begins executing. Therefore, these commands display exactly the same output that you see when DOS starts.

The DATE and TIME commands are useful in two situations: First, if you need to know either the date or the time, the computer will tell you. Second, sometimes the date or time may be set wrong and you will need to correct it.

You should have no trouble using the DATE and TIME commands because you have actually been using them all along; however, the examples that follow explain their operation again, in case you have any questions about the way they work.

Examples

1. Enter the TIME command now. You will see output similar to that shown here:

```
Current time is 14:14:24.10
Enter new time:
```

As you learned in Chapter 2, the system time is displayed using a 24-hour clock. This means that the time shown in this example represents 2:14 P.M. You must also enter the time using the 24-hour format. DOS does not recognize the symbols A.M. and P.M. It displays the time in this format:

hours:minutes:seconds.hundredths of a second

When you enter the new time, any field that you don't specify is treated as 0; therefore, if you enter 9:30, the time will be set to 9:30:00.00. If you enter an invalid time, DOS prompts you repeatedly until you provide a valid response.

To leave the time unchanged, simply press Enter.

2. Enter the DATE command now. You will see output similar to this:

```
Current date is Fri 11-24-1989
Enter new date (mm-dd-yy):
```

To leave the date unchanged, just press (Enter). To change the date, you must enter appropriate numbers for the month, the day, and the year. You may separate the parts of the date using either dashes (as shown), periods, or slashes (/). If you enter an invalid date, DOS will repeat the prompt until you provide a valid response.

Exercise

1. Try the DATE and TIME commands on your own, to verify that your computer does, indeed, have the correct date and time.

5.6 | MASTER VOLUME LABELS

When you list the directory of your DOS work disk, the first line looks like this:

```
Volume in drive A has no label
```

Traditionally, the DIR command refers to the disk as a volume. Although it would be much clearer to simply call a disk a disk, *volume* is the accepted term in this context. In DOS, the name you give a disk is called its *label*, or sometimes its *volume label*. Therefore, in plain English, the first line of the directory says "The diskette in drive A has no name."

Presently, DOS doesn't do anything with the volume label; however, in the future, it may be put to good use. For the time being, a volume label simply helps you identify a disk. For this reason, you should choose descriptive volume labels that reflect the disk's contents.

To give a disk a volume label, use the LABEL command, which has this general form:

LABEL *volume-label*

LABEL is an external command. A volume label can be from 1 to 11 characters long and it cannot contain characters that would not be acceptable in a file name. Both floppy disks and fixed disks can be given volume labels.

You can also execute the LABEL command by itself. If you do, DOS will display the current volume label (assuming one has been assigned) and will then prompt you for a new label. You can type a new label or just press Enter to maintain the current one.

If you just want to see what the volume label is, you can use VOL, an internal DOS command, instead of LABEL.

You can also give a disk a volume label when you format it by using another of FORMAT's options. Specify the /V option, and FORMAT will automatically prompt you for a volume label after the disk has been formatted.

Examples

1. Let's give your DOS work disk a volume label. Enter the following command:

```
LABEL WORKDISK
```

Once the DOS prompt returns, execute a DIR command. Notice that the top line now reads

```
Volume in drive A is WORKDISK
```

You can change the label of a disk that is not in the currently logged-in drive by placing a drive specifier in front of the new volume name. For example, this command would change the volume label of a disk in drive B to MYDISK:

```
LABEL B:MYDISK
```

One final point: The volume label is stored on the diskette, so you cannot change the label of a write-protected diskette. Write protection prevents DOS from writing a new label to the disk.

2. It is possible to execute LABEL without actually specifying a label. Try this now, and you will see the following lines:

```
Volume in drive A is WORKDISK
Volume label (11 characters, ENTER for none)?
```

The first line tells you the current volume label and the second asks for a new one. Since there is no reason to change the present label, just press ⏎. Next, you will see this message:

```
Delete current volume label (Y/N)?
```

If you don't enter a new label, LABEL checks to see whether you want the old one deleted or simply want to leave everything as it is. Type **N** to keep the present volume label.

3. To display—but not change—the volume label, use the VOL command. To see how this works, type **VOL** and press (Enter). You will see the following message:

```
Volume in drive A is WORKDISK
```

You can display the volume label of the disk in any drive by placing a drive specifier after VOL. For example, this command would report the volume label of the fixed disk:

```
VOL C:
```

4. Let's format a new diskette and give it a volume label at the same time. To do this, issue the following command:

```
FORMAT A: /V
```

After the formatting is complete, you will see this message, which is similar to the one displayed by LABEL:

```
Volume label (11 characters, ENTER for none)?
```

Enter MYDISK. Once the DOS prompt appears, enter the VOL command and you will see that the disk does, indeed, have MYDISK as its volume label.

Exercises

1. What command would change the volume label of the current disk to ACCOUNTING?

2. Is [MYDISK] a valid volume label?

3. What is the difference between VOL and LABEL?

4. What option causes FORMAT to request a volume label?

EXERCISES

MASTERY
SKILLS CHECK

At this point, you should be able to answer these questions and perform these exercises:

1. What command displays the contents of a text file? What specific command displays the contents of the file MYTEXT?

2. What command prints the contents of MYTEXT on the printer?

3. What PRINT option cancels the printing of all files currently in the print queue?

4. What happens if you press the F3 key when the DOS prompt is displayed?

5. If the previous DOS command was COPY A:*.* B:, what sequence of keystrokes would change it into COPY A:*.* C:?

6. What commands display the system date and time?

7. What is a volume label and how does a disk get one?

8. If the current volume label were MYDISK, what command changes it to WORDPROC?

9. What command compares the contents of two files called FILE1 and FILE2?

10. What command compares a disk in drive A with a disk in drive B?

EXERCISES

This section checks to see how well you have integrated the material in this chapter with that from earlier chapters.

1. After executing this command

```
RENAME MYTEXT MORE.COM
```

you see this error message:

```
Duplicate file name or File not found
```

Explain what each part of the message means and suggest possible ways to remedy the problem.

2. What command copies all files that start with ABC and have an extension that begins with X to the disk in drive B?

3. Can you copy a volume label using the COPY command?

4. When you use DISKCOPY to copy a disk, does the volume label get copied? (Hint: experiment and see if it does.)

5. What happens if you are printing a file using PRINT and you press the [PrtSc] key? (Hint: try it and see.)

Mastering Directories

►6◄

So far, you have only used a fraction of DOS's disk directory capabilities. In this chapter, you will learn to make full use of DOS's powerful tree-structured directory system. You will also learn several new commands that relate to directories.

For this chapter, have a blank, formatted diskette on hand. You will need it to follow along with the examples and exercises.

EXERCISES

SKILLS CHECK

Before proceeding you should be able to answer these questions and perform these exercises:

1. What command displays the contents of a text file on the screen?

2. What command prints a file called FORMLET.WP on the printer?

3. What does the COMP command do? What does DISKCOMP do?

4. What happens if you press the [F1] key at the DOS prompt?

5. What does the VOL command do?

6. What command gives a disk the label MYDISK?

6.1   UNDERSTAND TREE-STRUCTURED DIRECTORIES

Until now, we have discussed directories in the singular. By default, a disk has one directory, which is the *root directory* and it is created by the formatting process. There is only one root directory per disk; however, a disk may contain several different *subdirectories*. A *subdirectory* is essentially a directory within a directory. From a logical point of view, the outer directory encloses the subdirectory. Put differently, the subdirectory is *nested* within the outer directory.

A key point about DOS's directory system is that a subdirectory can, itself, contain subdirectories. In fact, any directory can contain a subdirectory. It is important to understand that the term subdirectory describes a relationship between that directory and its *parent*. Regardless of their *parent-child* relationships, all directories have the same capabilities. The only directory that does not have a parent is the root.

In general, subdirectories hold related files. How the files relate is up to you. For example, it is very common for one subdirectory to contain all word processing files. Or, a subdirectory may hold all files—no matter how diverse—that relate to a specific person. DOS does not care what files you keep in what subdirectory. However, to make subdirectories effective tools for managing your files, the files they hold must relate to each other in some way.

When you draw a system of subdirectories on paper, it resembles the root system of a tree. Because of this resemblance, DOS's directory system is called *tree structured*. Figure 6-1 shows the tree-structured directory system of a disk used in a small office. There are three subdirectories in the root, which are used for word processing, spreadsheets, and accounting. Word processing contains two more subdirectories, used by two employees, Larry and Janet. The accounting directory contains three subdirectories: one for the general ledger, one for accounts payable, and one for accounts receivable. The spreadsheet directory contains no further subdirectories.

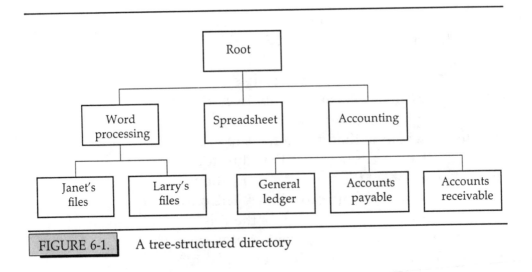

FIGURE 6-1.   A tree-structured directory

The theory behind tree-structured directories is
that related groups of files organized into subdirectories are treated as units of increasing specialization. If
directories are organized correctly, they will be more
specialized as you move from parent to child, and
more general as you move from child to parent. For
example, in Figure 6-1, there are two subdirectories
under word processing: Janet and Larry. These directories each hold files that relate to one individual;
thus, they are specialized directories. The word processing directory encloses both of them; hence, it is
more general. This directory could hold files used by
both Janet and Larry and also by other people. The
root is the most general directory of all because it
encompasses the entire disk.

A good way to understand tree-structured directories is by using the analogy of a file cabinet. The entire
file cabinet is analogous to the root directory. Each
drawer is similar to a subdirectory. Within each

drawer are folders, which are like subdirectories within a subdirectory. If you organize your disk directories along the lines of a file cabinet, you will be doing precisely the right thing.

As stated before, the term subdirectory only describes a relationship. Therefore, except in cases where the relationship is important, the term directory is used in this book to describe both subdirectories and the root directory.

To create a subdirectory, use the MD internal command, which has this general form:

MD *directory-name*

Here, *directory-name* is the name of the directory, which can be up to eight characters long. You can give a directory any name you want as long as you don't duplicate the name of another subdirectory under the same parent. Also, characters that are not acceptable in file names are not acceptable in directory names either.

DOS also lets you refer to MD as MKDIR. Use whichever form is easier for you to remember.

Directories are a little like disk drives in the sense that one directory is, by default, the focus of DOS commands. This is called the *current* directory. You can change the current directory using the CD internal command. Its simplest form is

CD *directory-name*

where *directory-name* is the name of the directory you want to make current. You can also refer to this command as CHDIR, if that is easier for you to remember.

Examples

In the examples that follow, you will create several directories. Put a blank, formatted disk into drive A and log in to that drive. You are going to create a directory structure that mirrors Figure 6-1. In the examples, we'll call the disk in drive A your *directories work disk*.

1. To create the first subdirectory, enter this command:

```
MD WP
```

Since WORD PROCESSING is too long to use as a directory name, the abbreviation WP is used. Most other directory names will be abbreviations as well.

Next, list the directory. It will contain only one entry, which will look like this (of course, the time, date, and number of free bytes will differ):

```
WP          <DIR>      11-24-89  4:00p
    1 File(s)     361472 bytes free
```

In the parent's directory, all subdirectories show <DIR> in place of the file size. Notice that DOS claims there is now one file in the root directory. This is because DOS actually stores the contents of a subdirectory in a file.

It is important to understand that the file DOS uses to store the contents of a subdirectory is not a user file. Commands like COPY, RENAME, ERASE, or TYPE cannot be applied to directories. Directories can only be accessed by DOS itself.

Now, let's create the other two subdirectories found in the root. To do so, issue these commands:

```
MD SPSHT
MD ACCTING
```

If you list the directory now, it will look like this:

```
Volume in drive A has no label
Directory of  A:\

WP          <DIR>     11-24-89    4:00p
SPSHT       <DIR>     11-24-89    4:01p
ACCTING     <DIR>     11-24-89    4:01p
        3 File(s)   359424 bytes free
```

Notice that the amount of free space diminishes each time a new subdirectory is created because some disk space is used to store the directory.

2. Issue this command next:

```
CD WP
```

Now, enter these two commands to create the JANET and LARRY subdirectories of the WP directory:

```
MD JANET
MD LARRY
```

Finally, list the directory again. It will be similar to that shown here:

```
Volume in drive A has no label
Directory of  A:\WP

.           <DIR>     11-24-89    4:00p
..          <DIR>     11-24-89    4:00p
JANET       <DIR>     11-24-89    4:04p
LARRY       <DIR>     11-24-89    4:04p
        4 File(s)   357376 bytes free
```

The JANET and LARRY directories appear as expected, but what are the . and .. directories? The . directory refers to the current subdirectory. The .. directory is the parent directory. You can use . and .. in various DOS commands. For example, this DIR command lists the contents of the root directory:

```
DIR ..
```

To list the contents of the current subdirectory, you could use this command:

```
DIR .
```

However, in actual practice you wouldn't use the previous command because DIR displays the current directory by default.

Notice the second line of the directory display.

```
Directory of  A:\WP
```

This is the name of the current directory. You can also see the name of the current directory by entering CD without specifying a directory. Try this now, and you will see the following output:

```
A:\WP
```

4. Enter this command now:

```
CD ..
```

This command makes the root directory current. As you learned in the previous example, the .. is DOS's way of referring to the parent directory, which in this case is the root. Next, enter this command so you can create the subdirectories in the ACCTING directory:

```
CD ACCTING
```

Now, issue these three commands:

```
MD GL
MD AR
MD AP
```

If you list the directory at this point, it will look similar to this:

```
Volume in drive A has no label
Directory of  A:\ACCTING

.           <DIR>      11-24-89       4:01p
..          <DIR>      11-24-89       4:01p
GL          <DIR>      11-24-89       4:05p
AR          <DIR>      11-24-89       4:05p
AP          <DIR>      11-24-89       4:05p
        5 File(s)    354304 bytes free
```

Return to the root directory by issuing this command:

```
CD ..
```

Exercises

1. If you have not done so, create a diskette as described in the previous examples. You will need it for subsequent sections.

2. What is the difference between a parent directory and its subdirectory?

3. How does the root directory differ from other directories?

4. What command creates a subdirectory? What command changes the current directory?

5. What command displays the current directory name?

6.2 | UNDERSTAND PATH NAMES

Before you learn more about using directories, you need to know about path names. In essence, a *path name* describes the route to a directory. For example, the path from the root directory to the AR subdirectory in ACCTING is root to ACCTING to AR. In DOS, this path would be represented as shown here:

```
\ACCTING\AR
```

The first backslash is DOS's symbol for the root directory. The second backslash is used as a separator. In general, use a backslash to separate subdirectories from each other in a path name.

You can use a path name with most DOS commands. For example, this command lists the contents of the JANET directory, which is in the WP directory:

```
DIR \WP\JANET
```

To switch to the JANET directory, you would use this command:

```
CD \WP\JANET
```

You can precede a path name with a drive specifier. For example, this command would display the directory of LARRY, if the directories disk were in drive B:

```
DIR B:\WP\LARRY
```

You can precede a file name with a path name. For example, this command copies a file called OLDFILE from drive B to the JANET directory and names the copy NEWFILE:

```
COPY B:OLDFILE   \WP\JANET\NEWFILE
```

Notice that the backslash separates the file name from the path name. When you use a path with a file name, the file name must always come last. In general, whenever you can use a file name, you can precede that file name with a path name.

Actually, file names and path names are not really separate entities—although it is helpful to think of them as separate for the sake of discussion. Every file name has an associated path name that describes the path to the directory where the file can be found. However, you don't always have to specify the full path name because DOS automatically prefixes the path to the current directory onto a file name when you don't supply a path.

Let's define two terms. A *full*, or *complete*, *path name* explicitly specifies the entire path beginning at the root. A *partial path name* assumes the path to the current directory and only specifies the remainder of the path.

As you know, assuming disk space is available, any directory can have a subdirectory. However, the longest path name DOS will accept is 63 characters, including any file name that may be specified.

Before you begin the examples for this section, a short digression is in order. Although you won't learn how to customize DOS until later in this book, there is one very useful customization that relates to directo-

ries and will make it much easier for you to manage
them. To see how this feature works, issue the following command:

```
PROMPT $P$G
```

This command causes the DOS prompt to display the
path to the current directory. For example, if the
current directory is JANET, the prompt will now look
like this:

```
A:\WP\JANET>
```

The advantage of this customization is that you
always know what directory you are using. Keep in
mind that you need to issue this command each time
you start DOS.

Examples

1. To begin, make the LARRY directory current by
   issuing this command:

   ```
   CD \WP\LARRY
   ```

   To move from LARRY to WP means, in this case,
   moving from the child to the parent. To do this, you
   can use either of these commands:

   ```
   CD ..
   CD \WP
   ```

   As you know, the .. refers to the parent of any
   subdirectory, so CD .. makes WP the current directory. The command CD \WP also works because it
   specifies the complete path to the WP directory.
   Execute one of these commands now.

At this point, you could use the following command to move to the JANET directory:

```
CD \WP\JANET
```

However, there is an easier way to move from the WP directory to the JANET directory. As stated previously, when you supply a partial path name DOS automatically adds the current directory's path name to the start of the specified path. Therefore, to move from WP to JANET you can also use this command:

```
CD JANET
```

This partial path relies on the fact that DOS automatically adds the \WP\ for you. Execute this command now.

It is important to understand that

```
CD JANET
```

is *not* the same as

```
CD \JANET
```

The path \JANET tells DOS that JANET is an immediate subdirectory of the root because the leading \ is DOS's name for the root. However, in fact, JANET is *not* a direct subdirectory of the root, so DOS will not find the JANET directory. Specifying the partial path JANET causes DOS to automatically prefix JANET with the current path name, \WP\. Now, DOS can find the JANET directory.

2. You can move to the root directory from any other directory by issuing this command:

```
CD \
```

Since \ is the name DOS gives the root directory, this command makes the root current. Try this command now.

3. At this time, move to the LARRY directory. (Use CD \WP\LARRY.) Now, create a text file using this command:

```
COPY CON: MYFILE
```

Next, enter this fragment of the First Amendment to the U.S. Constitution:

```
Congress shall make no law respecting an establishment
of religion, or prohibiting the free exercise thereof;
or abridging the freedom of speech. . .
```

After entering the three periods, press (Enter). Then press (Ctrl)-(Z) followed by (Enter).

If you list the directory at this point, you will see output similar to this:

```
Volume in drive A has no label
Directory of  A:\WP\LARRY

.            <DIR>       11-24-89    4:04p
..           <DIR>       11-24-89    4:04p
MYFILE              151  11-25-89    7:22a
    3  File(s)        353280 bytes free
```

To display MYFILE on the screen, use this command:

```
TYPE MYFILE
```

Since the current default path is \WP\LARRY, there is no need to specify the entire path name, although it is not wrong to do so. This command would achieve the same result as the previous one:

```
TYPE \WP\LARRY\MYFILE
```

The key point is that most DOS commands operate relative to the current disk and directory by default. Therefore, when you access a file that is in the current directory, there is no need to specify the complete path to that file.

4. At this time, return to the root directory (use CD \). Now, if you wish to display the contents of MYFILE in the LARRY directory, you need to specify the complete path to that file using this command:

```
TYPE \WP\LARRY\MYFILE
```

Because the root directory rather than the LARRY directory is now active, you must specify the full path to the file.

The same TYPE command displays the contents of MYFILE no matter what directory you are in. For example, switch to the AR directory using this command:

```
CD \ACCTING\AR
```

Now, execute the previous TYPE command. Because the path to MYFILE is fully specified, DOS finds it and displays its contents.

Next, move to the WP directory using this command:

```
CD \WP
```

Now, display MYFILE by issuing this command:

```
TYPE LARRY\MYFILE
```

Because \WP\ is the default path, DOS automatically adds that prefix to the partial path specified in this command. Thus, DOS finds MYFILE and displays it on the screen.

5. You can copy a file from one directory to another using the COPY command. For example, use this command to copy MYFILE into the AR directory.

```
COPY \WP\LARRY\MYFILE \ACCTING\AR
```

You may be wondering why this command works and does not produce a "Duplicate file" error message, because now the disk contains two files named MYFILE. Although DOS cannot have two files with the same name in the same directory, two files can share the same name if they reside in different directories. The automatic prefix of the path name to the file name effectively gives the files different names. For example, in this particular case the full path name of the original file is \WP\LARRY\MYFILE, while the copy's full name is \ACCTING\AR\MYFILE.

Exercises

1. If you have not done so, perform the previous examples at this time.

2. In general, what is a path name and what function does it perform?

3. Given the directory structure of the directories work disk that you created in the previous section,

and assuming that the root is the current directory, what command would copy MYFILE from AR into the SPSHT directory?

4. What command would display the contents of MYFILE in the AR directory, no matter what directory was current?

5. What command causes a parent directory to become current?

6. What command causes the root directory to become current?

LEARN TO DISPLAY THE DIRECTORY STRUCTURE   6.3

As you begin using DOS in your day-to-day work, you may find that the directory structure of your work disks becomes fairly complex, especially if you use a fixed disk, which can easily hold over a hundred directories. When this happens, it can be difficult to remember in what directory a specific file is "hiding." To help solve this problem, DOS supplies the TREE command, which displays the directory structure of a disk. TREE is an external command. It has this general form:

TREE *drive-specifier*

The *drive-specifier* determines which drive is used. Of course, you don't need to use a drive specifier if the default disk is the one you want.

By default, TREE displays only the directory names. However, if you specify the /F option, the files in each directory are also displayed.

DOS provides a second way for you to display the structure of a disk's directory system by using a special option with the CHKDSK command. When you specify the /V option, CHKDSK displays a disk's directory structure along with a list of the files in each directory.

Before you can use TREE or CHKDSK to display the directory structure of the directories disk, you must copy TREE.COM and CHKDSK.COM to your directories work disk. If you have two diskette drives, put your DOS work disk in drive B. If you have only one diskette drive, have your DOS work disk ready because you will be prompted to swap diskettes. On drive A, make sure that the root directory is active. (To move to the root from any directory, execute CD \.) Also, drive A should be the active drive. Now, execute these commands:

```
COPY B:CHKDSK.COM
COPY B:TREE.COM
```

Examples

1. Execute the TREE command now. (Type **TREE** and press (Enter).) Output similar to that in Figure 6-2 will show the tree-structured directories on your directories work disk. The directory information will scroll off the screen, so use (Ctrl)-(S) or Pause if you want to examine the output.

    Execute TREE a second time, using the /F option. As you can see, the file names are now displayed.

2. A second way to display the directory structure of a disk is by using the /V option of CHKDSK. Try this command now:

```
CHKDSK /V
```

You will see output similar to that shown in Figure 6-3. Notice that both the directory names and the file names are displayed.

One advantage of using CHKDSK to display the directory structure of a disk is that its output is more compact than that produced by TREE.

```
        DIRECTORY PATH LISTING

        Path: \WP
        Sub-directories:    JANET
                            LARRY

        Path: \WP\JANET
        Sub-directories:    None

        Path: \WP\LARRY
        Sub-directories:    None

        Path: \SPSHT
        Sub-directories:    None

        Path: \ACCTING
        Sub-directories:    GL
                            AR
                            AP

        Path: \ACCTING\GL
        Sub-directories:    None

        Path: \ACCTING\AR
        Sub-directories:    None

        Path: \ACCTING\AP
        Sub-directories:    None
```

FIGURE 6-2.   Output from the TREE command

```
Directory A:\
Directory A:\WP
Directory A:\WP\JANET
Directory A:\WP\LARRY
        A:\WP\LARRY\MYFILE
Directory A:\SPSHT
Directory A:\ACCTING
Directory A:\ACCTING\GL
Directory A:\ACCTING\AR
        A:\ACCTING\AR\MYFILE
Directory A:\ACCTING\AP
        A:\CHKDSK.COM
        A:\TREE.COM

   362496 bytes total disk space
     8192 bytes in 8 directories
    16384 bytes in 4 user files
   337920 bytes available on disk

   654336 bytes total memory
   601184 bytes free
```

| FIGURE 6-3. | Output from CHKDSK using the /V option. |

Exercises

1. If you have not done so, try the previous examples.

2. What command would display the directory structure of the fixed disk?

6.4 UNDERSTAND MORE ABOUT PATHS

This section further explores paths and subdirectories. Make sure that your directories work disk is in drive A and that drive A is current.

To copy a file from a subdirectory to the root directory, use this form of the COPY command:

COPY *file-name* \

Since the backslash is DOS's name for the root directory, this command causes a file to be copied to the root from any other directory.

    If you want to change the target file's name when copying to the root, use this form of the COPY command:

COPY *file-name* *new-name*

To copy a file from the root while in a subdirectory, use this general form of COPY:

COPY *file-name*

You can execute a program that resides in one directory from another directory by specifying the full path name to the program. For example, if you have a program called MYPROG.EXE in the AR directory, and the SPSHT directory is current, this command will execute MYPROG.COM.

```
\ACCTING\AR\MYPROG
```

The number of directories a disk can hold is limited only by the amount of space on the disk, and except for the root, a directory can hold as many files as available disk space will allow. However, if you have more than a hundred or so files in a directory, you should think about creating a subdirectory to hold some of them, because directories that contain a large number of files may be difficult to manage effectively.

    The number of files the root directory can hold is fixed and varies with the storage capacity of a disk-

TABLE 6-1.	Directory Capacity of Various Diskettes

Diskette capacity (in bytes)	Maximum files in root directory
180K	64
360K	112
720K	112
1200K	224
1440K	224

ette. Table 6-1 shows the most common sizes. The root directory of a fixed disk can hold 512 entries.

One important point to remember about subdirectories is that they exist largely to provide a means of organizing the files on a disk. In general, you should store related files in their own subdirectory. As stated at the start of this chapter, files can be related in different ways. Therefore, the way a computer is used (and how many people use it) will largely dictate how you organize your directories. Also, keep in mind that directories use disk space, so you should not create an unnecessarily large number of subdirectories. Further, subdirectories that are deeply nested have long path names, which slow DOS's access to the files they contain.

Examples

1. Move to the LARRY directory and execute this command:

```
COPY \TREE.COM
```

This copies the TREE command into the LARRY directory. Now, execute TREE. Notice that even when TREE is executed from a subdirectory, it still displays the structure of the entire disk.

2. From the LARRY directory, you can execute CHKDSK in the root using this command:

```
\CHKDSK
```

Go ahead and try this command now.

3. Switch to the SPSHT directory. (You can do this using CD\SPSHT.) Now, execute TREE in the LARRY directory using this command:

```
\WP\LARRY\TREE
```

Exercises

1. What command would copy MYFILE from \WP\LARRY to \ACCTING\GL?

2. Assume that CHKDSK.COM is in the SPSHT directory and some other directory is current. What command will execute CHKDSK?

3. How many files can a subdirectory hold?

LEARN TO REMOVE A DIRECTORY

6.5

From time to time, you may find that you no longer need a directory. Since directories use disk space, when a directory is no longer being used, it is a good idea to delete it. To remove a directory, use the RD internal command. It has this general form:

RD *directory-pathname*

Here, *directory-pathname* must specify the path to the directory that you want to remove. RD can also be specified as RMDIR, if this is easier to remember.

Three restrictions apply to removing a directory. First, the directory must not contain any files or subdirectories (except the . and .. directories). When you list the contents of the directory only the . and .. entries should be present. Second, you cannot remove the current directory. Finally, you cannot under any circumstances delete the root directory.

Examples

1. At this time, move to the \ACCTING\AP directory. If you have been following the examples carefully, this directory contains no files. Use the DIR command to check that the directory is empty. If it does contain any files, erase them now. Next, move to AP's parent directory and issue this command:

   ```
   RD \ACCTING\AP
   ```

   Now, list the directory of ACCTING and you will see that the AP directory is no longer shown. Re-create the AP directory at this time.

The ACCTING directory should still be current. If it is not, make it current now. Since DOS automatically adds the path to the current directory onto any path specified, and since ACCTING is the current directory, you can actually use this shorter form of RD to remove the AP directory:

```
RD AP
```

DOS will automatically supply the \ACCTING\ prefix. Once again, re-create AP before you go on.

Now, move to the root directory and try this command:

```
RD \AP
```

This command tells DOS to remove a directory called AP that is an immediate subdirectory of the root. However, AP is actually a subdirectory of ACCTING, so this command will fail and will cause the following error message to appear:

```
Invalid path, not directory,
or directory not empty
```

To remove the \AP directory from the root, you must specify its full path using this command:

```
RD \ACCTING\AP
```

This command deletes the AP directory. It *does not* remove the ACCTING directory. The RD command removes only the *last* directory of the specified path.

2. Move to the WP directory and try removing the LARRY directory using this command:

```
RD LARRY
```

Because LARRY contains the files MYFILE and TREE.COM, DOS cannot remove the directory, and it displays the same error message you saw in the previous example.

3. Go back to \ACCTING\AP and try this command:

```
RD AP
```

Because AP is the current directory, this command will fail. You cannot remove the current directory.

Exercises

1. What two conditions prevent a subdirectory from being deleted?

2. What command would remove the AR subdirectory of ACCTING assuming the current directory is \WP\JANET?

3. Assume that the AP, AR, and GL subdirectories of ACCTING are all empty. What command sequence would be necessary to remove the ACCTING directory from the disk? (Hint: ACCTING must be empty to be removed.)

EXERCISES

MASTERY
SKILLS CHECK

At this point, you should be able to answer these questions and perform these exercises:

NOTE: These exercises assume the directory structure of your directories disk.

1. What is a subdirectory?

2. DOS directories are tree structured. Explain what this means.

3. What command creates a subdirectory called MYDIR?

4. What command changes the current directory?

5. If a program called COMP.COM is in the \WP directory, what command executes this program when the \SPSHT directory is current?

6. What command copies MYFILE from the \WP\LARRY directory into \ACCTING\GL?

7. Assuming SPSHT is empty, what command removes it?

8. Show two commands that display the directory structure of a disk.

EXERCISES

This section checks how well you have integrated the material in this chapter with material from earlier chapters.

INTEGRATING SKILLS CHECK

1. Assuming the root directory of your directories work disk is current, what command displays the contents of MYFILE in the \WP\LARRY directory?

2. What command compares MYFILE in \WP\JANET with MYFILE in \ACCTING\AR?

3. Although you cannot have two files with the same name in the same directory, explain why two files can have the same name as long as they are in different directories.

4. Like most DOS commands, ERASE accepts full path names. What ERASE command removes MYFILE from the LARRY directory?

5. On your own, try using path names with other DOS commands that you know.

Master Batch Commands

▶7◀

As fast as your computer is, it will still take a fair amount of time to complete some tasks. In fact, some tasks take so long that you will want to give DOS a list of commands and then let the computer run unattended while you do other things. For example, you might want to run a payroll program, followed by a monthly general ledger, followed by an invoicing program, without having to wait around to start each task as the previous one finishes. Also, you might need to execute a particular sequence of commands repeatedly and want to avoid typing the same command sequence over and over again. The solution to both of these problems is the topic of this chapter: Here, you will learn how to give DOS lists of commands.

In this chapter you will create several text files. To do this you will need to use a word processor or text editor. If you have one of these programs and know how to use it, go ahead with this chapter. If you have a word processor but don't know how to use it, take a little time to learn about it now. If you don't have your own word processor, you will have to use EDLIN, DOS's text editor, which is described in Appendix A. After you've learned how to use EDLIN, continue with this chapter.

Be sure your DOS work disk is in drive A; or, if you have a fixed disk, you can use drive C.

EXERCISES

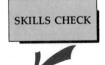

SKILLS CHECK

Before proceeding you should be able to answer these questions and perform these exercises:

1. What is a path name?

2. Assuming the directory structure of your directories work disk, how would you make the GL directory current?

3. What command do you use to create a subdirectory?

4. What command do you use to remove a subdirectory? Do any restrictions apply to deleting a directory?

5. What command would make the \WP\JANET directory current?

6. How long can a path name be?

UNDERSTAND BATCH FILES

7.1

DOS allows you to create a list of commands using a batch file. A *batch file* is simply a text file that contains one or more DOS commands and/or the names of your application programs. All batch files use the extension .BAT. Once you have created a batch file, you can have DOS execute the commands listed in the file by specifying the name of the batch file at the DOS prompt.

In essence, a batch file is a custom DOS command that you create. In fact, batch files are sometimes called *batch commands*. Thus, batch files allow you to enhance and extend the capabilities of DOS.

When you execute a batch command, DOS finds that command on disk, reads the list of commands it contains, and performs them one after another in the order in which they appear in the file. After the last command is executed, DOS is ready to accept another command from you.

You must be careful not to give any batch file a filename that duplicates that of any DOS command or application program. The reason is that when you enter a command at the DOS prompt, DOS first checks to see if it is an internal DOS command. If it isn't, DOS then checks files with the .EXE and .COM extensions to see if your entry is an external DOS command or an application program. (Remember, external DOS commands and application program files use the .EXE or .COM extension.) Only if none of these match the name you entered at the DOS prompt does DOS check all files using the .BAT extension. Therefore, if you called a batch file COMP.BAT, for example, that batch file would never be executed, because DOS would find COMP.COM first.

Examples

1. For a simple first example, create a file called MYBAT.BAT that contains these two commands:

```
CLS
VER
```

   Next, execute this batch file by entering **MYBAT** at the DOS prompt. As you can see, the screen is cleared and the DOS version number is displayed. Keep in mind that a batch file is executed one command at a time starting at the top and working toward the bottom.

2. For a second example, change MYBAT.BAT so that it contains these commands:

```
DIR
VER
```

   Execute this file now. As you can see, first the directory is listed and then the DOS version is displayed.

3. You can cancel the execution of a batch command by pressing either [Ctrl]-[C] or [Ctrl]-[Break]. Try this now by executing MYBAT again and canceling the

command before the DIR command finishes. You will see the following prompt:

```
Terminate batch job (Y/N)?
```

Whenever you cancel a batch command, DOS displays this prompt. The reason for this double check is that by pressing Ctrl-C or Ctrl-Break, you actually cancel only the command that is currently executing (in this case, DIR), so DOS does not know whether you want to cancel that single command or the entire batch file. If you type **Y** in response to the prompt, the entire batch file is terminated. If you type **N**, the command that was executing when you pressed Ctrl-C or Ctrl-Break is terminated, but any commands left in the batch file are executed.

At this time, type **Y**. As you can see, the entire batch file is canceled and the VER command is not executed. Execute MYBAT a second time, again canceling the DIR command. This time type **N** when the prompt appears. Now the DIR command is canceled, but the VER command is still executed.

4. One very common use for batch files is to back up important files. For example, a disk might contain several data files that share the .DAT extension, some text files that use the .TXT extension, and a mailing list file called MLIST.INF. By putting these commands into a batch file called BKUP.BAT, you only need to execute BKUP to copy all these files. The batch file would look like this:

```
COPY *.DAT B:
COPY *.TXT B:
COPY MLIST.INF B:
```

Exercises

1. What extension must a batch file have?

2. Create a batch file that checks the current disk, shows the current directory structure using the TREE command, and then copies all files that begin with an R to drive B.

3. Create a batch file that will copy the files ACCOUNTS.DAT, PAYROLL.INF, and FORMLET .TXT to drive A.

7.2   MASTER BATCH FILE PARAMETERS

Very often you will find that two batch files differ only slightly from each other. For example, here are two similar batch files:

File 1	File 2
COPY *.TXT B:	COPY *.TXT A:
COPY *.DAT B:	COPY *.DAT A:
COPY *.EXE B:	COPY *.EXE A:

As you can see, the only difference between the two files is that the first batch file copies the files to drive B while the second one copies the same files to drive A. In cases like this it seems there should be some way to combine these two files—and indeed, there is. In this section you will learn to create batch commands that can accept command line arguments.

A *command line argument* is information that is specified on the DOS command line after the name of a DOS command, program, or batch file. You have been using command line arguments since Chapter 1. For example, this COPY command has two arguments:

```
COPY MYFILE YOURFILE
```

Here, the two arguments are MYFILE and YOURFILE.

A batch file accesses command line arguments using special *replaceable parameters* (sometimes called *dummy parameters*), which receive the value of each argument. These parameters are called %0 through %9. The %0 parameter always contains the name of the batch file and is of little interest in most cases. The remaining nine parameters receive the command line arguments. Specifically, the %1 parameter is replaced by the first command line argument, %2 is replaced by the second argument, and so on.

In DOS, command line arguments must be separated by spaces, tabs, commas, or semicolons. For example, to DOS this is one argument, not four:

```
this-is-a-test
```

Examples

1. For a first example of a batch file that takes a command line argument, modify MYBAT.BAT so that it contains these commands:

```
DIR %1
CHKDSK %1
TREE %1
```

Now, try this command:

```
MYBAT A:
```

This command causes DOS to substitute A: for the %1 parameter. This means that MYBAT executes as if it contained these commands:

```
DIR A:
CHKDSK A:
TREE A:
```

Now, try this command (use C: in place of B: if you have a fixed disk and only one diskette drive):

```
MYBAT B:
```

Now, DOS substitutes B: for the %1 parameter.

2. The two slightly different batch files discussed earlier can be combined into one batch command by adding parameters as shown here:

```
COPY *.TXT %1
COPY *.DAT %1
COPY *.EXE %1
```

3. Here is a batch file that is useful when you are copying very important files:

```
COPY %1 %2
COMP %1 %2
```

This batch file automatically copies the file specified as the first parameter to the second parameter and then compares the files to verify that an accurate copy has been made. For example, if the previous batch file were called VCOPY.BAT, the following command would copy MYFILE to MYFILE.BAK and then compare the two files.

```
VCOPY MYFILE MYFILE.BAK
```

Here, %1 would contain MYFILE and %2 would contain MYFILE.BAK.

Exercises

1. What are the batch file parameters called?

2. What does %0 contain?

3. Show the contents of a batch file that displays a specified text file on the screen and then prints it on the printer.

4. Show how these two batch files could be combined:

File 1
```
DIR A:
DISKCOPY A: B:
DISKCOMP A: B:
DIR B:
```

File 2
```
DIR B:
DISKCOPY B: A:
DISKCOMP B: A:
DIR A:
```

MASTER SOME SPECIAL BATCH FILE COMMANDS

7.3

DOS supports several batch file commands that increase the power and scope of batch files. In fact, if you use these commands, your batch files will be somewhat similar to programs. The special batch file commands are shown in Table 7-1. In this section we examine ECHO, REM, PAUSE, and GOTO. The remaining commands are examined in later sections.

The ECHO command has two uses. First, you can use it to display a message on the screen. To do so, use this general form:

ECHO *message*

| TABLE 7-1. | The Special Batch File Commands |

Command	Synopsis
CALL	Executes another batch file
ECHO	Displays a message on the screen and can also be used to prevent screen output
FOR	Allows a command sequence to be repeated
GOTO	Causes execution of a batch file to jump to a specified place in the file
IF	Allows conditional execution of a command
PAUSE	Temporarily stops execution of a batch file
REM	Allows a remark to be embedded in a batch file
SHIFT	Enables more than nine command line arguments to be used

The second way you can use ECHO is to control whether the commands that comprise the batch file are displayed as they execute. You may have noticed in the previous section that when each command of a batch file is executed, its name is shown on a prompt line as if you had typed it. You can prevent each command from being displayed by using this form of the ECHO command:

ECHO OFF

To cause commands to be displayed once again, use

ECHO ON

There is a second way to keep a command from being displayed on the screen: You can precede the command with an at (@) sign. The @ command affects only the line it is on.

You can embed a comment inside a batch file using REM, which has this basic form:

REM *comment*

REM lines are skipped when the batch file is executed, so DOS ignores whatever comes after the REM command on the same line. A comment can be up to 123 characters long. Comments have several uses. For example, a comment can be used to identify the author of a batch file. Comments can also explain how to operate the file. You should include comments in complex batch files to remind yourself how the file operates.

The PAUSE command temporarily halts the execution of a batch file, prints this message,

```
Strike a key when ready . . .
```

and waits for a keypress. If you press Ctrl-C or Ctrl-Break, you terminate the batch file. If you press any other key, execution resumes.

If you like, you can specify a prompting message after the PAUSE command. However, this message will only show if ECHO is on because it is not actually output by PAUSE itself.

The GOTO command allows execution to occur in a way other than the strict top-down flow that the previous examples have shown. The GOTO command requires a label. Its general form is

GOTO *label*

.

.

.

:label

In DOS, a label begins with a colon. However, the label that follows the GOTO command does not need to be preceded by a colon, although using the colon causes no harm. All commands that lie between the GOTO and its target label are bypassed. Furthermore, GOTO can be used to jump forward or backward in the file.

A label can be up to 123 characters long, but only the first 8 characters are significant. This means, for example, that as far as DOS is concerned, these two labels are the same:

```
:ThisLabel
:ThisLabelIsTheSameToDOS
```

Note that you cannot use a period as part of a label.

Examples

1. Modify MYBAT.BAT so that it contains the following commands:

```
ECHO This will be printed
ECHO OFF
ECHO This will be printed too,
ECHO but ECHO will not.
VER
```

Execute this file now. You will see the following output:

```
A>mybat

A>ECHO This will be printed
This will be printed

A>ECHO OFF
This will be printed too,
but ECHO will not.

IBM Personal Computer DOS version 3.30
```

As you can see, after the ECHO OFF command is executed, DOS does not display command names.

One important point: You don't have to turn ECHO on after a batch file terminates; DOS does this automatically.

2. You can output any character using ECHO. However, if the message contains any character that cannot be used as part of a file name, that character must be surrounded by double quotes. For example, this command prints a greater than sign (>):

```
ECHO This prints a ">"
```

Unfortunately, DOS displays the quotation marks when it displays this message. However, not enclosing the > between double quotes would cause an error.

3. Here is a batch file that uses the PAUSE command to let you insert a diskette into drive B before the TREE command is executed:

```
PAUSE Insert diskette into drive B
TREE B:
```

Another handy batch file that uses PAUSE is shown here:

```
ECHO OFF
ECHO Erasing %1. Are you sure? (Ctrl-C to cancel)
PAUSE
ERASE %1
```

This batch file gives you a chance to change your mind about erasing a file. For example, if you called the previous batch file ER.BAT, you could use the following command to erase MYFILE:

```
ER MYFILE
```

As a result, you would see this output on the screen:

```
A>ER MYFILE

A>ECHO OFF
Erasing MYFILE. Are you sure? (Ctrl-C to cancel)
Strike a key when ready . . .
```

If you then pressed [Ctrl]-[C] (or [Ctrl]-[Break]), the file would not be erased, but pressing any other key would erase the file. A batch file like this can be very useful to someone who is just beginning to learn DOS, because it helps prevent accidental erasures.

4. In this version of ER.BAT, the @ is used to prevent the commands from being displayed:

```
@ECHO Erasing %1. Are you sure? (Ctrl-C to cancel)
@PAUSE
@ERASE %1
```

5. In the next version of ER.BAT, comments are added.

```
ECHO OFF
REM This batch file provides a double check
REM before a file is erased.
REM Usage:
REM          ER filename
REM
```

```
REM Written by: Herbert Schildt
REM
ECHO Erasing %1. Are you sure? (Ctrl-C to cancel)
PAUSE
ERASE %1
```

In this example, the comments explain what the batch file does, how to invoke it, and who wrote it. If your computer is used by several coworkers, it is a good idea to include comments similar to those just shown with every batch file you write.

6. Here is a simple example that uses GOTO:

```
GOTO AROUND
ECHO This will not be executed.
:AROUND
ECHO This will be displayed.
```

Be careful when you use GOTO because it is easy to create an *infinite loop*. For example, consider this batch file:

```
:MYLABEL
ECHO This will print over and over again
ECHO until you press Ctrl-C or Ctrl-Break
GOTO MYLABEL
```

In this case, GOTO causes the ECHO commands to be repeated until you terminate the batch file by pressing Ctrl - C or Ctrl - Break.

You will see how useful GOTO can be in the next sections.

Exercises

1. What command prevents commands from being displayed when a batch file executes?

2. What does the PAUSE command do?

3. What command outputs this message: "Backing up files"?

4. How do you embed a comment in a batch file?

5. Write a batch file that repeatedly checks the disk and, at the start of each pass through the loop, asks users if they want to stop by pressing [Ctrl]-[C] or [Ctrl]-[Break]. (Hint: Use GOTO.)

6. What effect does the @ have in a batch file?

7.4 LEARN ABOUT THE IF COMMAND

In this section you will learn how to use the IF batch file command.

Sometimes, you will want a command in a batch file to be executed only if some condition is true. For example, you may not want a copy operation to proceed if the target disk already contains files with the same names as those that are about to be copied. To allow conditional execution of a command, DOS provides the IF command. It has this general form:

IF *condition command*

If the *condition* is true, then the *command* will be executed. If the *condition* is false, then the *command* will be skipped and execution will pick up at the next line.

The IF command can evaluate three types of conditions: It can check for the existence of a file; it can compare two strings for equality (a *string* is simply a group of characters); and finally, it can check to see if the previous program executed normally.

To check for the existence of a file, use this form of the IF command:

IF EXIST *file-name command*

The *file-name* may include a drive specifier and path name. You may also include wildcard characters in the file name.

To compare two strings for equality, use this form of the IF command:

IF *string1* = = *string2 command*

In this situation, DOS differentiates between upper- and lowercase letters. For example, it recognizes the string "Hello" as different from "HELLO". Note that neither of the strings being compared may contain spaces.

When a program finishes execution, it can set an internal DOS variable that indicates whether the program terminated normally or because of an error. For the sake of this discussion, let's call this the *error variable*. If a program terminates normally, the error variable is set to zero. If the program terminates abnormally, the error variable is set to something other than zero. Although knowing the exact value of the error variable may be useful to programmers, generally you will only need to know whether it is zero or nonzero.

You can test the value of the error variable by using this form of the IF command:

IF ERRORLEVEL *n command*

where *n* is a number greater than or equal to zero. If the value of the error variable is greater than or equal to *n*, this form of the IF will be true and the command will be executed. Otherwise, the condition will be false and execution of the batch file will resume on the following line.

All three types of conditions may be preceded by a NOT, which effectively reverses true and false. For example, this statement is true when MYFILE does not exist on drive B:

```
IF NOT EXIST B:MYFILE ECHO File not found
```

Examples

1. To see a simple example of the EXIST condition, try this batch file:

```
IF EXIST SORT.EXE ECHO SORT.EXE is on the disk
```

Assuming this batch file is on your DOS work disk, DOS will display the message "SORT.EXE is on the disk".

Remember, you can use wildcard characters in the file name. For example, this IF command simply checks to see whether any .EXE files are on the disk.

```
IF EXIST *.EXE ECHO .EXE files on disk
```

2. Sometimes, you will want to be sure a file is not copied from one disk to another if the target disk already contains the same file. You can accomplish this by using this batch file:

```
ECHO OFF
IF EXIST %2%1 ECHO File already on target disk
IF NOT EXIST %2%1 COPY %1 %2
```

To use this batch file, specify the name of the file you want to copy as the first command line argument and the target drive specifier as the second. For example, assuming the batch file is called CHKCOPY.BAT, to copy MYFILE from the current drive to drive B, you would use this command:

```
CHKCOPY MYFILE B:
```

After substituting the arguments, the batch command would look like this:

```
ECHO OFF
IF EXIST B:MYFILE ECHO File already on target disk
IF NOT EXIST B:MYFILE COPY MYFILE B:
```

3. You can create many useful batch files using the IF string comparison. For example, if you were going out of town on business, you might create a file like this to leave instructions for your assistant:

```
ECHO OFF
IF %1 == MON ECHO Confirm meeting with Jack
IF %1 == TUE ECHO Request Inventory report
IF %1 == WED ECHO Run General Ledger
IF %1 == THU ECHO Run payroll, write checks
IF %1 == FRI ECHO Back up all files
```

Assuming you named this file DAY.BAT, your assistant need only enter the day of the week each morning. On Tuesday your assistant would enter

```
DAY TUE
```

to receive Tuesday's instructions. Since one and only one IF statement will be true each day, this file will provide instructions for the entire week.

4. Another very good use for an IF string comparison is to provide a generalized backup batch command. Assume that a computer is used by four people, each with a separate subdirectory. For example, imagine that Mary does financial forecasting, Ralph does accounting, Ted does word processing, and Sherry handles insurance claims. This single batch file would allow all four coworkers to back up their files:

```
ECHO OFF
IF %1 == MARY   COPY  \MARY\*.*  B:
IF %1 == RALPH  COPY  \RALPH\*.*  B:
IF %1 == TED  COPY  \TED\*.*  B:
IF %1 == SHERRY  COPY  \SHERRY\*.*  B:
```

Assume this file is called BKUP.BAT. To back up his or her files, each person could simply specify his or her name as an argument. For example, this command would back up Sherry's files:

```
BKUP SHERRY
```

5. You can check to see whether the previous program terminated normally by using this command:

```
IF ERRORLEVEL 1 ECHO Abnormal Program Termination
```

Remember, the condition will be true if the error variable is one or greater. Since zero indicates normal program termination, the message will only be displayed if the previous program terminated because of an error.

If you have two diskette drives, you can see how ERRORLEVEL works in actual practice by using this batch file:

```
CHKDSK B:
IF ERRORLEVEL 1 ECHO Abnormal Program Termination
```

Before you execute this batch file, open drive B's door. Now, execute the file. After a while, you will see this message:

```
Not ready error reading drive B
Abort, Retry, Fail?
```

When this prompt appears, type **F** for Fail. This response causes the error variable to be set to something other than zero, indicating abnormal termination of the CHKDSK command. This, in turn, causes the IF statement to be true and the message "Abnormal Program Termination" appears on the screen.

6. You can create blocks of commands that are conditionally executed by using the GOTO statement. For example, this file lets you either print a file on the printer or display it on the screen:

```
ECHO OFF
IF NOT %1 == PRINT GOTO NEXT
  REM This prints a file on the printer
  ECHO Make sure printer is on
  ECHO and has paper in it.
  PAUSE
  PRINT %2
:NEXT
IF NOT %1 == TYPE GOTO DONE
  REM This displays the file on the screen
  TYPE %2
:DONE
```

Call this file SHOWFILE.BAT. You can execute it using either of these two forms:

SHOWFILE   TYPE   *file-name*
SHOWFILE   PRINT   *file-name*

If you elect to print the file, DOS prompts you to turn on the printer and make sure it contains paper. Otherwise, DOS displays the file on the screen.

Exercises

1. What IF command checks for the existence of SORT.EXE on drive A and then, if it exists, copies it to drive B?

2. How are two strings compared using the IF command?

3. What IF command reports whether the previously run program set the error variable to a value of three or greater?

7.5   MASTER MORE BATCH FILE COMMANDS

In this section, you will learn about the three remaining batch file commands: FOR, SHIFT, and CALL.

The FOR command allows commands to be automatically executed. Its general form is

FOR %%*var* IN (*argument list*) DO *command*

Here, *var* is a single letter. The *argument list* contains a list of values that will be given to *%%var*. The arguments must be separated by spaces, tabs, or commas. The FOR repeats the *command* as many times as there are arguments in the *argument list*. The FOR assigns *%%var* values from the *argument list* moving from left to right.

As you learned earlier in this chapter, there are only 10 command line parameters: %0 through %9. It is possible, however, to specify more than 10 arguments on the command line. To access arguments number 11 and up you must use the SHIFT command. Each time SHIFT is executed, the contents of the parameters move down one position. This means that the content of %1 is moved to %0, %2 is moved to %1, and so on. It also means that the content of %0 is lost and that %9 contains a new argument. For example, given these 11 command line arguments,

EXAMPLE A B C D E F G H I K

%0 contains EXAMPLE and %9 contains I. After the SHIFT command is executed, %0 will contain A and %9 will contain K.

The final batch file command is CALL. It is used to execute one batch file from within another. Its general form is

CALL *batch-file-name*

where *batch-file-name* is the name of the batch file you want executed. After the called file has executed, the

calling batch file resumes execution at the line immediately following the CALL command. This procedure
is like inserting the second batch file within the first.

It is important to understand that you can execute
one batch file from within another without using the
CALL command. You simply use the file's name as
though it were a command. There is a difference,
however: If you don't use the CALL command, when
the second batch file finishes, DOS does *not* resume
the first batch file; it simply redisplays the DOS
prompt. Therefore, when you want the original batch
file to continue, you must use the CALL command.

Examples

1. Let's look at an example of the FOR command.
   Modify MYBAT.BAT so that it contains this line:

   ```
   FOR %%X IN (DIR TREE VER) DO %%X
   ```

   When you run this batch file, it will display the
   directory, execute TREE, and then run VER. It
   works like this: The first time through the FOR,
   %%X is assigned DIR. After the DIR command has
   executed, the FOR repeats, only this time the %%X
   contains TREE. After TREE executes, %%X is given
   the value VER. Once VER has completed, there are
   no further arguments, so the FOR command terminates.

2. This FOR command displays the first three command line arguments with which it is executed:

   ```
   FOR %%X IN (%1 %2 %3) DO ECHO %%X
   ```

3. Modify MYBAT.BAT so that it contains these commands:

```
ECHO OFF
FOR %%X IN (%0 %1 %2 %3) DO ECHO %%X
SHIFT
ECHO After shift
FOR %%X IN (%0 %1 %2 %3) DO ECHO %%X
```

Now, execute this file using the following command:

```
MYBAT ONE TWO THREE FOUR
```

You will see this output:

```
MYBAT
ONE
TWO
THREE
After shift
ONE
TWO
THREE
FOUR
```

As you can see, after the SHIFT command executes, the contents of the parameters shift down one location.

4. To see how the CALL command works, create two batch files called BAT1.BAT and BAT2.BAT. Put these commands in BAT1.BAT:

```
ECHO OFF
ECHO In BAT1
CALL BAT2
ECHO Back in BAT1
```

BAT2.BAT should contain this command:

```
ECHO Inside BAT2
```

Now, execute BAT1. You will see this output:

```
In BAT1
Inside BAT2
Back in BAT1
```

As you can see, once BAT2 has finished, execution resumes in BAT1.

Now, change BAT1 so it looks like this:

```
ECHO OFF
ECHO In BAT1
REM Here, BAT2 is executed, not CALLed
BAT2
REM Now, the next line is never executed
ECHO Back in BAT1
```

Now, BAT2 is executed by BAT1 without using the CALL command. This means that when BAT2 finishes, execution does not resume in BAT1. Instead, the DOS prompt is displayed.

5. You can pass arguments to a called batch file by specifying them after the batch file's name. As an example, change BAT2.BAT so it looks like this:

```
ECHO In BAT2, argument is %1
```

Now, change BAT1.BAT so it calls BAT2.BAT using this command:

```
CALL BAT2 Hello
```

When BAT2 executes, Hello will be passed to it in its %1 parameter.

Exercises

1. What FOR command reports whether the files SORT.EXE and PRINT.COM are on the disk in drive A?

2. What does the SHIFT command do?

3. What does the CALL command do?

4. On your own, experiment with all the batch file commands.

CREATE AN AUTOEXEC.BAT FILE

7.6

Very often, you will want DOS to perform a series of commands when it starts. For example, you may want it to check the disk, install the resident part of the PRINT command, and then clear the screen. Also, you will usually want customization commands, which you will learn about later, to be executed when DOS starts running.

For commands to be executed when DOS starts, you must put them into a special batch file called AUTOEXEC.BAT. When DOS begins executing, it looks for AUTOEXEC.BAT on the DOS disk. When AUTOEXEC.BAT is found, DOS automatically executes it. If AUTOEXEC.BAT is not on the disk, DOS automatically executes the DATE and TIME commands. However, when AUTOEXEC.BAT is present, DATE and TIME are no longer automatically executed, so you may want to include these commands in your AUTOEXEC.BAT file.

The AUTOEXEC.BAT file must be in the root directory of the disk for DOS to find it.

Examples

1. Here is a short but effective AUTOEXEC.BAT file:

```
DATE
TIME
PROMPT $P$G
CLS
```

Create this file on your DOS work disk and then restart the computer by simultaneously pressing [Ctrl], [Alt], and [Del]. When it starts, you'll see that DOS finds the AUTOEXEC.BAT file and executes it.

In Chapter 6, you learned that PROMPT PG displays the path to the current directory. This is an extremely useful customization when you are working with subdirectories. If you include it in the AUTOEXEC.BAT file, you no longer have to change your prompt manually each time you start the computer.

2. Another way you can use the AUTOEXEC.BAT file is to display instructions, information, or identification. For example, this AUTOEXEC.BAT file warns unauthorized people not to use your computer:

```
ECHO OFF
CLS
ECHO Warning: This computer may be used
ECHO only by employees of Widgit Corp.
ECHO Unauthorized use is strictly prohibited!
```

Exercises

1. Create an AUTOEXEC.BAT file that performs the following functions: requests the time and date, displays the following message,

```
Prepare to back up files
Strike a key when ready . . .
```

and finally, copies all the files from the root directory of the disk in drive A to the disk in drive B.

You might use an AUTOEXEC.BAT file like this to ensure that people who use the computer back up their disks every day.

2. On your own, create an AUTOEXEC.BAT file that meets your specific needs.

EXERCISES

At this point, you should be able to answer these questions and perform these exercises:

MASTERY
SKILLS CHECK

1. In general, what is a batch file?

2. Create a batch file called SAMPLE.BAT that clears the screen, checks the disk, displays the directory, and then waits for a keypress.

3. What effect does this batch file command have?

   ```
   ECHO OFF
   ```

4. What command allows you to embed comments in a batch file?

5. What are a batch file's replaceable parameters? Create a batch file that displays the first two command line arguments.

6. Using a FOR command, create a batch file that checks to see whether four files specified on the command line exist on drive B.

7. What does the GOTO command do? Show a simple example by creating a batch file that contains only three lines. Make one line an ECHO statement that is never executed.

8. What makes AUTOEXEC.BAT special?

9. What command executes one batch file from within another?

10. What does the SHIFT command do?

EXERCISES

INTEGRATING
SKILLS CHECK

These exercises check how well you have integrated the material in this chapter with that from earlier chapters.

1. Create an AUTOEXEC.BAT file that requests the time and date and then waits for you to insert your directories work disk (from Chapter 6) into your drive A.

2. Create a batch file called RENEXT.BAT that accepts two command line arguments, both of which specify file name extensions. Have RENEXT.BAT change all files with extensions that match the first argument to the extension specified in the second argument. However, it should rename files only after checking to make sure that no file by the new name already exists.

3. As you learned in previous chapters, the FORMAT

command destroys any preexisting information on a disk during the formatting process. Thus, accidentally formatting the wrong disk can be a disaster. Create a batch file called FMT.BAT that checks to be sure there are no files on the target diskette and gives the user a chance to cancel the FORMAT command if files are found. This batch file will be a valuable addition to your DOS work disk.

4. Extra challenge: Using the IF, GOTO, and SHIFT commands, it is possible to create a batch file that will accept an arbitrary number of command line arguments. The key is to make the last argument signal the end of the list. Create a batch file that accepts a variable number of file names as command line arguments. Have the file copy the specified files from drive A to drive B. To signal the end of the list, use the word *END*.

Learn to Redirect I/O

▶8◀

Your computer receives information from *input devices*. The most commonly used input device is the keyboard. Your computer outputs data using *output devices*. The two most used output devices are the monitor and the printer. Some devices are capable of both input and output. For example, disk drives and tape backup units can perform both input and output operations. No matter what the device, the transfer of information to or from a device is referred to as an *input/output,* or I/O, operation. In this chapter you will learn how to use DOS to redirect the flow of data to the various devices attached to your computer.

Make sure that your DOS work disk is in drive A and that A is logged in. (If you have a fixed disk, you can use drive C instead.)

EXERCISES

SKILLS CHECK

Before proceeding you should be able to answer these questions and perform these exercises:

1. What command formats and installs the DOS system files on a diskette in drive B?

2. What is the AUTOEXEC.BAT file?

3. What does the following batch file command do?

   ```
   IF NOT EXIST MYFILE.DAT ECHO File not found
   ```

4. Imagine you are the office manager of a small insurance company and you want your employees to receive their daily instructions from the computer. Create a batch file called JOB.BAT that contains instructions for three employees: Jon, Rachel, and Sherry. Make JOB.BAT accept an employee's name on the command line and then display that person's instructions. (You can use any instructions that you like.)

5. What command creates a subdirectory called MYDIR?

6. What is a disk volume label?

8.1 REDIRECT I/O TO DISK FILES

Most DOS commands do not communicate directly with the keyboard or the screen. In fact, most commands don't "know" where their input comes from or where their output goes. The reason for this seemingly odd situation is that most DOS commands communicate using two *psuedo devices* called *standard input* and *standard output*. Standard input and output act as switches that route information to or from actual physical devices like the keyboard or the monitor screen.

By default, when DOS begins execution, standard input is connected to the keyboard and standard output is connected to the screen. However, it is possible to connect standard input and output with other physical devices instead. For example, it is not uncommon to link standard input or output (or both) to a disk file. You can visualize standard input and output as depicted in Figure 8-1. In this section you will learn to redirect I/O to files. The next section describes re-directing I/O to other devices.

It is possible to redirect input and output operations to a disk file when you execute a DOS command and some application programs. To allow this, DOS includes three special I/O operators: >, >>, and <. Let's see how these operators work.

NOTE: For ease of discussion, this chapter uses the term *command* to refer to both DOS commands (internal or external) and application programs.

To redirect the output of a DOS command to a file instead of the screen, execute the command this way:

command > *file-name*

This form causes all output to be sent to the specified file. Be careful what file name you specify: If you choose the name of a file that already exists, that file is

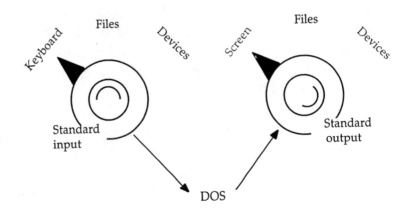

Keyboard   Files   Devices   Screen   Files   Devices

Standard
input

Standard
output

DOS

Figure 8-1.   A depiction of standard input and standard output

erased and a new one is created. If the file does not
exist, it is automatically created.

You can cause output to be appended to the end of
an existing file if you execute a command using this
general form:

command >> file-name

If the specified file exists, its current contents are
preserved and the new output is appended to the
end. If the file does not exist, DOS creates it.

Although it is less common to redirect input than output, input to a command can be redirected to a disk file if the command is executed using this general form:

command < *file-name*

Of course, the specified file must exist. Furthermore, it must contain all information required by the command, including carriage returns and responses to Yes/No prompts. If the file doesn't contain sufficient information to satisfy the command, the computer will lock and you will have to restart DOS.

It is important to understand three points: First, in general, error messages are output to the screen even when output is directed to a file. Second, redirected input and/or output does not affect I/O operations that are unrelated to standard input and output. For example, the COPY command still copies one file to another, even if its output is redirected. In essence, redirecting standard input or output does not change the function of a command. Third, not all application programs use DOS's standard input and output. In an attempt to achieve higher performance, some programs bypass DOS and perform I/O operations directly on the hardware devices in the computer. In this case, I/O cannot be redirected using the <, >, or >> operator. You may have to experiment to determine which applications allow I/O redirection and which do not.

Examples

1. To see the effect of the > operator, try this command:

```
DIR TREE.COM > OUT
```

As you can see, no output appears on the screen. Instead, DOS writes all output to the OUT file. If you enter **TYPE OUT** at the DOS prompt, you will see output similar to that shown here:

```
 Volume in drive A has no label
 Directory of  A:\

TREE      COM      3571   3-17-87  12:00p
         1 File(s)      54272 bytes free
```

Now, try this command:

```
DIR CHKDSK.COM > OUT
```

Examine the OUT file and you will see that it now contains this output:

```
 Volume in drive A has no label
 Directory of  A:\
CHKDSK    COM         9850   3-17-87  12:00p
         1 File(s)         54272 bytes free
```

As you can see, the original contents of OUT were overwritten by the second DIR command. Remember, the > operator causes DOS to erase any existing file with the specified name and create a new one. Thus, the original contents of the file are lost.

2. To append information to the end of an existing file, use the >> operator. For example, try this command:

```
DIR TREE.COM >> OUT
```

Now, display the contents of OUT. They will be similar to that shown here:

```
Volume in drive B has no label
Directory of  B:\

CHKDSK    COM     9850   3-18-87  12:00p
        1 File(s)      54272 bytes free

Volume in drive B has no label
Directory of  B:\

TREE      COM     3571   3-17-87  12:00p
        1 File(s)      54272 bytes free
```

This time, the original contents of OUT are preserved and the new output appears at the end of this file.

3. Now try redirecting input to a file. First, create a file called IN that looks like this:

```
12:00
```

Make sure you press [Enter] after you type **12:00**. Next, execute this command:

```
TIME < IN
```

Now, as it executes, the TIME command will read the file IN for input. It will no longer wait for you to enter the time at the keyboard, as you'll see when you run the command.

4. You can redirect both input and output at the same time. Try executing the TIME command like this:

```
TIME < IN > OUT
```

In this example, input for TIME is read from IN and output from TIME is written to OUT.

1. What is the difference between the > and >> operators?

2. What command sends the output of CHKDSK to a file called CHKDSK.OUT?

3. Assume you have two files—FILE1.DAT and FILE2.DAT—on a disk, and you want to compare them by executing this command:

   ```
   COMP < IN
   ```

   What must the contents of IN be? (Hint: Think about the information the COMP command requests.)

8.2   ROUTE I/O TO OTHER DEVICES

In addition to redirecting I/O operations to disk files, you can redirect them to other devices connected to the computer, such as a printer. To accomplish redirection of this sort, you must use some special DOS device names. A *device name* is the name DOS gives a device. These names are shown in Table 8-1.

As the table indicates, DOS can accommodate up to three printers and up to four asynchronous serial ports attached to the computer. An *asynchronous serial port* (generally just called a *serial port*) is a device that allows transmission of data to another serial port. Serial ports are quite common and are often used to connect two computers for file transfers or networks.

Table 8-1.	The DOS Device Names

Name	Device
CON	The console, either keyboard or screen
AUX	The first asynchronous serial port
COM1	Same as AUX
COM2	The second asynchronous serial port
COM3	The third asynchronous serial port
COM4	The fourth asynchronous serial port
PRN	The first printer (output only)
LPT1	Same as PRN
LPT2	The second printer (output only)
LPT3	The third printer (output only)
NUL	A nonexistent device programmers use to test software

Serial ports are both input and output devices. Virtually all DOS-based computers come with at least one serial port.

You use the DOS device name to refer to a device. For example, earlier in this book, you used the command

```
COPY CON MYFILE
```

to copy characters that you typed at the keyboard to a file called MYFILE. The name CON refers to either the keyboard or the screen, depending on the context.

Because of the way DOS was originally written, a DOS device name may have a colon appended to it—that is, both PRN and PRN: are valid device names; however, nothing is gained by adding the colon, so this book will not do so.

Examples

1. Create a small text file, called MYFILE (it can contain anything you like). Now, try this command:

```
COPY MYFILE CON
```

As you can see, the contents of MYFILE are displayed on the screen. The previous command is equivalent to

```
TYPE MYFILE
```

As stated before, context determines whether CON refers to the keyboard or to the screen. When CON is used as an output device, it refers to the screen. When it is used as an input device, it refers to the keyboard.

2. You can copy MYFILE to the printer using this command:

```
COPY MYFILE PRN
```

This command provides an alternative to PRINT. However, unlike PRINT, it does not operate in the background.

3. Keep in mind that you can redirect the standard input and output of commands to other devices using the <, >, and, >> operators. For example, another (albeit unusual) way to print MYFILE is to redirect the TYPE command, as shown here:

```
TYPE MYFILE > PRN
```

Here is a more practical example of redirecting output to the printer:

```
DIR > PRN
```

This command prints the disk directory. Remember this command because it is an easy way to obtain a "hard-copy" listing of the directory.

4. You can use the next command to make your computer act something like an electric typewriter.

```
COPY CON PRN
```

This command routes your keystrokes to the printer. If you want to stop typing, press [Ctrl] - [Z].

NOTE: Depending on the type of printer connected to your computer, output to the printer may be *line buffered,* which means that nothing is actually printed until you press [Enter] at the end of each line. Also, for some printers, nothing is printed until you terminate the COPY command.

Exercises

1. How would you print the directory structure of a disk on the printer using the CHKDSK /V command?

2. What does COPY CON CON do? How would you terminate the command?

3. Give two DOS names for the first asynchronous serial port.

8.3   LEARN TWO FILTER COMMANDS

Three special DOS commands act as filters. In DOS, a *filter* reads standard input, performs some manipulation on the data it reads, and then writes its output to standard output. The three filter commands are MORE, FIND, and SORT. All three commands are external. This section examines the first two. The SORT command is discussed in the following section.

The MORE command reads text data from standard input, displays 24 lines on standard output (usually the screen), and then waits for a keypress. Every time you press a key, another 24 lines are displayed until the end of the file is reached. MORE works much like the /P option to DIR. A common form of the command is shown here:

MORE < *file-name*

Remember, though, that MORE reads standard input, so it can be redirected to take input from any standard device.

The FIND command searches one or more files for a specified string. Each line in which the string is found is written to standard output, which is usually the screen. The general form of FIND is

FIND "*string*" *file-list*

Notice that *string* must be enclosed in double quotes. You may specify one or more files to be searched;

however, unfortunately you cannot use wildcard characters in the file names. You must specify each file name explicitly.

Unlike most DOS commands, FIND is case sensitive; FIND recognizes "HI" and "hi" as different strings.

FIND has three options that alter its behavior: /C, /N, and /V. These options must be specified immediately after FIND and before the string.

If you specify the /C option, FIND does not display the lines in which the specified string is found. Instead, it simply displays the number of lines in which a match occurs.

Specifying the /N option causes FIND to display the line number of each line in which a match occurs.

Specifying the /V option causes FIND to display all lines in which *no* match is found. The /N and /V options are mutually exclusive.

Examples

1. To see how MORE works, first create a file called ALPHA that contains the letters of the alphabet, with only one letter per line. For example, the first five lines would look like this:

```
A
B
C
D
E
```

Now, try this command:

```
MORE < ALPHA
```

You will see the first 24 lines of the file followed by this message:

```
-- More --
```

When you press any key, the rest of the alphabet will appear and MORE will terminate.

You will see additional uses for the MORE command later in this chapter.

2. To get some practice using the FIND command, create a file called MYTEXT that contains the following lines:

```
THIS is a sample text file.
It contains the word
"this" in both upper- and
lowercase. It also contains
the word "is" twice and the
word "contains" three times
```

Be sure to enter the text exactly as it is shown.

Now, try this command:

```
FIND "contains" MYTEXT
```

This output will result:

```
---------- MYTEXT
It contains the word
lowercase. It also contains
word "contains" three times
```

As you can see, DOS displays the three sentences that include the word "contains." The fact that one of the "contains" is enclosed within double quotes does not matter.

3. Now, try this FIND command:

```
FIND "is" MYTEXT
```

This time, you'll get this output:

```
---------- MYTEXT
THIS is a sample text file.
"this" in both upper- and
the word "is" twice and the
```

As you can see, the previous command finds the word "is" in three different lines, even though it only appears twice. This happens because FIND searches for matching character sequences, not for words. Therefore, the "is" at the end of "this" in the second line also causes a match. Remember this important point: Even if the string that matches the search string is within a larger word, FIND will still consider it a match.

4. To FIND, upper- and lowercase are different. Try this command to see an example:

```
FIND "this" MYTEXT
```

This FIND command outputs only the following match:

```
-----------MYTEXT
"this" in both upper- and
```

In the first line "THIS" is not matched, because it is capitalized.

5. FIND can display the line number of each matching line if you use the /N option. For example, try this command:

```
FIND /N "is" MYTEXT
```

The resulting output will look like this:

```
---------- MYTEXT
[1]THIS is a sample text file.
[3]"this" in both upper- and
[5]the word "is" twice and the
```

6. You can also make FIND display just the number of lines in which a match is found by using the /C option. For example, try this command:

```
FIND /C "is" MYTEXT
```

DOS will display this output:

```
---------- MYTEXT: 3
```

7. To display all lines that do not contain a match, use the /V option to FIND. For example, try this command:

```
FIND /V "is" MYTEXT
```

You will see the following output:

```
---------- MYTEXT
It contains the word
lowercase. It also contains
word "contains" three times
```

8. You can also specify a list of files when you use FIND. For example, this FIND command would search the files LETTER1, LETTER2, and LETTER3 for the string "overdue":

```
FIND "overdue" LETTER1 LETTER2 LETTER3
```

Exercises

1. What does the MORE command do?

2. Is this a valid FIND command?

```
FIND " " MYTEXT
```

(Hint: Experiment to find out.) If the command is valid, what lines would it match?

3. What FIND command searches for occurrences of the phrase "and the" in MYTEXT and reports the line number of any matches?

MASTER SORT

8.4

The SORT command sorts a text file on a line-by-line basis. It takes this general form:

SORT < *input* > *output*

If you don't specify *input*, DOS uses the keyboard, which is generally not very helpful. If you don't specify *output*, DOS uses the screen.

SORT sorts each line according to the internal representation of each character, from least to greatest. For letters of the alphabet, SORT sorts in alphabetical order. However, other characters may have internal representations that are either greater or less than the internal representations of the letters of the alphabet. Furthermore, SORT is not case sensitive, so "X" and "x" are the same as far as SORT is concerned.

SORT has two options. The first, /R, causes output to be sorted in reverse order. The second is /+*n*, where *n* specifies the position in the line at which sorting should begin. Sometimes, you will want SORT to skip the first few characters in each line and begin sorting somewhere in the middle. For example, you might have a table that contains several columns of data and want to sort the table on the third column. You can do so by using the /+*n* option.

Examples

1. As a simple first example, try the following command (you will need the MYTEXT file that you created in the previous section):

```
SORT <MYTEXT
```

This command displays the following output on the screen:

```
"this" in both upper- and
It contains the word
lowercase. It also contains
the word "is" twice and the
THIS is a sample text file.
word "contains" three times
```

Because no specific output device was specified, the output is displayed on the screen by default.

2. To output the MYTEXT file in reverse order, use this command:

```
SORT /R <MYTEXT
```

This display will result:

```
word "contains" three times
THIS is a sample text file.
the word "is" twice and the
lowercase. It also contains
It contains the word
"this" in both upper- and
```

3. A good way to use SORT is to obtain a sorted listing of your directory. You can do so by issuing these two commands:

```
DIR >OUTDIR
SORT <OUTDIR
```

If you execute these commands using your DOS work disk, you will see output similar to that shown

```
           33 File(s)       52224 bytes free
        Directory of  B:\
        Volume in drive B has no label
        APPEND   EXE      5825   3-17-87   12:00p
        ASSIGN   COM      1561   3-17-87   12:00p
        ATTRIB   EXE      9529   3-17-87   12:00p
        BACKUP   COM     31913   3-18-87   12:00p
        BASIC    COM      1063   3-17-87   12:00p
        BASIC    PIF       369   3-17-87   12:00p
        BASICA   COM     36403   3-17-87   12:00p
        BASICA   PIF       369   3-17-87   12:00p
        CHKDSK   COM      9850   3-18-87   12:00p
        COMMAND  COM     25307   3-17-87   12:00p
        COMP     COM      4214   3-17-87   12:00p
        DEBUG    COM     15897   3-17-87   12:00p
        DISKCOMP COM      5879   3-17-87   12:00p
        DISKCOPY COM      6295   3-17-87   12:00p
        EDLIN    COM      7526   3-17-87   12:00p
        FIND     EXE      6434   3-17-87   12:00p
        FORMAT   COM     11616   3-18-87   12:00p
        GRAFTABL COM      6128   3-17-87   12:00p
        GRAPHICS COM      3300   3-17-87   12:00p
        JOIN     EXE      8969   3-17-87   12:00p
        LABEL    COM      2377   3-17-87   12:00p
        MORE     COM       313   3-17-87   12:00p
        MORTGAGE BAS      6251   3-17-87   12:00p
        MYTEXT            168   12-06-89    1:54p
        OUTDIR              0   12-06-89    3:45p
        PRINT    COM      9026   3-17-87   12:00p
        RECOVER  COM      4299   3-18-87   12:00p
        RESTORE  COM     34643   3-17-87   12:00p
        SHARE    EXE      8608   3-17-87   12:00p
        SORT     EXE      1977   3-17-87   12:00p
        SUBST    EXE      9909   3-17-87   12:00p
        TREE     COM      3571   3-17-87   12:00p
        XCOPY    EXE     11247   3-17-87   12:00p
```

Figure 8-2.   A sorted directory listing of the DOS work disk

in Figure 8-2. The three lines at the top are out of order because they contain leading spaces. As represented internally by the computer, spaces are lower in value than the letters of the alphabet, so lines that start with spaces are placed before lines that start with letters.

In the next section you will see an easier way to obtain a sorted directory listing.

4. You can sort your directory by extension instead of by filename if you use this command:

```
SORT /+10 < OUTDIR
```

This command works because file extensions begin on the tenth character. When you specify the /+10 option, SORT sorts each line beginning with the tenth character.

5. You can route the output of the SORT command to a file. For example, this command would write the sorted directory to a file called SORTDIR:

```
SORT <OUTDIR >SORTDIR
```

Exercises

1. What command sorts a file that is called INVTRY.DAT?

2. How do you sort a file in reverse order?

3. What command sorts the directory listed in OUTDIR by creation date?

4. On your own, try to think of several uses for SORT.

UNDERSTAND PIPES

8.5

You can route the output of one command into the input of another as long as both commands use standard input and output. This process is called *piping* because you can envision data flowing from one command to the next via a pipe. DOS uses the vertical bar to represent a pipe. To pipe the output of one command to the input of the next, use this basic form:

command1 ¦ *command2*

Here, the output of *command1* is fed into the input of *command2*.

You can pipe more than two commands together. In fact, you can connect as many commands as will fit on the command line.

Each time a pipe is used, DOS creates a temporary disk file to hold the output of one command until it can be fed into the input of another. After all the data has been piped to the second command, the temporary disk file is erased. It is important to understand that there must be enough free disk space on the current drive to hold the output of the first command.

Examples

1. A simple, yet effective, use of a pipe is to feed the output of the DIR command as input to MORE. To do so, use this command:

   ```
   DIR ¦ MORE
   ```

   Try it, and you'll see that the directory listing is

paged. (Of course, you can accomplish the same thing using DIR's /P option.)

2. Using a pipe, it is possible to list a disk's directory in sorted order using only one command, as shown here:

DIR ¦ SORT

As you can see, this method is more efficient than the two-command sequence described in the previous section.

3. You can pipe more than two commands together. For example, this useful command displays a sorted directory, one page at a time:

DIR ¦ SORT ¦ MORE

You can visualize this series of pipes as shown in Figure 8-3.

4. A very useful command can help you find a "lost" file. It is easy to store a file in the wrong subdirectory by accident, especially if you have a fixed disk. If you have many directories and many files, it can be quite difficult to find the file manually. However, you can find the file automatically by using this command:

CHKDSK /V ¦ FIND *"file-name"*

Here *file-name* is the name of the file that you want to find. This command works because executing CHKDSK with the /V option displays the contents of all directories, using this form:

drive:path\file-name

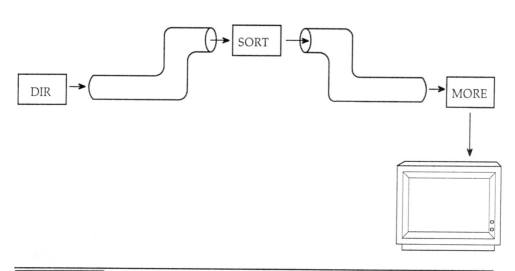

Figure 8-3.   A representation of the DIR ¦ SORT ¦ MORE command

Therefore, when the FIND command matches the file name the entire line is displayed and you can read the path to the directory in which the file is stored.

You can try this using your DOS work disk by issuing this command:

```
CHKDSK /V ¦ FIND "SORT.EXE"
```

Because SORT.EXE is on your DOS work disk, this line will appear on your screen:

```
A:\SORT.EXE
```

Exercises

1. What does a pipe do?

2. What command displays the output of the TREE command, one screen at a time?

3. What command displays a sorted list of all the files on a disk, regardless of what directory they are in?

EXERCISES

At this point, you should be able to answer these questions and perform these exercises:

1. How do standard input and output differ from your keyboard and screen?

2. What command routes the output of the TREE command to a file called TREE.OUT?

3. What is the difference between the > and >> operators.

4. Name DOS's three filter commands.

5. What command sorts a file that is called PHONE.DAT and writes the sorted output to a file called PHONE.SRT?

6. What command searchs a file called FORMLET for the phrase "On your behalf"?

7. What does the MORE command do?

8. What does a pipe do? Using a pipe, combine CHKDSK with FIND to display only the amount of free disk space.

EXERCISES

This section checks how well you have integrated the material in this chapter with that from earlier chapters.

INTEGRATING SKILLS CHECK

1. Create an AUTOEXEC.BAT file that requests the time and date and then checks the disk. Also, have the output of CHKDSK appended to a log file called CHKDSK.LOG, so that a record of disk errors can be kept.

2. Create a batch file that accepts three command line arguments. Using the FOR batch file command, have FIND search for each argument in a file called MYTEXT.

3. What is wrong with the following command?

```
FIND "somestring" CHKDSK.COM
```

4. What command sends the output from the TREE command to the printer?

5. What is wrong with this command?

```
COPY PRN MYFILE
```

More DOS Commands

►9◄

By now, you have learned enough about DOS to run your day-to-day applications without any trouble. The commands you have learned up to this point are those you will use most commonly. This chapter presents several new DOS commands that you will use less frequently, although they are indispensable in certain situations. This chapter also explores a few new ways to use several commands that you already know.

Make sure your DOS work disk is in drive A and that A is logged in. (If you have a fixed disk, you can use drive C instead.)

EXERCISES

SKILLS CHECK

Before proceeding you should be able to answer these questions and perform these exercises:

1. What does the RD command do?

2. What command prints the contents of the disk directory on the printer?

3. Assuming you have a text file that is called OVERDUE.TXT, what command sorts that file in reverse order and writes the sorted output to a disk file called OVERDUE.SRT?

4. What is wrong with the following batch file?

```
AGAIN
ECHO Check another disk (Ctrl-C to stop)
PAUSE
CHKDSK B:
GOTO AGAIN
```

5. What three conditions can the IF batch file command check?

6. What is the difference between ERASE and DEL?

7. What is the difference between the next two commands?

```
COPY A:*.* B:
DISKCOPY A: B:
```

VERIFYING DISK WRITE OPERATIONS

9.1

Although it doesn't happen frequently, it is possible for data to be incorrectly written to a disk file. This might occur for several reasons: A power surge can cause the disk drive to malfunction temporarily. A static electricity discharge to the computer can cause a temporary problem. Excessive heat or cold can cause a disk drive to misbehave. Whatever the reason, if the integrity of your data is crucial, you will want some way to verify that all disk write operations are accurate. To accomplish this goal, you can use the VERIFY internal command.

The VERIFY command turns on or off a DOS feature that confirms each disk write operation. The command takes this general form:

VERIFY ON/OFF

By default, VERIFY is off. To check its status, enter **VERIFY** by itself.

You should only turn VERIFY on when you are dealing with extremely important files because it takes about as much time to verify the contents of a file as it does to actually write the data to the file. This means programs that perform many disk write operations will take about twice as long to run. So, to avoid degrading your computer's overall performance, use VERIFY wisely.

Examples

1. Enter the following command to see whether VERIFY is on or off.

```
VERIFY
```

2. To turn VERIFY on, use this command:

```
VERIFY ON
```

3. To see how VERIFY affects performance, create a batch file called VTEST.BAT that contains these commands:

```
VERIFY OFF
COPY CHKDSK.COM TEST.COM
VERIFY ON
COPY CHKDSK.COM TEST.COM
VERIFY OFF
```

When you run this batch file, you will notice that the second COPY command takes longer than the first because the second time DOS is confirming the contents of TEST.COM. Before you move on, erase TEST.COM.

Exercises

1. If you haven't already done so, try Example 3 now.

2. On your own, think about the work you do with your computer. Are there some applications for which VERIFY should be turned on?

9.2 | LEARN MORE ABOUT COPY

COPY has two additional features that you may use from time to time. The first is the /V option, which verifies that information is accurately written to the target file. The /V option causes DOS to check the contents of the target file in exactly the way VERIFY does. The advantage of using /V is that the extra checking process is only in effect for the duration of the COPY command, and will not affect the performance of your other programs.

With COPY, it is possible to combine two or more text files. To do so, use this general form:

COPY *file1 + file2 + . . . + fileN target-file*

If you don't specify a target file name, the first source file will be used and it will contain the contents of all other specified files. You can use the wildcard characters in the source file names.

Although you can combine any type of file with any other type of file, generally only text files can be meaningfully combined. Combining two program files, for example, does not produce a meaningful result. (In fact, attempting to execute combined program files is likely to crash your computer!) Also, combining data files does not generally produce a meaningful outcome. The reason is that most programs expect data files to be in a specific format. Combining two or more data files does not produce a format that is acceptable to most programs.

Examples

1. This COPY command verifies that TEST.COM actually contains an accurate copy of TREE.COM:

```
COPY TREE.COM TEST.COM /V
```

Erase TEST.COM before you move on.

2. At this time create two text files called TEXT1.TXT and TEXT2.TXT. Type the following line in TEXT1.TXT.

```
This is the first text file.
```

Press (Enter) at the end of the line. Type this line in TEXT2.TXT:

```
This is the second text file.
```

Again, be sure to press (Enter) at the end of the line.
Now, issue this command to combine the two files:

```
COPY  TEXT1.TXT+TEXT2.TXT  TEXT3.TXT
```

Next, enter **TYPE TEXT3.TXT**. You will see that TEXT3.TXT contains these two lines:

```
This is the first text file.
This is the second text file.
```

3. As stated before, you can use the wildcard characters to combine groups of files. For example, first erase TEXT3.TXT (created in the preceding example), and then try this command:

```
COPY  *.TXT  TEXT3.TXT
```

When you examine TEXT3.TXT, you will see that it does, indeed, contain TEXT1.TXT combined with TEXT2.TXT.

One thing to keep in mind when you use wildcards in specifiers is that you will not necessarily know the order in which the files will be combined. If the order is important, you will have to specify it explicitly using complete file names.

Exercises

1. What COPY command copies a file that is called MYDATA.DAT to a file called BACKUP.DAT and verifies that the copy operation was successful?

2. What COPY command combines all files that begin with MARY and have the WP extension into a file called MARY.OUT?

3. Show a command that combines these three files in this order: FILE1.WP, FILE3.WP, and FILE2.WP. Call the target file FILE.OUT.

USE THE ATTRIB COMMAND

9.3

Every file on a disk has a set of attributes associated with it. Most file attributes are for DOS's internal use, and you cannot examine or change their settings. However, the external command ATTRIB allows you to examine and/or modify the *read-only* and *archive* file attributes. Before you learn to use ATTRIB, it will be helpful for you to learn what these two attributes do.

The setting of the read-only attribute determines whether a file can be modified or erased. If read-only is off (which it is by default), a file may be read and written to. This means, in short, that the contents of that file can be changed. If read-only is on, the file may be read, but no write operations are allowed; thus, the file cannot be modified in any way or erased. (Erasure implies changing the contents of the file.)

There are many reasons to make a file read-only. For example, you might do so to protect the file from unauthorized tampering or accidental erasure.

DOS's archive attribute makes backing up files easier—especially if you have a fixed disk. Although we won't look closely at the backup procedure until later in this book, a brief discussion is in order now, to show the importance of the archive attribute. For the following discussion, keep in mind that DOS has special commands for backing up a disk.

Each time you create or modify a file, DOS automatically turns on the archive attribute. The backup procedure turns off the archive attribute. Further, it is possible, when backing up a disk, to tell DOS to copy only those files that have their archive attributes turned on. In this way, subsequent backups will only need to copy those files that are new or that have changed since the last backup.

You can use the ATTRIB command to display or change the state of the archive and read-only attributes. Its general form is

ATTRIB *attribute file-name*

If *attribute* is not present, the current status of the specified file is displayed. You can use wildcard characters in the file name. The following four values are valid for *attribute*:

+R   Turns on read-only attribute
−R   Turns off read-only attribute
+A   Turns on archive attribute
−A   Turns off archive attribute

By specifying the /S option, you can have ATTRIB operate on all files in the current directory as well as on all files in any subdirectories of the current directory.

Examples

To follow along with the examples, you will need to create a short file called MYFILE on your DOS work disk. It doesn't matter what the file contains.

1. First, try this command:

```
ATTRIB MYFILE
```

DOS will respond like this:

```
A        A:\MYFILE
```

The A indicates that the archive attribute is on. Because no attribute was specified, DOS only examines and displays the current attribute settings; it does not change anything.

2. Now, make MYFILE read-only using this command:

```
ATTRIB +R MYFILE
```

Next, execute this command:

```
ATTRIB MYFILE
```

You will see the following output:

```
A   R  A:\MYFILE
```

This time, both an A and an R are displayed. The R indicates that the file is read-only. In general, when a letter is displayed, it means that that attribute is on. When the attribute is off, no letter appears.

3. To see the effect of making a file read-only, try this command:

`ERASE MYFILE`

DOS responds with this message:

`Access denied`

Since MYFILE is read-only, you cannot erase it.

4. Try this command:

`DIR > MYFILE`

This command attempts to write the contents of the disk directory to MYFILE. However, since MYFILE is read-only, DOS responds with the following message:

`File creation error`

As you know, the > operator erases any preexisting file with the specified name and creates a new one. This, of course, would modify the file, which is not allowed, because it is read-only.

5. To return MYFILE to read-write mode, use

`ATTRIB -R MYFILE`

Now, execute this command:

`ATTRIB MYFILE`

This time, the R is no longer shown. This means that you can now perform read and write operations on MYFILE.

6. As stated previously, you can use wildcard characters in the file name when using ATTRIB. For example, this command would display the attributes of all files that have the .EXE extension:

```
ATTRIB *.EXE
```

Be careful when you use wildcard characters to alter the state of an attribute, because you might change more files than you intend. It is best to issue a DIR command using the same wildcards first, to be certain no unexpected files are selected.

7. You can examine or alter the attributes of files in the current directory as well as those in any subdirectories to the current directory by using the /S option. For example, the following command would turn on the archive attribute for all files in the current directory and in any subdirectory that has the .DAT extension.

```
ATTRIB +A *.DAT /S
```

Exercises

1. What command displays the attributes for all files in the current directory?

2. Can a read-only file be copied? (Hint: try it!)

3. What command turns off the read-only attribute for all files that have a .COM extension in the current directory and in all subdirectories?

9.4 | MASTER XCOPY

As useful as the COPY command is, it lacks certain desirable features: It cannot copy all files in the current directory and in any subdirectories, nor can it selectively copy only files that have their archive attributes set. In addition, COPY cannot prompt you before it copies a file. Finally, COPY cannot selectively copy a file based on its creation date. To address these shortcomings, DOS provides the external XCOPY command.

The general form of XCOPY is

XCOPY *source-file target-file options*

In its simplest form, using no options, XCOPY operates just like COPY. However, it is the options to XCOPY that make the command so powerful. Let's take a look at them now.

The /A option allows you to copy only those files that have their archive attributes set. This option does not turn off the archive attribute. The /M option is the same as /A except that it does turn off the archive attribute. You can use these options to help you back up a disk. However, later in this book you will learn about the BACKUP and RESTORE commands, which are designed expressly for this purpose.

The /D option allows you to copy only those files that have creation dates equal to or later than the date you specify. This option takes the general form

/D:*mm-dd-yy*

You can have XCOPY copy all files from the specified directory and from any subdirectories using the /S option. If no directory is explicitly specified, the default directory is used. If the target diskette does not contain the same directory structure, XCOPY creates it. However, empty subdirectories are not created. If you wish to have empty subdirectories created on the target disk, you must also include the /E option.

Using the /P option causes XCOPY to ask you before it copies each file.

The /V option makes XCOPY verify that the contents of the target file are the same as those of the original.

Since XCOPY is an external command, it might not be on the disk that you want to copy. Using the /W command causes XCOPY to display this message and then wait for a keypress:

```
Press any key to begin copying file(s)
```

This pause gives you an opportunity to switch diskettes.

One restriction does apply to XCOPY: It cannot be used to copy from or to any devices other than files. You cannot use XCOPY to copy a file to a printer, for example.

Examples

The examples that follow use the directories disk that you created in Chapter 6. This disk must be inserted into drive A. You will also need a blank formatted diskette. If the directories disk is not available, create a new directories disk now. If you have your old directories disk, erase all the files on it, but retain the directory structure. Now, copy XCOPY.EXE into the root of the directories disk. Finally, in the \WP\LARRY directory, create a short text file called MYFILE that contains the sentence "This is a test."

1. Make the root directory of drive A current. If you have two diskette drives, put the blank diskette into drive B. If you only have one diskette drive, you will need to swap diskettes. Now, try this command:

   ```
   XCOPY A:*.* B: /S
   ```

   The remaining examples assume that you have two diskette drives. Make appropriate substitutions if this is not the case.

   As the XCOPY command executes, you will see the following output:

   ```
   Reading source files(s). . .
   A:XCOPY.EXE
   A:\WP\LARRY\MYFILE
           2 File(s) copied
   ```

   After the command terminates, log in to drive B and list the contents of the root directory. You will see that it contains two items: XCOPY.EXE and the WP directory. Go to the \WP\LARRY directory. Here, you will find MYFILE.

XCOPY automatically creates any necessary directories when you specify the /S option. Return to the root directory of drive B and again list its contents. Notice that neither the SPSHT or ACCT-ING directories are on the disk in B. The reason is that those directories are empty and XCOPY does not create empty directories on the target disk unless you specify the /E option. To see how this works, return to A drive and try this command:

```
XCOPY A:*.* B: /S /E
```

After the command terminates, examine the contents of the disk in drive B. You will find that all directories have been created, empty or not.

One final point about the commands in this example: The *.* is technically unnecessary because XCOPY assumes *.* if nothing else is specified. Thus, the following command is equivalent to the previous one.

```
XCOPY A: B: /S /E
```

2. Using the /D command, you can cause XCOPY to selectively copy only files with creation dates equal to or later than the date specified. For example, try this command (substitute today's date, however):

```
XCOPY A: B: /S /D:01/12/90
```

This command copies MYFILE, but not the XCOPY.EXE command itself. This is because XCOPY.EXE has an earlier creation date than the one you specified. However, since you just created MYFILE, its date is equal to the one specified and the file is copied.

3. At this time, copy ATTRIB.EXE to the root directory of the diskette in drive A. Now execute this command:

```
ATTRIB *.* /S
```

The following output will result:

```
A          A:\WP\LARRY\MYFILE
A          A:\XCOPY.EXE
A          A:\ATTRIB.EXE
```

As you can see, the archive attribute of all three files is on. For this example, turn off the archive attribute of ATTRIB.EXE using this command:

```
ATTRIB -A ATTRIB.EXE
```

Now, try this XCOPY command:

```
XCOPY A: B: /S /A
```

As you can see, only XCOPY.EXE and MYFILE are copied. When you specify the /A option, XCOPY only copies files that have their archive attributes on. As stated earlier, the archive attribute is automatically turned on when a file is created or modified. The /A option does not turn off the archive attribute, but the /M option does. To observe this in action, try the next command:

```
XCOPY A: B: /S /M
```

After this command has finished, reexamine the attributes of the files. You'll find that the archive attribute has been turned off.

4. Using the /P option, you can have XCOPY prompt you before it copies each file. Each file name will be displayed, and you must respond by typing either **Y** to copy the file or **N** to skip it. Try this command now:

```
XCOPY A: B: /P
```

Notice that this command does not contain the /S option. This means that its scope is restricted to the current directory, which, in this case, is the root. Therefore, you will only be prompted about the files XCOPY.EXE and ATTRIB.EXE.

5. Using the /W option gives you a chance to switch diskettes. Try this command to see the prompt:

```
XCOPY A: B: /W
```

Since there is no reason to actually change diskettes, press any key to start the copy process.

Exercises

Many of these exercises assume the directory structure of the directories disk.

1. What command copies all files in the ACCTING directory and all files in all of its subdirectories to a disk in drive B? (If you want to experiment, simply create files in the GL, AR, and AP directories.)

2. Assuming the root directory of drive A is current, what command copies all the files in that directory to drive B and verifies that an accurate copy is made?

3. What is one reason you might want to copy selected files based on their creation date? What command copies, from drive A to drive B, all the files that

begin with R, use the .EXE extension, and are created or last modified on or after January 20, 1990?

4. Create a command that copies from drive A to drive B only files that have their archive attributes set. Have XCOPY clear the archive attribute of each file in the process.

5. What does the /P option do when it is applied to XCOPY?

9.5   UNDERSTAND REPLACE

There are two special situations that neither COPY nor XCOPY can handle. The first situation occurs when you want to replace files on the target disk with files from the source disk that have the same file names. For example, you might receive an upgrade to an application program and need to replace the old files with the new ones. The second situation is more or less the opposite of the first one. It arises when you want to add files to a disk only if they do not already exist on the target disk. To handle these two situations, DOS includes the REPLACE command.

The REPLACE command has this general form:

REPLACE *source target options*

Here, *source* is the name of the file on the source disk, while *target* specifies the target drive and, if necessary, the directory. The *options* specified govern exactly what REPLACE does.

By default, when no option is specified, REPLACE copies files from the source disk only if they also exist on the target disk. This means, for example, that if a file called SAMPLE exists on the source disk but not on the target disk, it would not be copied.

To add only files that do not already exist to the target disk, specify the /A option. This option prevents files that already exist on the target disk from being replaced.

By default, REPLACE only examines the current directory on the target disk. However, if you specify the /S option, REPLACE examines all subdirectories of the current directory of the target disk. It is important to understand that the /S option does not cause REPLACE to search subdirectories of the source disk. It applies only to the target disk. Note that you cannot use the /A and /S options together.

Using the /P option causes REPLACE to prompt you before it copies each file. This option allows you to replace selected files. The /W option causes RE-PLACE to wait until you press a key, which gives you a chance to change diskettes.

Finally, the /R option allows read-only files on the target disk to be replaced. Remember, read-only files cannot usually be modified. The /R option temporarily overrides the read-only attribute.

Examples

The examples that follow require the directories disks that you used in the preceding section. Copy REPLACE.EXE into the root directory of the diskette in drive A.

1. Try this command:

   ```
   REPLACE A:*.* B:
   ```

   This copies the files XCOPY.EXE and ATTRIB.EXE to drive B. However, since REPLACE.EXE does not exist on the diskette in drive B, it is not copied.

2. Because the /A option is specified, the next command copies only the file REPLACE.EXE to drive B.

   ```
   REPLACE A:*.* B: /A
   ```

   If you try this command a second time, no files will be copied because all the files on the disk in drive A already exist on the disk in drive B.

3. Now, try this command:

   ```
   REPLACE A:*.* B: /P
   ```

   This causes REPLACE to ask you before it replaces a file.

4. To learn how the /S option works, first try this command:

   ```
   REPLACE A:*.* B: /S
   ```

   As you can see, only the three files in the root directory of A are copied to drive B. MYFILE in \WP\LARRY is not copied. The reason is that the /S option applies only to the target diskette.

   Now, copy MYFILE into the root directory of the disk in drive A and retry the previous command. This time, REPLACE also replaces MYFILE in \WP\LARRY on the target disk in drive B.

The point here is that with /S, REPLACE replaces the correct files in the correct subdirectory, but the replacement files must be in the current directory of the source disk. The way this option is implemented may seem a little weird to you. If it does, don't worry; this is simply the way REPLACE works.

5. You can use wildcard characters in the file name when you use REPLACE. For example, this command causes any file that begins with X and has the .EXE extension to be replaced:

```
REPLACE A:X*.EXE B:
```

6. You can specify a path name with REPLACE. For example, this command causes MYFILE in \WP\LARRY to be replaced on the target disk:

```
REPLACE A:\WP\LARRY\*.* B: /S
```

Exercises

1. What command causes all files that exist in the root of drive C to be replaced by those on the diskette in drive A?

2. What command causes all files on drive A to be added to the root of drive C provided they do not already exist there?

3. What does the /P option do?

4. What does the /R option do?

9.6 LEARN THE RECOVER COMMAND

From time to time a disk file may become damaged. If this happens DOS will display an error message indicating that the file contains a bad sector when you try to access it. If the damaged file is a text file, you can use the RECOVER command to recover the information from any good sectors that are part of the file. RECOVER is an external command.

The RECOVER command has two general forms. Use this one to recover a specific file:

RECOVER   *file-name*

Should a disk's directory become damaged, use this form of the RECOVER command to recover all files on the disk:

RECOVER *drive-specifier*

Here, the disk to be recovered is specified by the *drive specifier*. When you use this second form, RECOVER recovers all the files that it finds and gives each file a name that begins with FILE followed by four digits and has the extension .REC. For example, the first recovered file would be called FILE0001.REC, the second FILE0002.REC, and so on.

Although technically RECOVER can recover the usable parts of any kind of damaged file, it only makes sense to use it on text files. The reason is that losing even a small portion of a program file can cause the program to seriously malfunction. Therefore, there is virtually no point in recovering a program file because the resulting file simply will not work. The same is true of data files because, in general, a program expects a data file to have a specific structure. If part of the file is missing, the structure will not be intact. However, if a small amount of text from a text file is lost, it can often be replaced by simply typing the missing characters again.

Examples

1. Put your directories disk in drive A, then copy RECOVER to the root directory of this disk, and log in to drive A. Now, try this command:

    ```
    RECOVER ATTRIB.EXE
    ```

    You will see the following message:

    ```
    Press any key to begin recovery of the
    file(s) on drive A:
    ```

    This prompt gives you a chance to switch diskettes in situations that require it.

    Press any key to begin the recovery process. Since the ATTRIB.EXE file is not damaged, RE-COVER will be able to recover it all. Once it has done so, it prints this message:

    ```
    9529 of 9529 bytes recovered
    ```

    If you happen to have a damaged file, try the RECOVER command on it and then watch what happens.

2. Make sure that your directories disk is in drive A and that drive A is logged in. Further, make sure that the copy of the directories disk that you made using XCOPY in a previous section is available, because the next RECOVER command effectively destroys the disk in drive A.

This command recovers all files on the directories disk in drive A:

RECOVER A:

Once again, you are instructed to press a key when ready. Go ahead and do so now.

When RECOVER terminates, examine the contents of the directory. You will see that all files and subdirectories have been turned into files with names like FILE0001.REC. (Remember, subdirectories are held in special disk files, so RECOVER recovers them along with the other files.)

Be very careful when recovering all files from a disk because accidentally specifying the wrong disk can be a catastrophe.

Exercises

1. If you have not already done so, try the previous examples.

2. What command recovers a file called INFO.DAT from drive B?

3. What command recovers a file called MYFILE in the \WP\LARRY subdirectory?

9.7   LEARN TO PRINT GRAPHICS IMAGES

Aside from DOS version 4, which uses graphics images in a limited way, DOS is a character-based operating system. However, it is still possible to run programs that use graphic screen output under DOS if your computer has a graphics video adapter. If it does, you will probably have programs that use your computer's graphics capabilities. A graphics image is simply an image that is comprised of lines, dots, circles, boxes, and so on. Common examples are business bar graphs and paint programs that allow you to create freestyle "drawings" on the screen with a mouse.

Often, you may find that you want to print a copy of what is on the screen. When the screen is in text mode, this is easily accomplished by simply pressing the (PrtSc) key. However, when your computer is displaying graphics, (PrtSc) will not work unless you first execute the GRAPHICS external command.

The GRAPHICS command is one of the few installable external commands. When executed, it loads into memory a program that lets DOS print graphic images from the screen on the printer. (Keep in mind that you can still print text screens after executing GRAPHICS.) GRAPHICS is not built in because it increases the size of DOS by about 2300 bytes. Since not everyone wants to print graphics screens, the designers of DOS decided to make GRAPHICS an installable command.

The general form of the GRAPHICS command is

GRAPHICS *printer options*

Both *printer* and *options* are optional. If one or both are not specified, GRAPHICS supplies defaults.

Several types of printers can be connected to your computer.

For a graphics image to be printed correctly, DOS needs to know what kind of printer you have. Here are the valid names for *printer:*

Printer type	Printer name
IBM Personal Graphics Printer	GRAPHICS
IBM ProPrinter	GRAPHICS
IBM PC Convertible Printer	THERMAL
IBM Compact Printer	COMPACT
IBM Color Printer with black ribbon	COLOR1
IBM Color Printer with red, green, blue, and black ribbon	COLOR4
IBM Color Printer with cyan, magenta, and yellow ribbon	COLOR8

If no printer name is specified, the IBM Personal Graphics Printer is assumed. Epson printers are quite commonly used with microcomputers, and they are also specified using the GRAPHICS printer name.

If you have a color printer, your printout will have color if the screen graphics images do. For noncolor printers, colors will print as shades of gray.

By default, graphics output is printed inversely on paper; that is, white (or any color) prints as black, and black as white. The reason is that the most common background color for a screen graphics image is black, and the most common paper color is white. However, you can cause the printed output to resemble the screen by specifying the /R command. Frankly, this option seldom produces acceptable printed copy and cannot be recommended.

If you have a color printer, you can cause the background color to be printed by specifying the /B option.

The last GRAPHICS option is /LCD. You must use this option if you have an IBM PC Convertible Liquid Crystal display.

NOTE: From time to time, advances in computer hardware outpace those in computer software. As graphics hardware advanced, new ways of producing high-quality graphics images developed. It is possible (even likely) that your computer can produce certain graphics images that will not be able to be printed even after executing GRAPHICS, so if you get a garbled printout, this is most likely the reason.

Examples

1. If you have an Epson MX or LX printer or an IBM ProPrinter or Personal Graphics Printer, use this command to load the GRAPHICS command:

```
GRAPHICS
```

2. To print graphics screens on an IBM Personal Computer Color Printer without reversing black and white, use this command:

```
GRAPHICS COLOR1 /R
```

Exercises

1. Why is the GRAPHICS command needed?

2. It is not possible for most versions of DOS to produce a graphics image; therefore, no concrete example of printing a graphics screen image to the printer can be shown. However, if you have a program that does use graphics, try printing a graphics screen just to see what you get.

9.8 | USE THE SYS COMMAND

After you have formatted a diskette, if you have not specified the /S option, there is no DOS system on the disk. However, you can put a system on a disk at a later date as long as the disk's directory is completely empty. The disk must be empty because the DOS system files must be the first directory entries. Keep in mind that the DOS system is stored in hidden files, so you won't see the directory entries.

Actually, in some cases you can install the system on a disk that already contains files. If a disk was formatted using the /B FORMAT option, space for the DOS system is reserved in its directory. Therefore, even if there are files on the disk, the system can still be installed.

To install the DOS system files, use the SYS command, whose general form is

SYS *target-drive-specifier*

Keep in mind that the default drive must contain a disk that contains the system files.

SYS has one quirk that you need to know about. Part of the DOS system is the nonhidden file called COMMAND.COM. COMMAND.COM displays the command prompt. It is sometimes referred to as a *command interpreter*. For some reason, SYS does not copy this file to the target disk. You must do this manually using the COPY command. If you neglect this step, you will see this message when you try to use the disk to load DOS:

```
Bad or missing command interpreter
```

The main reason you may need to install a system is simple: DOS is a copyrighted program. This means that although you can make copies of it for your own use, you cannot give it away or sell it. Therefore, you may receive a disk that has room for the system, but does not actually contain it. In this case, you must copy the system files to the disk.

Example

1. Format a diskette at this time. Don't specify the /B or /S option. Now, copy CHKDSK.COM to the newly formatted diskette. If you have two diskette drives, put the new diskette in drive B and your DOS work disk in drive A. If you have only one diskette drive, remove the newly formatted diskette

and insert your DOS work disk into drive A. In either case, log in to A and execute this command:

```
SYS B:
```

(If you only have one diskette drive, you will be prompted to swap disks.) DOS responds with this message:

```
No room for system on destination disk
```

This message appears because you copied CHKDSK.COM to the newly formatted disk, which prevents SYS from making the DOS system files the first directory entries.

Now erase CHKDSK.COM from the target diskette and try the command a second time. This time the command works and DOS responds with this message:

```
System transferred
```

Exercises

1. Even though SYS transfers the DOS system files, what must you do to enable a disk to be used as a DOS Startup disk?

2. In what case is it impossible to transfer the DOS system to a disk?

EXERCISES

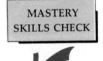

MASTERY
SKILLS CHECK

At this point, you should be able to answer these questions and perform these exercises:

1. What command causes DOS to double-check each disk write operation for accuracy?

2. Assume that you have two text files called TEXT1 and TEXT2. What command combines these files into a file called MORETEXT?

3. What does the /V COPY option do?

4. What command turns off the archive attribute of a file called SAMPLE.DAT?

5. What XCOPY command copies the entire directory structure and all files from a disk in drive A to a disk in drive B?

6. What XCOPY command copies all files created after February 28, 1990 from the current directory of the disk in drive A to a disk in drive B?

7. What command copies files from drive A to drive B only if the disk in drive B already contains files by the same names?

8. What does RECOVER do?

9. What command must you execute before you can print graphics images on the printer?

10. What does the following command do? (Assume that drive A is current.)

```
SYS B:
```

EXERCISES

This section checks how well you have integrated the material in this chapter with that from earlier chapters.

1. What command displays the names of all read-only files in a directory. (Hint: Use FIND and a pipe.)

2. The next command creates a disk that contains the same information as the original. What command creates an exact copy of the original disk?

    ```
    XCOPY A: B: /S /E
    ```

3. Although REPLACE is a very convenient command in certain situations, it is not technically necessary. To illustrate this point, create a batch file that copies a file called MYFILE from drive A to drive B only if it does not already exist on drive B.

4. Using XCOPY, you can automatically duplicate a disk's directory structure. Unfortunately, there is no complementary command that removes a disk's directory structure (unless you reformat the disk, of course). If you wish to remove a subdirectory, what procedure must you follow?

Configuring DOS

►10◄

There have been hints throughout this book about the many ways you can configure and customize DOS to best suit your individual computing environment. Now it is time to look directly at this topic.

To follow along with the examples in this chapter, you need to have your DOS work disk in drive A.

EXERCISES

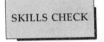

SKILLS CHECK

Before proceeding you should be able to answer these questions and perform these exercises:

1. What command displays the file attributes for all files in the default directory?

2. What command outputs a sorted directory listing?

3. What does the /E option to the XCOPY command do?

4. What command installs the DOS system files on a disk?

5. What do the > and >> operators do?

6. What command copies from a disk in drive A to a disk in drive B all files on A that do not already exist on B?

7. What command attempts to recover damaged files?

8. What command clears the computer screen?

9. What does the VERIFY command do?

10.1 | CUSTOMIZE THE DOS PROMPT

As you learned in Chapter 6, DOS can display the current directory path as part of its prompt. In this section you will learn other ways to customize the DOS prompt.

To customize the DOS prompt, use the PROMPT command, which has this general form:

PROMPT *prompting-message*

Whatever message you specify after the PROMPT command becomes the new DOS prompt. If you enter PROMPT without specifying a message, DOS returns the prompt to its default setting.

There are some characters that you cannot enter as part of the prompting message. For example, the I/O redirection operators > and < cannot be included in the message because DOS will think that you are redirecting input or output to some file. Certain other characters, such as the backspace and the carriage return, usually can't be included in the message either. To allow these types of characters to be part of the DOS prompt, PROMPT recognizes several character sequences called *meta-strings*, which you can substitute for the character that will actually show as part of the prompt. All meta-strings begin with a dollar sign ($), which is followed by a single character. The character may be either upper- or lowercase. The PROMPT meta-strings are shown in Table 10-1. If you follow a $ with an invalid character, PROMPT will ignore the meta-string altogether.

TABLE 10-1.	The PROMPT Codes

Code	Meaning
$$	dollar sign
$b	¦ character
$d	system date
$e	escape character
$g	> character
$h	backspace
$l	< character
$n	current drive letter
$p	current directory path
$q	= character
$t	system time
$v	DOS version number
$_	carriage return-linefeed sequence

Examples

1. The DOS prompt can be anything you like. For example, try this command:

   ```
   PROMPT What next?
   ```

   As you can see, the DOS prompt now becomes "What next?".

2. Looking at Table 10-1, you can understand why the command

   ```
   PROMPT $P$G
   ```

   causes the DOS prompt to display the directory path. The $P is the meta-string for the current path, and $G is the meta-string for the > symbol.

3. One handy DOS prompt displays the system time,

the current path name, and the > symbol. To generate this prompt, use the following command:

```
PROMPT $T $P$G
```

Now, whenever DOS displays its prompt, it also outputs the current time. Therefore, if you want to know what time it is, you simply press [Enter] at the prompt, and DOS redisplays the prompt using the current time.

4. Although the DOS prompt can have as many as 128 characters, long prompts tend to be distracting. For example, try this command:

```
PROMPT $D $T $V $P$G
```

As you can see, it causes the date, time, DOS version number, current directory path, and > operator to be displayed. In theory, this might seem like a good idea, but in practice it produces a very unattractive prompt.

In general, prompts should be no longer than 15 to 20 characters. However, if you really need a long prompt, the best way to handle it is to divide the prompt between two lines. For example, try this prompt:

```
PROMPT $D $T $V$_$P$G
```

By issuing a carriage return after the DOS version number, only the path name and > symbol are displayed on the second line of the prompt.

Exercises

1. What prompt command creates a prompt that looks like this:

```
¦<
```

2. What command displays this prompt?

   Drive A:

3. What command returns the DOS prompt to its default form?

10.2 USE THE MODE COMMAND

As you know, your computer is comprised of several different devices, all of them under DOS's control. These devices have various modes of operation. When DOS begins execution, it initializes all devices to a default state. For example, the screen is initialized to 80-column text mode, even though other video modes exist. Often, DOS's default setting for a device is fine. However, from time to time, you may find that you need to change the way some device operates, perhaps to accommodate the needs of a new application program. To change the way a device works, use the external command MODE.

The MODE command has several forms and uses. We will examine the most common ones in this section.

One very common use of MODE changes the way DOS displays information on the screen. There are two general categories of video adapters: monochrome and color/graphics. The monochrome video adapter can only display text in a single color. The color/graphics adapter can display text or graphics in more than one color. Further, it can display text in two sizes: 40 or 80 columns wide. If you have a

Code	Effect
40	Sets color/graphics adapter display width to 40 columns
80	Sets color/graphics adapter display width to 80 columns
BW40	Activates the color/graphics adapter; sets the width to 40 columns and the display mode to black and white
BW80	Activates the color/graphics adapter; sets the width to 80 columns and the display mode to black and white
CO40	Activates the color/graphics adapter; sets the width to 40 columns and the display mode to color
CO80	Activates the color/graphics adapter; sets the width to 80 columns and the display mode to color
MONO	Activates the monochrome adapter; fixes display width at 80 columns

TABLE 10-2.   The MODE Video Codes

color/graphics adapter attached to your computer, you can use this form of the MODE command to change the way text is displayed:

MODE *video-mode*

Table 10-2 shows the valid video modes.

Another common use for the MODE command is to configure the asynchronous serial port. DOS uses the serial port (as it is commonly referred to) to send and receive information to and from devices such as modems, plotters, and mice. It is also used to transfer information between two computers. Although most commercial programs that use the serial port configure it automatically, you may need to configure certain parameters manually.

DOS transfers information into or out of a serial port one bit at a time. Since a byte is eight bits long, a series of eight bits must be sent to transfer each byte (thus, the name *serial port*). The rate at which bits are transferred is measured in *bits per second*, or *baud*. For one serial port to communicate with another, both must have the same rate of transmission. To set the baud rate of a serial port, use this general form of MODE:

MODE COM*x:baud-rate*

As you may remember from Chapter 8, up to four serial ports can be connected to your system, and their DOS device names are COM1, COM2, COM3, and COM4. In the previous command, you must substitute the proper number (from 1 through 4) for *x*.

The value of *baud-rate* must be one of the following values (moving from slowest to fastest): 110, 150, 300, 600, 1200, 2400, 4800, 9600, or 19200. Although your computer may be capable of faster transmission rates, 19200 is as fast as DOS can send or receive data.

In addition to the baud rate, four other features of the serial port can be configured using the MODE command. While a complete understanding of these features requires a background in computer engineering, it is important that you have a general idea of their significance. The first feature is parity. During data transmission, it is possible for an error to occur. To help detect transmission errors DOS transmits one additional bit, called the *parity bit*. The value of the parity bit is determined by the value of the preceding data bits. The parity bit is set so that the sum of the bits having the value 1 will be either even or odd, depending on which transmission scheme is used. The receiving port checks each parity bit to see if it is set appropriately. If it is not, then one or more bits have been transmitted incorrectly. Clearly, for this system to work, both ports must use the same approach to parity checking: If the sending port uses even parity and the receiving port uses odd parity, every byte transmitted will appear to be in error. By default, DOS uses even parity. It is also possible to turn off parity altogether.

The second feature you can set on the serial port is the number of data bits transmitted for each byte. Although bytes are eight bits long, the eighth bit is not needed when only text is being transmitted. This is because the entire set of upper- and lowercase letters plus punctuation and digits all fit into the first seven bits. Therefore, if only text is being transmitted, it is not necessary to send the eighth bit, although it is not wrong to do so. Not sending the eighth bit increases the effective transfer rate by about one eighth. For this reason, you can specify that either seven or eight data bits be transmitted. Again, though, for two ports to communicate, they must agree on the number of data bits being sent. By default, DOS transmits seven data bits.

The third feature of the serial port that you can configure with MODE is the number of stop bits sent between each set of data bits. To mark the end of each byte, the serial port transmits either 1 or 2 nondata bits, or *stop bits*. For two ports to communicate, they must be sending the same number of stop bits. By default, DOS uses 1 stop bit, except for 110-baud transmission.

Retry, the fourth feature you can set on the serial port, may not affect you. However, if you have a printer attached to a serial port, then for technical reasons, you must tell DOS to continually retry sending a byte if an error occurs. Retry is off by default. To turn Retry on, specify a P as the last argument to MODE.

The general form of the MODE command that allows all features of the serial port to be set is

MODE COMx:*baud-rate, parity, data-bits, stop-bits, retry*

If you don't specify one or more items, the defaults are used. (You must specify *baud-rate,* however.) The value for *parity* must be either E for even, O for odd, or N for no parity. The *data-bits* must be either 7 or 8 and the *stop-bits* must be 1 or 2. If a value is present for *retry*, it must be the letter P.

The next MODE command we will discuss determines the number of characters per line and the number of lines per inch the printer will print. If your printer is connected to the computer in the normal way, DOS initializes it to print 80 characters per line and 6 lines per inch. If you want to fit more characters on a line, you can specify 132 characters per line; however, the characters will be smaller and harder to read. You can also specify 8 lines per inch. The general form of the MODE command is

MODE LPTx:*chars-per-line, lines-per-inch*

The final form of the MODE command we will examine allows you to redirect printer output to a serial port. The general form of this command is

MODE LPT# = COM#

where # is 1 through 3 for LPT and 1 through 4 for COM. Once you redirect printer output, all information is automatically sent through the specified serial port.

Examples

1. If you have a color/graphics adapter, try this version of MODE:

```
MODE 40
```

This command sets the screen to 40-column mode. As you can see, the characters are now twice as wide as they were in 80-column mode. To return to 80-column mode, use this command:

```
MODE 80
```

2. This command sets COM1's baud rate to 4800:

```
MODE COM1:4800
```

MODE responds with the following message:

```
COM1: 4800,e,7,1,-
```

As you can see, when you specify only the baud rate, DOS gives the other parameters their default values.

Actually, the first two digits of each baud rate are sufficient to tell DOS which baud rate is desired. Therefore, this command would have the same effect as the previous one:

```
MODE COM1:48
```

3. This command sets COM1 to 9600 baud, odd parity, 8 data bits, and 2 stop bits:

```
MODE COM1:96, 0, 8, 2
```

4. The next command sets COM1 to 1200 baud, even parity, 7 data bits, and 2 stop bits:

```
MODE COM1:12, , , 2
```

Notice that you must still enter a comma when you don't specify a value for a field.

5. If you have a printer, create a short text file called MYFILE that contains anything you like. Now, try this series of commands:

```
PRINT MYFILE
MODE LPT1:132, 8
PRINT MYFILE
MODE LPT1:80, 6
```

Compare the way the file is printed each time. You will see that the second command causes the characters to be smaller and closer together, thus allowing more characters per line and more lines per page.

6. This MODE command redirects all printer output to the second serial port.

```
MODE LPT1=COM2
```

Exercises

1. What command puts the screen in 80-column color mode?

2. What command configures COM1 for 19200 baud, no parity, 8 data bits, and 1 stop bit?

3. What command causes the printer to print 132 characters per line and 6 lines per inch?

4. On your own, check the user manuals for your application programs. Do any of them request that you configure a device using MODE? If they do, have you done so?

APPLY THE PATH COMMAND

10.3

When you execute an external command, program, or batch file, it either must exist in the current directory or you must specify the full path name to the directory in which it does exist. However, using the DOS PATH command you can tell DOS to automatically search one or more directories for a file when that file is not found in the current directory. The general form of the internal PATH command is

PATH *pathname1;pathname2;. . .;pathnameN*

were *pathname* is the path to a directory were DOS will search for an executable file if it does not find the specified command, program, or batch file in the current directory. You may specify 1 or more search paths, but the longest single path cannot exceed 63 characters, and the entire semicolon-separated list cannot exceed 128 characters.

One important point: No spaces may occur anywhere in the path name or names, including after a semicolon.

To see the current search path, enter the PATH command without arguments. To reset the current path, enter the PATH command followed by a single semicolon. Each time you enter a new path using the PATH command, it overwrites any existing paths.

REMEMBER: PATH can only be used to locate files that end in .EXE, .COM, or .BAT.

Examples

The following examples assume the directory structure of the directories disk that you created in Chapter

6. To follow along, insert your directories disk into drive A. Then erase all files in the directories on the disk, but leave the directory structure intact.

1. Copy the file CHKDSK.COM into the directory \ACCTING\AR. Then log into the root directory and issue this command:

```
CHKDSK
```

Because CHKDSK.COM is not in the current directory, DOS responds with the message "Bad command or file name." Now, enter this PATH command:

```
PATH \ACCTING\AR
```

Next, retry the CHKDSK command. This time, when DOS does not find CHKDSK.COM in the current directory, it automatically searches the directory \ACCTING\AR. Since CHKDSK.COM does exist in this directory, the command is now executed.

2. To see the current PATH, you enter **PATH** with no arguments. For example, enter **PATH** now, and you will see the following message:

```
PATH=\ACCTING\AR
```

3. To complete this exercise, copy TREE.COM to the \WP\JANET directory. Enter this command:

```
PATH \ACCTING\AR;\WP\JANET
```

Finally, enter this command sequence:

```
CHKDSK
TREE
```

Because the PATH command contains two paths, DOS finds and executes both of these commands, even though they reside in different directories.

4. In general, it is best to include a drive specifier with the paths you specify using the PATH command. Then, no matter what drive you are currently using, DOS will find your commands. For example, here is the best way to describe the paths shown in the preceding example:

```
PATH A:\ACCTING\AR;A:\WP\JANET
```

5. To cancel the PATH command enter

```
PATH ;
```

Exercises

1. What PATH command allows DOS to look for executable files in the \SPSHT directory?

2. Assume that the GL directory contains the CHKDSK.COM command and that the following PATH command has just been entered using drive A:

```
PATH \ACCTING\GL
```

Can you execute CHKDSK from any drive other than drive A? If not, how could you alter the PATH command so that it works correctly, no matter what drive is current?

3. What command clears all paths?

USE THE APPEND COMMAND

The APPEND command is virtually the same as the PATH command except it works for files that have extensions other than .EXE, .COM, and .BAT. In other words, APPEND allows DOS to access a file in a directory other than the current one. Its general form is

APPEND *path1;path2;. . .;pathN*

where *path* is the path to the directory that holds the file or files you want to access. As with PATH, no spaces can exist anywhere in the path name or names—even after a semicolon.

APPEND is both an internal and an external command. The first time it is executed, DOS installs it in memory. After that, it is not reloaded.

You can view the current APPEND path by entering APPEND without any arguments. To clear the APPEND path or paths, enter **APPEND** followed by a semicolon. Each time you enter a new APPEND path, the old path or paths are overwritten and thus lost.

There is one option to APPEND that you might want to use. It is the /E option, which causes APPEND to find executable files. Using the /E option essentially eliminates any need to use the PATH command. Be aware, however, that you can only specify the /E option the first time APPEND is executed.

Examples

The following examples assume the directory structure of the directories disk. Before you go on, copy APPEND.EXE to the root directory of your directories disk.

1. Create a short text file called MYFILE in the \WP\ JANET directory. It can contain anything you want. Now, make the root directory current and execute this command:

TYPE MYFILE

As you can see, DOS does not find the file.
   Next, execute this command:

APPEND \WP\JANET

Now, retry TYPE MYFILE. This time, because you added the APPEND command, DOS finds and displays the contents of MYFILE.

2. If you have been following the examples, you should have the file TREE.COM in the \WP\JANET directory. Make sure the root directory is current, and then try this command:

TREE

As you can see, DOS does not find the TREE.COM file in \WP\JANET. The reason is that APPEND cannot execute a program or command in another directory without the /E option.

To see the effect of the /E option, you need to restart DOS. Do so now by pressing [Ctrl], [Alt], and [Del] simultaneously. When DOS begins running, execute this series of commands:

```
APPEND /E
APPEND \WP\JANET
TREE
```

This time, DOS executes the TREE command.

You had to restart DOS to try this example because APPEND is an installed command, and the /E option can only be specified the very first time APPEND is executed.

3. Once you have APPENDed a directory path, you can access the files in that path from any directory. For example, switch to \ACCTING at this time and then enter this command:

```
TYPE MYFILE
```

As you can see, DOS displays the file on the screen.

4. You can specify more than one path when using APPEND. For example, this command tells DOS to search the \WP\LARRY and \WP\JANET directories if it can't find a file in the current directory:

```
APPEND \WP\JANET;\WP\LARRY
```

Remember, spaces are not allowed in the path names or after a semicolon.

Exercises

1. What command appends the path to the GL directory of ACCTING?

2. What command appends the paths to the GL, AR, and AP subdirectories of ACCTING?

3. What command clears all APPENDed paths?

10.5   UNDERSTAND THE SET COMMAND

The SET command links a string to a name that becomes part of DOS's environmental parameters. Although it is unlikely you would use SET just to run DOS, you might have an application program that requires it. For this reason, we look briefly at the SET command here.

The general form of SET is

SET *name* = *string*

where *name* is the name that is placed into DOS's environment and *string* is the string linked to that name.

Once a name and its string have been entered into the DOS environmental parameters table, an application program can look up the name and then read the string. This is mainly useful for defining directory paths. For example, a word processor might look up the name WP to find the directory the word processing files are in.

To remove a name from the environment, use this general form:

SET *name* =

To see all environmental names, enter the SET command without arguments. Note that DOS adds to the environment the path or paths defined by PATH and any PROMPT commands.

Examples

1. This command creates the DOS environmental name LARRYDIR and links it to the string named \WP\LARRY:

```
SET LARRYDIR=\WP\LARRY
```

Enter the previous command and then execute SET using no arguments. You will see something similar to this:

```
COMPSEC=A:\COMMAND.COM
LARRYDIR=\WP\LARRY
```

DOS has automatically entered the COMSPEC name into the environment. It tells DOS what directory contains the command processor. (Remember, the command processor displays the DOS prompt.) Note that you may see other entries in addition to those shown here.

2. To remove LARRYDIR, use this command:

```
SET LARRYDIR=
```

Exercises

1. What command creates the environmental name MYDIR and links it to the string that is named C:\MYFILES\WORK?

2. On your own, see if any of your application programs require or would benefit from the SET command.

10.6   LEARN ABOUT THE CONFIG.SYS FILE

A number of DOS options must be determined when DOS first begins execution. The reason is that some aspects of DOS are fundamental to its operation and cannot be changed while the program is running. To set one or more of DOS's startup options, you must use special *configuration commands,* which are placed in a file called CONFIG.SYS. This file must be in the root directory of the disk you use to load DOS. When DOS begins execution, it reads the contents of this file if it is present and executes the commands.

IMPORTANT: The CONFIG.SYS file does not take the place of the AUTOEXEC.BAT file, or vice versa. These files perform different functions. The only similarity between them is that both are executed when DOS starts running. If both files exist on a disk, CONFIG.SYS is processed first.

There are two general types of configuration commands: those used mostly by programmers or system integrators and those you might want or need to use on your own. It is the latter type that we will examine in this section. Keep one thing firmly in mind: If you have a fixed disk, a CONFIG.SYS file will probably be on the disk already. If you experiment with any of the configuration commands in this section, be sure you add them to the preexisting commands found in the file on your hard disk. However, it will probably be best if you use your DOS work disk for these examples rather than modifying the CONFIG.SYS file on your fixed disk. Also, remember that DOS only reads CONFIG.SYS when the program begins execution, so any changes you make to this file will only take effect when you restart DOS.

The first configuration command we will look at is BREAK. The BREAK command determines how frequently DOS checks to see if you have pressed Ctrl-Break or Ctrl-C. By default, DOS only checks for a Ctrl-Break when it performs a standard input or output operation. However, some programs may not perform a standard input or output for extended periods. For example, a program that is sorting a large database may not perform any standard I/O operations for several minutes. In this case, you cannot cancel the program until it finishes. To solve this problem, you can instruct DOS to check for Ctrl-Break more frequently. The BREAK command takes this form:

BREAK ON

Although BREAK is a configuration command, it can also be entered at the command line. When it is used at the command line, BREAK takes this general form:

BREAK ON/OFF

You can check the current BREAK status by entering **BREAK** without arguments.

There are three configuration commands you may need to use because an application program instructs you to do so. These commands are BUFFERS, FILES, and FCBS. All three affect the performance and capabilities of the DOS file system. Although a detailed description of these commands is beyond the scope of this book, each is discussed briefly so you'll know what each does and how it affects your system.

The BUFFERS command determines the number of disk buffers DOS sets aside in memory. A disk buffer is a region of memory that is large enough to hold one complete sector of information. As you learned earlier in this book, the smallest accessible unit of disk storage is the sector. Thus, when DOS accesses a file, it reads an entire sector and puts the information into a disk buffer. The same is true when information is written to a disk. DOS stores the information in a disk buffer until a sector's worth of data has been output; only then is the buffer actually written to disk.

The default number of buffers varies between 2 and 15, depending on the capacity of the disk and the amount of memory in your system. However, you can specify the number of buffers needed by an application program. The general form of the BUFFERS command is

BUFFERS = *num-buffers*

where *num-buffers* is a number between 1 and 99.

Another attribute of DOS's file system that you might be required to change is set using the FILES configuration command. This command determines the number of files that can be in use, or *open*, at the same time. The FILES command takes this general form:

FILES = *num-files*

By default, 8 files can be open at any one time. However, the value of *num-files* can be anywhere between 8 and 255.

An application program uses *file control blocks* (FCBS) to access disk files. File control blocks are created and maintained by DOS. They are regions of memory used to hold various pieces of information about each file currently in use. By default, DOS allows 4 file control blocks; however, you can specify from 0 to 255. The only time you won't use the default value is when an application program requires additional blocks. The general form of the FCBS command is shown here:

FCBS *total, permanent*

As stated before, *total* may be between 0 and 255. The value of *permanent* determines the number of file control blocks that cannot be automatically reused. By default, this value is 0, but it can be between 0 and 255. Remember, you should use the FCBS command only if the instructions for your application program specifically request it.

Another configuration command that you may need to use is LASTDRIVE. By default, the maximum

6

number of drives DOS will recognize in your computer is 5 (A through E). However, if you install more
drives or if you install one or more virtual disks
(virtual disks are covered in the next section), you
may have to instruct DOS to recognize more drives.
To do so, you can add a LASTDRIVE command to
your CONFIG.SYS file. LASTDRIVE has this general
form:

LASTDRIVE = *drive*

The *drive* argument can be a letter from A to Z.

Remember, because the commands in the CON-
FIG.SYS file are only processed when DOS begins
execution, any changes you make to the CONFIG.SYS
file take effect only after you restart DOS.

Examples

For these examples, make sure your DOS work disk is
in drive A.

1. The following CONFIG.SYS file tells DOS to reserve
   room for 20 concurrently open files, 10 disk buffers,
   and 8 FCBS, none permanent. It also turns on
   extended Ctrl - Break checking.

```
FILES = 20
BUFFERS = 10
FCBS = 8, 0
BREAK ON
```

2. If you enter an invalid value or command in the
   CONFIG.SYS file, DOS displays this message when
   it encounters the unacceptable element:

```
Unrecognized command in CONFIG.SYS
```

Unfortunately, DOS doesn't tell you which command is in error, so it may take some experimentation to find the problem.

For example, if you change the line

```
BUFFERS = 10
```

to

```
BUFFERS = -10
```

DOS will report an error when it restarts. (Remember, the only valid values for BUFFERS are 1 through 99. Negative numbers are not allowed.)

3. As has been stated previously, when both an AUTOEXEC.BAT and a CONFIG.SYS file exist on the same disk in the root directory, DOS processes both files, but CONFIG.SYS is executed first. To confirm this, try creating a CONFIG.SYS file that contains an error and an AUTOEXEC.BAT file that has this first line:

```
ECHO Inside AUTOEXEC.BAT
```

When you restart the system, you will see the message caused by the error in the CONFIG.SYS file before you will see the message displayed by AUTOEXEC.BAT.

4. If your system has seven disk drives, this command must appear in your CONFIG.SYS file:

```
LASTDRIVE = G
```

Exercises

1. In general, what kind of commands go into a CONFIG.SYS file?

2. What command tells DOS to allow up to 15 disk buffers?

3. What does BREAK ON do?

4. Can BREAK be executed from the command line?

5. Is the following statement true or false? If both CONFIG.SYS and AUTOEXEC.BAT are present, only CONFIG.SYS is processed.

6. What command tells DOS that there are only three disk drives attached to your computer?

10.7   INSTALL DEVICE DRIVERS USING CONFIG.SYS

There is one more very important configuration command that you need to know about. It is the DEVICE command, which is used to install various device drivers. In general terms, a *device driver* controls a specific hardware device. For example, DOS already contains device drivers to control the screeen, keyboard, disk drives, and printer. However, depending on how your computer is used, there are two reasons why you may need additional device drivers. First, you may add a new device to your computer that requires a device driver of its own. A mouse is a common example. Second, you may need to access an existing device in a new way.

No matter what the reason, to add a device driver to DOS, you use this general form of the DEVICE command within your CONFIG.SYS file:

DEVICE = *device-driver*

Here, *device-driver* is the name of the file that contains the desired device driver.

In addition to any device drivers you might need to supply for special hardware devices, DOS includes five device drivers of its own, which you can use to alter or enhance the operation of certain devices. These device drivers are

```
ANSI.SYS
DRIVER.SYS
PRINTER.SYS
DISPLAY.SYS
VDISK.SYS
```

PRINTER.SYS and DISPLAY.SYS have been added since DOS version 3.30 to increase DOS's support of non-English-speaking environments. If you work in an English-speaking environment, you won't need to use these device drivers, and if you live in a non-English-speaking country, it's likely that your computer is already properly configured; therefore, we won't spend time on these two device drivers.

The DRIVER.SYS file is very complicated, and is better left to programmers and system configuration specialists. Let's go on now to examine the remaining two device drivers.

Perhaps the most important device driver included with DOS is VDISK.SYS, which is used to create a virtual disk drive, or *RAM-disk,* in memory. A virtual disk simulates the operation of a disk drive, using memory instead of a magnetic disk surface to store information. To your programs, a virtual disk behaves like a regular disk drive. For example, you can copy files to and from it. You can also load application programs onto it and execute them. However, there is one big difference between an actual disk and a virtual disk: Virtual disks are much faster because they transfer information to and from "disk" files at the speed of the computer's memory, which is much faster than the transfer rate of an actual disk drive.

The advantage of a virtual disk is its speed. The disadvantage is that, depending on how much memory your computer has and how it is configured, a virtual disk may seriously impact the amount of available system memory. Often this is not a problem; however, some application programs require so much memory that you cannot use a virtual disk with them.

One very important point to remember is that when the power is turned off or the computer is restarted, the contents of the virtual disk are lost. You must be sure to copy all important files to an actual disk before you turn off the computer or restart DOS with Ctrl-Alt-Del.

The general form of the VDISK.SYS command is

DEVICE = VDISK.SYS *total-size sector-size entries*

where *total-size* is the size of the virtual disk in kilobytes. The default value is 64K, but this is usually too small to be of any use. If you specify a value larger than can be allocated, VDISK automatically adjusts it to the largest amount that will fit in memory. The *sector-size* specifies how large the sector should be. It must be one of these values: 128, 256, or 512. Usually the best choice is 128 because this size makes the most efficient use of memory. This is also the default value. The *entries* argument specifies the number of directory entries to be allowed by the virtual disk. By default, this value is 64, and that is generally a good choice; however, you can specify any number that is between 2 and 512.

Some computers have extended memory. *Extended memory* is memory that is not directly usable by DOS but can be used by programs running under DOS. DOS can only use the first 640K of the computer's memory. If you have more memory than that, then you probably have extended memory. In this case, you can use extended memory for the virtual disk by specifying the /E option at the end of the VDISK command. When you use the /E option, the virtual disk does not reduce the amount of memory available to your application programs. The general form of the /E option is

/E:*transfer-size*

If the *transfer-size* is not specified, then VDISK transfers eight sectors at a time when transferring information to or from extended memory. However, you can specify transfers of between one and eight sectors if you wish. (Generally, you will want to use the default.) A virtual disk can occupy up to four megabytes of extended memory in your computer.

Another DOS device driver that you might need to install is ANSI.SYS. The ANSI.SYS driver provides an alternative method by which an application program can control the position of the cursor on a text screen. ANSI.SYS does not give you any additional features or control; it just makes it easier for some types of application programs to control the screen. If an application program requires this device driver, its user manual will tell you so.

Examples

1. Put the following command into your CONFIG.SYS file. It creates a virtual disk that allocates 256K of storage, has sectors 128 bytes long, and allows up to 64 directory entries.

```
DEVICE = VDISK.SYS 256 128 64
```

When you restart the computer, this message will appear when the virtual disk is created (of course, the actual drive letter may vary, depending on how many drives you have in your system):

```
VDISK Version 3.30 virtual disk E:
   Buffer size:        256 KB
   Sector size:        128
   Directory entries:   64
```

Once you see the DOS prompt, execute the CHKDSK command and examine its output. Specifically, notice the last two lines, which report total system memory and total bytes free. They will look similar to this:

```
654336 bytes total memory
338272 bytes free
```

The reason for the large difference between the two totals is the amount of memory used by the virtual disk.

2. If you have extended memory, put this configuration command into CONFIG.SYS and then start DOS:

```
DEVICE = VDISK.SYS 256 128 64 /E
```

If you run CHKDSK now, you will find that no memory space DOS can address is used by the virtual disk.

3. To install ANSI.SYS, put this command in the CONFIG.SYS file:

```
DEVICE = ANSI.SYS
```

4. A very common device driver called MOUSE.SYS is not included with DOS. It provides the drivers that operate a mouse. If you have a mouse, you will need to add this command to your CONFIG.SYS file:

```
DEVICE = MOUSE.SYS
```

Exercises

1. What is a device driver?

2. What is a virtual disk?

3. What command would you put into the CON-FIG.SYS file to create a 128K virtual disk that uses 128 byte sectors and allows 32 directory entries?

4. What command loads the ANSI.SYS device driver?

EXERCISES

MASTERY
SKILLS CHECK

At this point, you should be able to answer these questions and perform these exercises:

1. What command would display the following prompt:

   [path]

   where *path* is the path to the current directory?

2. What PROMPT meta-string displays the current time?

3. What command sets the screen to 40-column color text mode?

4. What command sets the first serial port to 1200 baud, 2 stop bits, 8 data bits, and no parity?

5. What command causes the printer to print 132 characters per line and 8 lines per inch?

6. What does PATH do?

7. What command adds to DOS's search path for commands and programs the path /MIKE/WORK /SPSHT?

8. What does APPEND do and how does it differ from PATH?

9. What does the FILES command do? If it is used, in what file should the FILES command be placed?

10. How would you create a virtual disk that has 384K of storage, uses 256 byte sectors, and has 48 directory entries?

EXERCISES

This section checks how well you have integrated the material in this chapter with material from earlier chapters.

INTEGRATING SKILLS CHECK

1. Create a batch file called PR.BAT that prints a file. This batch file should take two arguments. The first argument is the name of the file to be printed. If the second argument is NORM, then the file should print using 80 characters per line and 6 lines per inch. However, should the second argument be CONDENSED, the file should print using 132 characters per line and 8 characters per inch.

2. If you have placed all your application programs in a directory called \APS, all your DOS external commands in the \DOS directory, and all your word processing files in the \WP directory, what PATH and APPEND commands would you include in your AUTOEXEC.BAT file so that you could access all commands, programs, and files from any directory?

3. On your own, add your favorite DOS prompt to your AUTOEXEC.BAT file so that each time your system starts, that prompt will automatically be displayed. Also, should you want to use a virtual disk, add the appropriate command to your CONFIG.SYS file.

Managing Your System

►11◄

Congratulations! If you have worked through the preceding ten chapters, you are now definitely proficient at using DOS. This final chapter presents some important commands and techniques that will help you manage your computer more effectively. Among the new skills you will learn here are backing up and restoring the fixed disk.

EXERCISES

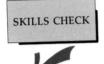

SKILLS CHECK

Before proceeding you should be able to answer these questions and perform these exercises:

1. What command creates a virtual disk that is 128,000 bytes large, uses 128 byte sectors, and has 32 directory entries?

2. What command prints a sorted directory listing on the printer?

3. What does the PATH command do?

4. What command attempts to recover a damaged file called MYDATA.DAT?

5. What command would make TREE.COM read-only?

6. What command would combine two files called FILE1 and FILE2 into a single file called OUTFILE?

7. How many subdirectories can be created on a disk?

8. What command creates a prompt that looks like this (but displays the current time, of course):

```
<12:43:40:12>--->
```

BACK UP YOUR FIXED DISK

11.1

This and the following section are for fixed disk users only. If you do not have a fixed disk in your computer, go on to section 11.3.

NOTE: If you have a tape backup system attached to your computer, you will probably want to use it to back up your fixed disk. If this is the case, refer to the tape backup system's user manual for details of its operation.

Backing up a fixed disk is more complicated than backing up a floppy disk. The reason is easy to understand: A fixed disk holds at least ten times more information than a floppy does. Thus, it takes several floppy disks to store the information on a fixed disk. Although you could conceivably back up your fixed disk using XCOPY in some situations, this is not the most error-free approach. In any case, XCOPY cannot copy a file from the fixed disk to a floppy if the file is larger than the capacity of the floppy. To aid in the fixed disk backup procedure, DOS includes the BACKUP external command.

The general form of the BACKUP command is

BACKUP *source target options*

Here, *source* specifies the drive, path, and file name of the fixed disk to be copied to the *target* drive. You may use the wildcard characters in the source file name. BACKUP supports several options, which we will look at now.

Perhaps the most commonly used BACKUP option is /S, which copies all subdirectories of a specified directory. This option makes it possible to back up the entire fixed disk using one command.

If the diskettes you are using to receive the information have not been previously formatted, you will want to specify the /F option, which causes BACKUP to automatically format each target diskette. (This option is available only in DOS versions 3.30 or later.)

Since backing up the entire contents of a high-capacity fixed disk can be a lengthy procedure, BACKUP includes the /M option. When you specify this option, BACKUP only copies files that have their archive attribute set. This is a good way to save time when only a few files have been created or changed since the last backup was performed. The BACKUP command automatically turns off the archive attribute of each file it backs up.

If you want to append one or more files to the target disk or disks, use the /A option.

You can copy only those files created or last modified on or after a specified date using the /D option. The /D option takes this general form:

/D:*mm-dd-yy*

Similarly, you can copy only files that have times equal to or later than a specified time on a specified date using the /T option. The /T option takes this general form:

/T:hours:minutes:seconds

You need not specify the time precisely. For example, you wouldn't specify the seconds in most situations. You must specify the time using the 24-hour (military style) method, however. Although you can use the /T option by itself, it is most commonly used with the /D option.

The last BACKUP option is /L, which creates a log file where DOS records the path and file name of each file backed up and the target diskette where each backup is stored. The option's general form is

/L:file-name

If you don't specify a file name, BACKUP automatically uses the name BACKUP.LOG. Either way, the log file is always written to the root directory of the source disk.

If a log file by the specified name already exists, the new output is appended to the end of the original file. If the file does not exist, DOS creates it.

Table 11-1 summarizes the seven BACKUP options.

One important point: Since the backup operation uses several diskettes, you must number each diskette, starting with 1. This is important because the recovery process must be performed in the same order as the backup.

Examples

Since the directory structure and contents of every fixed disk differ, the examples in this section are

TABLE 11-1.	The BACKUP Options

Option	Meaning
/A	Add files instead of overwriting the backup diskettes
/D	Copy files with dates on or after the specified date
/F	Format each backup diskette before writing to it
/L	Create a log file
/M	Copy only those files that have been created or changed since the last backup
/S	Back up all subdirectories starting with the specified path
/T	Copy files with times equal to or later than the time specified

"thought experiments" only. Do not actually try the commands. For the examples, imagine that the directory structure of your fixed disk is organized as shown in Figure 11-1.

1. To back up the entire contents, including all subdirectories, of the fixed disk in drive C to diskettes in drive A, you would use this command:

```
BACKUP C:\*.* A: /S
```

As you can see, the /S option is specified. If it were omitted, only the files in the root directory of C would be copied.

As BACKUP began execution, you would see this message:

```
Warning! Files in the target drive
A:\ root directory will be erased
Strike any key when ready

*** Backing up files to drive A: ***
```

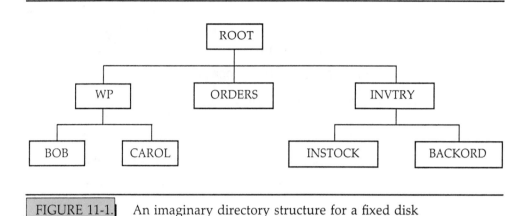

An imaginary directory structure for a fixed disk

As the backup process continued, you would be prompted to insert additional diskettes. Be sure to insert the diskettes in the order in which you numbered them.

2. Keep in mind that you can back up any portion of the fixed disk. For example, this BACKUP command would back up all files in the WP, BOB, and CAROL subdirectories, and format the target diskettes in the process:

```
BACKUP C:\WP\*.* A:/S/F
```

Many computers are used by several people. In this situation, it makes sense for each person to back up only those directories and files that he or she uses and maintains. A command like the previous one is a good way for the person in charge of word processing to back up all word processing files, leaving other parts of the disk for someone else to back up.

3. This command would back up all files in the \INVTRY\INSTOCK directory that were created or last modified on or after March 20, 1990:

```
BACKUP C:\INVTRY\INSTOCK\*.* A: /D:03-20-90
```

By adding a /T option, you could further limit the backup to only those files in the directory \INVTRY\INSTOCK that also were created after 12 noon. The command would look like this:

```
BACKUP C:\INVTRY\INSTOCK\*.* A: /D:03-20-90 /T:12:00
```

4. The next BACKUP command would back up all files in the ORDERS directory that have their archive attribute set. In the process, it would turn off the archive attribute.

```
BACKUP C:\ORDERS\*.* A: /S /M
```

5. The following command would back up all files on the fixed disk and create a log file called MYLOG containing a list of all files that were backed up and the target diskette on which they reside.

```
BACKUP C:\*.* A: /S /L:MYLOG
```

The previous command would create MYLOG if it did not already exist. If it did exist, the original contents would be preserved and the new information appended. On its first line, the log file shows the date and time the backup was begun. Subsequent lines show each file backed up and the number of the target diskette on which it was written. For example, if you backed up the files FILE1, FILE2, and FILE3 on 03-27-90 beginning at 4:30 P.M., you would see a log file that looked like this:

```
03-27-90    16:30:00
001    \FILE1
001    \FILE2
001    \FILE3
```

Log files are very useful because they tell you what diskette a file is on. This makes things much easier when you need to restore only one file, because you don't have to search each diskette, looking for that file.

6. This command would add FORMLET.23 from CAROL's directory to the existing backup diskettes:

```
BACKUP C:\WP\CAROL\FORMLET.23 A: /A
```

Exercises

1. What command backs up all files in the \WP\BOB directory?

2. What command backs up all files on drive C that were created on or after Jan. 10, 1991?

3. What BACKUP option causes only files that have their archive attribute set to be backed up?

4. What option creates a log file?

5. In general, why must you use BACKUP to back up the fixed disk instead of COPY, XCOPY, or DISKCOPY?

6. Since backing up a fixed disk generally requires several diskettes, how must you label the target diskettes?

11.2   LEARN TO RESTORE FILES

One key point to understand about the BACKUP command is that it does not store files on the target diskettes in the normal way. Instead, the files are stored in a special, compressed format designed to minimize the number of diskettes required to back up a fixed disk. Thus, when you need to restore a file, you cannot do so by simply finding the appropriate file and copying it to your fixed disk. In fact, if you look at the directories of the target disks, you will see that they contain only two files each: one called BACKUP.*num* and one called CONTROL.*num* (where *num* is the number of the diskette.) To recover a file you must use DOS's RESTORE external command. Its general form is shown here:

RESTORE *source target options*

The drive that contains the backup diskettes made using BACKUP is specified by *source*. The drive, path, and file name of the file to restore are specified by *target*. Like BACKUP, RESTORE supports several options.

There is one important point to remember about using RESTORE: You must always restore a file to the same subdirectory that held it when it was backed up using BACKUP. If you attempt to restore a file to another directory, RESTORE will issue an error message and will not copy the file.

Table 11-2 summarizes the RESTORE options. Let's look at each of them now.

TABLE 11-2.	The RESTORE Options

Option	Meaning
/A	Restore all files modified on or after the specified date
/B	Restore all files modified on or before the specified date
/E	Restore all files modified at or earlier than the specified time on a given date
/L	Restore all files modified at or later than the specified time on a given date
/M	Restore all files that have been modified or deleted since the last backup
/N	Restore only files that do not exist on the fixed disk
/P	Prompt before restoring a file
/S	Restore all subdirectories

Using the /S option, you can restore all files in the specified directory as well as all files in any subdirectories it may have.

The /P option makes RESTORE prompt you before it overwrites a file that has been modified since the last backup or that is read-only. This option gives you a chance to prevent important information from being accidentally overwritten.

The RESTORE command has several options that allow you to selectively restore files based on their creation (or last modification) dates and times. The /B option lets you restore files created or modified on or before a specified date. The /A option restores files created or modified on or after a specified date. The /B and /A options take the following general forms.

/B:*mm-dd-yy*
/A:*mm-dd-yy*

(If you live in a non-English-speaking country, your date format may be different, but the concept is the same.)

To restore files created or modified on or after a specified time, use the /L option. To restore files created or modified on or before a specified time use the /E option. The /L and /E options have these general forms:

/L:*hours:minutes:seconds*
/E:*hours:minutes:seconds*

You need not specify minutes or seconds. If you don't, RESTORE automatically defaults those fields to 0. Remember, you must specify all times using the 24-hour method.

To restore only files that have been modified or deleted from the target disk since the last backup was made, use the /M option.

If you use the /N option, RESTORE restores only files that don't exist on the target.

Keep one point in mind: RESTORE does not restore the DOS system files or COMMAND.COM. You must copy these files by hand.

Examples

The examples that follow assume the same hypothetical fixed disk structure described in the preceding discussion of BACKUP.

1. To restore the entire fixed disk in drive C, you would use this command:

```
RESTORE A: C:\*.* /S
```

Look carefully at this command. Remember, you must specify precisely what path and file names you want restored on the *target* not the source drive. This means that you must explicitly specify the C drive and the root directory. Also, to restore all files in all subdirectories, you have to use the /S option.

Keep in mind that RESTORE will only restore files to the same directory they were backed up from. This is why the directory path and file names are so important.

When RESTORE begins, you see this message:

```
Insert backup diskette 01 in drive A:
Strike any key when ready
```

This gives you a chance to change diskettes for the RESTORE process. You see a similar message each time RESTORE needs another backup diskette.

2. The next command restores only files that have been modified since the last backup.

```
RESTORE A: C:\*.* /S /M
```

3. You can restore files to a specific directory. For example, this command restores all files ending in .TXT to the BOB subdirectory:

```
RESTORE A: C:\WP\BOB\*.TXT
```

4. This command restores all files created or modified on or after 2-28-90:

```
RESTORE A: C:\*.* /S /A:02-28-90
```

You can use the /A and /B options together to specify a range. For example, the following command would restore all files created or modified on or before 3-30-90 and on or after 2-28-90:

```
RESTORE A: C:\*.* /S /A:02-28-90 /B:03-30-90
```

5. This command restores all files to the ORDERS directory that were modified or created on or after 9:00 A.M.:

```
RESTORE A: C:\ORDERS\*.* /L:9:00
```

6. The next command restores all files, but prompts before restoring a file that has been changed or deleted since the last backup.

```
RESTORE A: C:\*.* /S /P
```

Each time a file that has changed is encountered, you will see a message like this one:

```
Warning! File XXX
was changed after it was backed up
Replace the file (Y/N)?
```

To replace the file, type **Y** followed by [Enter]. To skip the file, type **N** followed by [Enter].

Exercises

1. Why can't you restore a file using COPY?

2. What command restores a file that is called INFO.DAT to the \INVTRY\BACKORD directory?

3. What does the /M option to RESTORE do?

4. What command restores all files created or last modified after 2:00 P.M. on 10-20-90?

5. What command restores all files created or last modified before 2:00 P.M. on 10-20-90?

KNOW WHEN TO BACK UP DISKS   11.3

As you know, the only sure way to protect against the loss of your data and programs is to make backup copies of each file. Although the backup procedure differs for floppy disks and fixed disks, the general concepts are the same.

If your system does not have a fixed disk, the best way to back up your floppies is with the DISKCOPY command. This approach is better than using either

COPY or XCOPY because it ensures that every file on the disk will be copied. DISKCOPY leaves no room for human error, such as forgetting to copy a file. As you learned in the preceding sections, you should use BACKUP to back up a fixed disk.

For backup copies to be useful, they must be up-to-date. Also, you should provide for both on-site and off-site backup copies. Without off-site copies, you would not be able to recover your data after a fire, for example. Although a fireproof safe may provide protection for paper documents, it may not protect diskettes adequately, so off-site copies are extremely important.

It is essential that you establish a backup routine. There are many acceptable backup procedures; the one described here is effective for floppy diskettes. For each work diskette, establish three backup diskettes. Label the backup diskettes using the names *daily*, *weekly*, and *monthly*. At the end of the day, copy your work diskette to the daily backup diskette. Every Friday, copy your work disk to the weekly diskette. At the end of each month, copy your work diskette to the monthly diskette and retire it—that is, at the end of each month, store the monthly backup diskette in a safe place. (Actually, to provide both on-site and off-site storage, you need two monthly diskettes.) The contents of the monthly diskettes are never modified.

The advantage of the backup system just described is that it provides immediate recovery if a work disk is damaged. You can copy the daily backup, which is never more than a few hours out-of-date. However, the system also provides protection against an error being propagated on every backup copy. An error may go unnoticed for several weeks, contaminating both the daily and the weekly backups. However, since the monthly backups are written to only once, the previous month's backup can be used as a pure starting point from which to recover.

If you have a fixed disk, you will want to follow the same general backup procedure that you use for floppy disks, except that on a daily basis, you would back up only files that had changed. Weekly, you would perform a full backup and monthly you would retire the last weekly backup diskettes.

If you do have to use a backup disk be sure to write-protect it first and then make a copy of it. Aside from using it to make a copy, you should never use a backup disk for any other purpose.

USE THE FASTOPEN COMMAND

11.4

It takes DOS longer to access a file located in a deeply nested subdirectory than a file located in the current directory. Beginning with DOS version 3.30, however, the FASTOPEN command alleviates this problem. Essentially, FASTOPEN causes DOS to memorize the path to a deeply nested directory so that it doesn't have to follow the path each time it accesses a file in that directory. FASTOPEN has this general form:

FASTOPEN *drive=num*

Here, *drive* is a drive specifier that indicates which drive will receive the benefit of FASTOPEN, and *num* specifies the number of files (10-999) DOS will remember the path to. If you do not specify a value, FASTOPEN uses the default value of 34. FASTOPEN can only be used with one drive.

FASTOPEN is an external command that installs itself when it is executed. For this reason, FASTOPEN can only be executed once.

FASTOPEN works by remembering the path to each file when the file is first accessed. The first access takes as long as usual, but subsequent accesses are much faster. If you access more files than FASTOPEN can remember, it simply removes the least recently used files and remembers the new path or paths.

It is probably best to use the default value of 34 for the number of files FASTOPEN can remember. If you specify too few files, you won't gain much benefit from FASTOPEN, but if you specify too many, FAST-OPEN may actually degrade performance rather than help it.

Examples

1. This command installs FASTOPEN for drive C, using the default value of 34.

   ```
   FASTOPEN C:
   ```

   If you have a fixed disk, try this command now. If you have a deeply nested subdirectory, create a small text file in it and then return to the root. Now, using TYPE, display the file you just created. You will hear the disk drive's head move about while it searches through the various subdirectories looking for your file. Next, try typing the file a second time. This time, the drive's movement is greatly reduced and the file is immediately displayed. DOS has memorized the file's location and no longer has to search each subdirectory for it.

2. This command installs FASTOPEN for drive C so that it can remember the paths to 100 directories or files:

```
FASTOPEN C:=100
```

Exercises

1. Assuming you have a fixed disk, try the first example if you have not already done so.

2. What command installs FASTOPEN for drive D and allows it to remember up to 45 files?

EXERCISES

At this point, you should be able to answer these questions and perform these exercises:

MASTERY
SKILLS CHECK

1. Why is it important to occasionally "retire" a backup diskette?

2. What command should you use to back up a floppy disk?

3. What command should you use to back up a fixed disk?

4. What command backs up the entire fixed disk in drive C to drive A?

5. What command restores a fixed disk?

6. What command backs up to drive A only files on the fixed disk in drive C that have been modified or created since the last backup?

7. What command restores all files created or last modified on or after July 20, 1990?

8. What does FASTOPEN do?

EXERCISES

INTEGRATING SKILLS CHECK

This section checks how well you have integrated the material in this chapter with the material from earlier chapters.

1. As you know, the log file produced by the BACKUP command using the /L option contains a complete list of all backed up files and of the target diskettes on which they reside. Assuming that the log file is called MYLOG, what command would tell you

whether a file called INFO.DAT had been copied and what disk it was on if it had been?

2. What command must you issue to have BACKUP and RESTORE automatically verify the success of each write operation?

3. If you have a fixed disk, put the FASTOPEN command into your AUTOEXEC.BAT file.

4. On your own, continue to explore your computer and DOS. The more you know about both, the better you will be able to use them.

EDLIN: The DOS Text Editor

This appendix explains how to use EDLIN, DOS's text editor, to create, modify, and maintain text files. If you have a different text editor or word processor and you know how to use it, you can skip this appendix; there is little point in learning to use EDLIN if you are already using a different editor.

Unless you are using a fixed disk, you will need your DOS work diskette in drive A to follow the examples in this chapter.

WHAT EDLIN IS AND ISN'T

EDLIN is a line-oriented text editor. It is not a screen-based editor, nor is it, in the proper definition of the term, a word processor. Its sole function is to allow the creation and modification of text files on a line-by-line basis. As text editors go, EDLIN is rather old-fashioned. It doesn't offer any flashy features, but it is sufficient for the examples in this book.

If you are new to microcomputers, keep in mind that EDLIN is not representative of the text editors in general use. It is a simple editor that is supplied with DOS so you can create and modify short text files that help you customize DOS and tailor it to your needs. EDLIN is not intended to take the place of a full-featured, screen-oriented text editor or word processor. If you need to perform extensive editing or word processing, you should invest in a high-performance package.

Today, most editors use the WYSIWYG (pronounced *wiz-ee-wig*) approach, which stands for "What you see is what you get." This means that files appear on the screen just as they look when they are printed. However, EDLIN does not follow this principle to a very great extent. With EDLIN, what you see on the screen is somewhat different from the printed file.

Another difference between EDLIN and most modern text editors is that EDLIN does not use the arrow keys to move around the screen. This is because EDLIN is not screen-oriented. Instead, EDLIN is line-oriented, which means it can only deal with one line of text at a time, not with a whole screenful.

EXECUTING EDLIN

EDLIN is an external command, so to use it you need a copy of EDLIN.COM on your work disk. To execute EDLIN, use this general form

EDLIN *file-name*

where *file-name* is the name of the text file you wish to edit. If *file-name* does not exist, EDLIN creates it. Remember that *file-name* may include a drive specifier and a path name.

SOME EDLIN BASICS

In this section, you will learn the essentials of EDLIN's operation including entering text, listing a file, saving the file, and exiting EDLIN. Once you understand EDLIN's basic operation, you'll be prepared for later sections in this chapter, which discuss EDLIN's commands in greater detail.

Creating a Text File

Execute EDLIN by entering

```
EDLIN EDTEST.TXT
```

When EDLIN begins executing, you will see the following:

```
New file
*_
```

As you might expect, the message "New file" simply means that the specified file did not exist and EDLIN has created it. The asterisk (*) is EDLIN's prompt. Whenever you see it, you know that EDLIN is ready to accept a command.

This is an important point: EDLIN operates a little like DOS itself. It displays a prompt and waits for a command. Each time you give EDLIN a command it performs the specific task, and when it is complete, another prompt appears.

Entering Text

As stated previously, when EDLIN displays its prompt, it is in command mode and is *not* ready to accept text. To prepare EDLIN to accept text you must issue it the I (Insert) command. (You may enter this and the other EDLIN commands in upper- or lower-case, as you like.) For example, enter the I command by typing **I** and then enter these lines of text:

Now is the time
for all good men
to come to the aid of their party.

Your screen will look like this:

```
*I
    1:*Now is the time
    2:*for all good men
    3:*to come to the aid of their party.
    4:*_
```

In Insert mode, EDLIN tabs in, displays the current line number and an asterisk (which in Insert mode indicates the currently active line), and waits for input. Each time you press (Enter) a new line number appears. Please remember that when the asterisk follows the line number, it is *not* a command prompt—it simply indicates the active line. (Initially, this is one of the most confusing aspects of EDLIN.)

The line numbers are not part of your file and will not be stored on the disk when the file is saved. Rather, they are supplied by EDLIN both as a convenience and as a means of referring to a line.

If you make a mistake while typing a line, you can use the same commands, functions keys, and control keys that DOS accepts to correct your mistake. However, once you have pressed (Enter), you must use special EDLIN commands to make corrections.

To stop entering text you press the (Ctrl)-(Break) key combination. Try this now. As you can see, a ^C is displayed and EDLIN's prompt reappears.

Listing a File

To list the contents of the file currently being edited, you use the L (List lines) command. To execute its simplest form, simply type **L** and press (Enter). Do so now, and you will see the text you just entered displayed like this:

```
1: Now is the time
2: for all good men
3: to come to the aid of their party.
```

Terminating EDLIN

There are two ways to terminate EDLIN. The one you will use most often is the E (End edit) command, which causes EDLIN to save the contents of the file and then terminate. The other is the Q (Quit edit) command, which causes EDLIN to abort without saving the file to disk.

Exit EDLIN using the E command at this time.

Reediting a File

EDLIN behaves a little differently when you are editing a preexisting file than when you are editing a new file. To begin, edit EDTEST.TXT once more by entering

```
EDLIN EDTEST.TXT
```

When EDLIN begins execution, you will see this message:

```
End of input file
*
```

The message "End of input file" is EDLIN's way of telling you that it has loaded the entire file into memory. The only time you would not see this message after loading a file is when the file is too large to fit into memory. In this case, EDLIN reads the file until 75 percent of the memory is used. To edit the remainder of a large file, you must use some special commands, which are discussed later. These commands write part of the file back to disk and then read more of the file from disk. In any case, it is unlikely you will ever have a file larger than will fit into memory.

Now list the file using the L command. It will look like this:

```
1:*Now is the time
2: for all good men
3: to come to the aid of their party.
```

Notice that the asterisk is at the start of line 1. Remember, this is EDLIN's way of telling you which line is current. The current line determines where certain commands will take effect. For example, if you enter the I command and begin inserting text now, the text that you entered would be inserted *before* line 1. Try this by typing **This is before line one**. Press [Enter] and then [Ctrl]-[Break]. List the file, and your screen will look like this:

```
1: This is before line one
2:*Now is the time
3: for all good men
4: to come to the aid of their party.
```

Notice that line 2 is now current. You'll learn more about the meaning and manipulation of the current line in the next section.

Enter the E command to save the EDTEST.TXT file to disk and exit the editor. At the DOS prompt, enter this command:

```
DIR EDTEST.*
```

Two files are displayed. One is EDTEST.TXT, as you might expect. The other is called EDTEST.BAK. This file contains the previous version of EDTEST.TXT. The .BAK extension stands for backup. Each time EDLIN saves text to an existing file, it first changes the extension of the existing file to .BAK and then writes the text to disk using the actual file name. In this way you always have the old version of your file in case you accidentally corrupt the current version. Periodically, you may want to erase backup files that you no longer need to gain additional disk space.

The Current Line

The concept of the current line is intrinsic to EDLIN's operation. You can think of the current line as the line you are "on." As stated earlier, EDLIN identifies the current line with the asterisk. When you begin editing a file, line one is current. As you will see shortly, a number of EDLIN commands change the current line.

When you insert text, EDLIN places it before the current line and the rest of the existing text moves down.

EDLIN'S COMMANDS

Now that you know the basics of EDLIN's operation, you're ready to study its commands in greater detail. EDLIN has 14 commands, which are summarized in Table A-1. Let's examine each of these commands more closely.

Inserting Text

To insert text at this point, edit EDTEST.TXT (use **EDLIN EDTEST.TXT**). Enter **2I**, type **this is new line two**, and press (Enter). Then press (Ctrl)-(Break). Use the L command to list the file. It will look like this:

```
1: This is before line one
2: this is new line two
3:*Now is the time
4: for all good men
5: to come to the aid of their party.
```

By placing a line number in front of the I command you told EDLIN to begin inserting text immediately before that line. The general form of the I command is

line-numI

where *line-num* is the number of the line before which you wish to add text. If you don't specify the line number, text is inserted before the current line.

To add text to the end of a file, simply specify a line number greater than the last line number of the file.

| TABLE A-1. | The EDLIN Commands |

Command	Meaning
A	Append lines from disk file
C	Copy lines
D	Delete lines
E	End edit and save file
I	Insert lines
L	List lines
M	Move lines
P	Display a page (23 lines)
Q	Quit without saving file
R	Replace text
S	Search text
T	Transfer lines (merges one file into another)
W	Write lines to file
line-num	Intra-line edit line *line-num*

For example, you could enter **6I** to add lines to the end of the EDTEST.TXT file. Try this now; then add these lines

Text editors
are fun to use
as long as you know the
right commands.

and press (Ctrl)-(Break). If you list the file, you will see that the lines have indeed been added to the end of the file.

Deleting Lines

To delete lines of text, use the D (Delete) command. The command has this general form:

*start-line, end-line*D

Start-line and *end-line* are line numbers. The Delete command deletes all lines from *start-line* to *end-line*. For example, using the EDTEST.TXT file, try this command:

3,5D

Now list the file. Your screen will look like this:

```
1: This is before line one
2: this is new line two
3:*Text editors
4: are fun to use
5: as long as you know the
6: right commands.
```

If you do not specify the starting line number, the Delete command deletes all lines from the current line to the ending line. You must start this form of the command with a comma, however. For example, this would delete lines 3 and 4 in the previous example.

```
,4D
```

You can delete any single line by simply specifying its line number. For example, this would delete line 2:

```
2D
```

Notice that no comma precedes this form of the command.

Finally, if no line number is specified, EDLIN deletes the current line.

Listing a File

So far, you have seen only the simplest form of the L command. Its general form is

*start-line, end-line*L

where *start-line* and *end-line* specify a range of lines to list on the screen. For example, to list lines 3 through 5, enter

```
3,5L
```

You'll see this display:

```
3:*Text editors
4: are fun to use
5: as long as you know the
```

If you omit the starting line number, EDLIN displays 11 lines before the current line and stops at the specified ending line. You must start this form of the command with a comma.

Omitting the ending line causes EDLIN to display 23 lines beginning with the specified line. If less than 23 lines remain, EDLIN displays lines until it reaches the end of the file. For example, issue this command, still using EDTEST.TXT:

```
4L
```

The following display will result:

```
4: are fun to use
5: as long as you know the
```

If no line numbers are specified, EDLIN displays 11 lines before and after the current line for a total of 23 lines, if there are that many in the file.

Editing Lines

To edit, or modify, an existing line in a file, enter its line number. EDLIN displays the specified line with the cursor positioned beneath the first character in the line. You can use any of the DOS editing keys to make changes to the line. The process of editing an existing line is called *intra-line editing*.

For example, enter **2** now, and you will see this:

```
2:*this is new line two
2: _
```

You may now edit this line exactly as you would the DOS command line. For example, press F1 until the cursor is positioned after the space following the word "is". Now, press Ins and type **a new addition to**. Then press F3 followed by Enter. When you list the file, line 2 will look like this:

```
2:*this is a new addition to new line two
```

Once you press Enter, any changes you have made to the line become part of the file. You can cancel the edit at any time before you press Enter by pressing either Esc or Ctrl - Break. Also, if you have not yet moved the cursor from the start of the line, pressing Enter cancels the intra-line editing process.

You can edit the current line by entering a period instead of its line number.

Copying Lines

The C (Copy) command is used to copy a range of lines. It has the general form

*start-line, end-line, dest-line, count*C

All the lines from *start-line* through *end-line* are copied in front of *dest-line*, *count* number of times. If *count* is not specified, the default is one.

For example, again using the EDTEST.TXT file, enter this command:

```
1,3,6L
```

The file will now look like this:

```
1: This is before line one
2: this is new line two
3:*Text editors
4: are fun to use
5: as long as you know the
6: This is before line one
7: this is new line two
8: Text editors
9: right commands.
```

REMEMBER: A copy duplicates lines. This means that the copied lines still appear in their original position as well as in the new location. The Move command, discussed next, is used to remove lines from one position and place them in another.

If you specify a count value, the specified lines are duplicated that many times. For example, try this command:

```
1,1,4,3C
```

Your file will now look like this:

```
 1: This is before line one
 2: this is new line two
 3: Text editors
 4:*This is before line one
 5: This is before line one
 6: This is before line one
 7: are fun to use
 8: as long as you know the
 9: This is before line one
10: this is new line two
11: Text editors
12: right commands.
```

Keep in mind that the destination line must be outside the range of the lines to be copied.

Moving Lines

The M (Move Lines) command is similar to the Copy command except it moves the specified range of lines from one spot in the file to another. Its general form is

*start-line, end-line, dest-line*M

Before proceeding, let's clean up the EDTEST.TXT file. First, delete all existing lines by entering **1,100D**. Now, insert the following lines:

one
two
three
four
five
six
seven
eight
nine
ten

Once this is done, try the following Move command:

```
2,5,8M
```

Now, list the file. It will look like this:

```
 1: one
 2: six
 3: seven
 4:*two
 5: three
 6: four
 7: five
 8: eight
 9: nine
10: ten
```

As you can see, the original lines 2 through 5 have been relocated to immediately precede line 8.

If you omit either the starting line, the ending line, or both, EDLIN uses the current line by default. For example, this command would move line 4 to the top of the file:

```
,,1M
```

As with the Copy command, the destination must not be within the range being moved.

Searching

To find a specific string in a file, use the S (Search) command. A *string* is simply a sequence of characters. The Search command takes this general form:

start-line, end-line, ? Sstring

The Search command searches the file between *start-line* and *end-line* looking for an occurrence of *string*. The ? is optional, and is used to find multiple occurrences.

To begin, delete all the lines in the EDTEST.TXT file and enter the following:

```
This is a test
of the search command.
From time to time,
you will find this command useful -
especially when the file is very large.
```

Once you have entered these lines, try this command:

```
1,5Stime
```

EDLIN displays the line that contains the specified string:

```
3: From time to time,
```

The line in which a match is found is also made current.

If you want to search for a specific occurrence of a string that appears more than once in the file, use the ? option. Without the ? option, EDLIN will only find the *first* occurrence. For example, enter this command:

```
1,5?Sthe
```

EDLIN responds

```
    2: of the search command.
O.K.? _
```

As you can see, the ? causes EDLIN to ask whether the desired occurrence of the string has been found. If it has, type Y or press (Enter); otherwise, press any other key. Type N this time, and EDLIN will find the second "the" in line 5 and will once again prompt you. Type N again. Since there are no more occurrences of "the" in the file, EDLIN prints the message "Not found".

The Search command is case-sensitive; it recognizes upper- and lowercase versions of the same character as different. For example, try entering

```
1,5?SThis
```

EDLIN finds the match with "This" in line 1, but does not report any other matches because in line 4 "this" begins with a lowercase *t*.

If you omit the first line number, the Search command begins with the line immediately following the current line. Omitting the second line number causes the search to continue through the last line in the file. If you omit the search string, EDLIN uses the previous search string, assuming there is one.

Go ahead and experiment with the Search command a few times before you move on.

Replacing Text

To replace one string with another you use the R (Replace) command. The general form of the Replace command is

start-line, end-line ?R*old-string* < F6 > *new-string*

The first two line numbers define the range over which the replacement will take place. The ? is optional. If you include it, EDLIN will prompt you prior to each replacement. *Old-string* is the string to be replaced by *new-string*. You must separate the old and new strings by pressing the F6 key.

Using the file you developed in the previous section, try the following command:

```
1,5Rtime<F6>day
```

Note that the F6 key displays as ^Z. This command changes line 3 from

```
From time to time
```

to

```
From day to day
```

If you do not want to change all occurrences of a string, use the ? option. EDLIN will prompt you to verify the change at each occurrence. For example, try using this command to change the sentences to past tense:

```
1,5?Ris<F6>was
```

The first thing you'll see is

```
     1: Thwas is a test
O.K.? _
```

As you can see, EDLIN found the "is" in "This". Since you do not want to change this "is" to "was", answer **N**. EDLIN then looks for other occurrences. The next one is the one you want to change. You will see

```
     1: This was a test
O.K.? _
```

Since you do want to change this "is", answer **Y**. This process will continue until EDLIN has searched all five lines.

You can use the Replace command to remove unwanted text by leaving the new string blank. For example, try this command:

```
1,5Ra<F6>
```

As you can see, every *a* is removed from the file. Pressing F6 is technically unnecessary in this case.

As with the Search command, omitting the first line number causes the replacements to begin with the line immediately following the current line. If the ending line number is not present, the replacement process ends with the last line in the file. If no strings are specified, EDLIN uses the strings from the previous R command.

If you wish, try using Replace on your own at this time.

Using the Page Command

The P (Page) command is used to list a block of lines on the display. It differs from the List command in that it resets the current line to the last line displayed. In its simplest form Page pages through a file 23 lines at a time. To use Page in this way, enter **P** repeatedly. The command's general form is

start-line, end-line P

If present, *start-line* and *end-line* specify a range of lines to display. If *start-line* is omitted, the line following the current line is used. If *end-line* is not specified, EDLIN lists 23 lines.

Using End Edit and Quit

As described earlier, End edit, E, terminates the editing process and saves the file. Quit, Q, terminates the editor but does not save what has been edited.

Transferring Text Between Files

EDLIN's T (Transfer) command allows you to merge the contents of a file on disk into the file you are currently editing. So that you can follow along, create two files called TEST1.TXT and TEST2.TXT. Enter these lines in TEST1.TXT:

```
one
two
three
four
```

In TEST2.TXT, enter

This is a test

Now, issue this command to edit TEST1:

```
3TTEST2.TXT
```

When you list the file, it will look like this:

```
one
two
This is a test
three
four
```

As you can see, the contents of TEST2 have been read into TEST1 immediately before line 3.

The Transfer command takes this general form:

line-numTfile-name

where *line-num* is the number of the line before which the text from the disk file will be placed. The *file-name* is the name of the file to read in. If no line number is specified, EDLIN adds the text before the current line.

There are three things to remember about the Transfer command. First, the text is read in immediately before the line specified. Second, if the specified file is not in the current directory, EDLIN displays the message "File not found". Third, the entire contents of the disk file are read in; you cannot transfer part of a file.

Using Append and Write

When you are editing a file that is too large to fit in memory, EDLIN reads in the file until 75 percent of free memory is used. You can tell EDLIN to read in more lines using the A (Append) command. The Append command has this general form

*num-lines*A

where *num-lines* is the number of additional lines to be read in. For example, 45A would read in 45 more lines. If no number is specified, EDLIN reads one additional line.

To edit the end of a very large file you may need to free memory by writing part of it to disk before you issue the Append command. To do this you use the W (Write) command, which has this general form:

*num-lines*W

Here, *num-lines* refers to the number of lines to write to the disk. If no number is specified, text is written until 75 percent of memory is free. The Write command writes lines from the top of the file, starting with line 1.

Quick Command Reference

This appendix contains a short summary of each DOS command. The commands are presented in alphabetical order. If you're not sure what a command does and need to find out quickly, or if you don't know which command you should use for some operation, this appendix can help. However, this appendix does not present a complete discussion of each command. If you need a full explanation, refer to the appropriate chapter earlier in this book.

The following notational conventions are used in this appendix: Items enclosed between square brackets ([]) are optional. Unless where explicitly noted otherwise, the term *path* refers to the full path name including an optional drive specifier. The term *file-name* may include a drive specifier and a path name. Finally, three periods (...)

indicate a variable length list, and two periods (..) indicate a range, such as 1..10.

For most commands, the complete general form of the command is shown. However, a few commands have very rarely used options, and these are presented in their most common form.

APPEND

The APPEND external command is used to join one directory to another. If directory B is joined to directory A, it will appear to the user that directory A contains all of A's and B's files. APPEND is an installed command. It is executed for the first time using one of these two forms:

APPEND *path1*[;*path2;..pathN*]

or

APPEND [/X] [/E]

The first form uses APPEND's default method of operation; you have access to the appended directory, but you cannot see the files in a listing of the appended directory, nor can you execute a command. The second form is used to install APPEND. The /X option causes all files in the appended directory to appear in a listing of the directory they are appended to. Also, it enables programs in the appended directory to be executed from within the appended to directory. The /E option causes the appended paths to be held in the DOS environment. APPEND allows access to data files in much the same way that PATH allows access to program files.

You can see the currently appended directories by simply entering the APPEND command without arguments. The following form disassociates any appended directories:

APPEND ;

Example This command appends the \WP directory:

```
APPEND \WP
```

ASSIGN

The ASSIGN external command redirects I/O operations from one disk drive to another. It takes this general form:

ASSIGN *drive1 = drive2* [*drive3 = drive4* . . .]

Example To reverse the assignments of drives A and B, you could use this command:

```
ASSIGN A=B B=A
```

All I/O operations for A would then go to B and all I/O operations for B would be redirected to A.

You reset the drives to their original assignments by entering **ASSIGN** without arguments.

ATTRIB

The ATTRIB external command allows you to set or examine the archive and read-only file attributes. It takes this general form:

ATTRIB [+R] [−R] [+A] [−A] [*file-name*] [/S]

where *file-name* is the name of the file or files for which you will set or examine attributes. Wildcard characters are allowed. The +R option turns on the read-only attribute; −R turns it off. The +A option turns on the archive attribute; −A turns it off. If one of these options is not present, ATTRIB displays the current state of the file attributes. The /S option tells ATTRIB to process files in the current directory plus any subdirectories.

Example   This command turns on the read-only attribute for all .EXE files in the current directory:

```
ATTRIB +R *.EXE
```

BACKUP

The external command BACKUP is used primarily to back up a fixed disk by copying its contents to several floppy diskettes. Used in this way, the command takes the general form:

BACKUP *source-drive*[*file-name*] *target-drive* [/A]
        [/D:*date*] [/F] [/L] [/M] [/S] [/T:*time*]

The *file-name* may include wildcard characters.

The meaning of each BACKUP option is shown here:

Option	Meaning
/A	Add files to existing target diskettes
/D:*date*	Copy only files that have dates the same or later than *date*
/F	Format the target diskette before copying
/L	Create and maintain a log file
/M	Copy only files that have been modified since the last backup
/S	Process all subdirectories
/T:*time*	Copy only files that have times equal to or later than *time* on the specified date

Example   Executed from the root directory of drive C, this command would back up the entire fixed disk:

```
BACKUP C: A: /S
```

BREAK

The internal BREAK command tells DOS to check more frequently for the [Ctrl]-[Break] key combination, which is used to cancel commands. BREAK takes this general form:

BREAK [ON] [OFF]

You may be tempted to set BREAK to ON as a matter of course; however, in general it is not a good idea to do so, because when BREAK is on, all commands and programs execute more slowly.

Example   This command tells DOS to check more frequently for the Ctrl - Break key combination:

```
BREAK ON
```

CALL

The CALL batch command is used to execute a batch file from within another batch file. The general form of CALL is

CALL *batch-file*

where *batch-file* is the name of the batch file you wish to execute.

Example   This command calls a batch file named COPYALL.BAT:

```
CALL COPYALL
```

CHCP

The internal CHCP command is used with code page switching for extended foreign-language and foreign-country support. It is a little-used command that is not generally required. Refer to your DOS manual for more information.

CHDIR

The internal CHDIR command (CD) is used to change the current directory. It takes this general form:

CHDIR *path*

where *path* is the path name of the directory you are changing to.

Example   This command makes the \WP directory current:

```
CHDIR \WP
```

CHKDSK

The CHKDSK external command reports the status of the specified drive and repairs certain types of disk errors. It takes this general form:

CHKDSK [*drive-specifier*][*file-name*][/F][/V]

If *drive-specifier* is absent, CHKDSK checks the current disk. The /F option instructs CHKDSK to fix any errors that it can. The /V option displays all files and their paths. Specifying a *file-name*, which may include wildcard characters, causes CHKDSK to report the number of noncontiguous, or nonadjacent, sectors used by the specified file or files.

Example   This command reports the status of drive A and attempts to fix any errors:

```
CHKDSK A: /F
```

CLS

The internal CLS command clears the computer's display monitor screen.

COMP

The COMP external command is used to compare two files. It has this general form:

COMP *first-file second-file*

where *first-file* and *second-file* are file names that may contain wildcard characters.

Example   This command compares the contents of the file ACCOUNTS.DAT on drive A to a file by the same name on drive B:

```
COMP A:ACCOUNTS.DAT B:ACCOUNTS.DAT
```

COPY

The internal COPY command is used to copy the contents of one file into another file. It takes this general form:

COPY source destination [/V]

where *source* is the name of the file to be copied into *destination*. Both file names may include wildcard characters. The /V option causes COPY to automatically verify that the information from the source file has been accurately copied to the destination file.

Example   This command copies to the C drive all files that begin with the extension .EXE.

```
COPY *.EXE C:
```

CTTY

The CTTY internal command is used to switch console control to a different device, such as a remote terminal. It takes this general form:

CTTY *device-name*

The *device-name* must be one of DOS's standard device names. Do not try this command unless there actually is another device attached to your computer that is capable of controlling it.

DATE

The internal DATE command is used to set the system date. It takes this general form:

DATE [*date*]

where *date* is the current date. You must use the proper date convention for the country that you live in. For the United States, the correct format is *mm-dd-yy*. If *date* is not specified on the command line, DATE reports its latest information about the current date and waits for you to either enter the correct date or press Enter indicating that you accept the date reported.

Example   This command sets the system date to June 26, 1991:

DATE 6-26-91

DEBUG

The external DEBUG command is used by programmers to help locate problems in programs. (You may not have DEBUG in your version of DOS.)

DEL

The DEL internal command erases files from a disk. It takes this general form:

DEL *file-name*

where *file-name* is the name of the file to be erased. You can use wildcard characters in the file name to erase groups of files. ERASE is another name for DEL.

Example This command would erase all files that begin with INV from the disk in drive B:

```
DEL B:INV*.*
```

DIR

The DIR internal command lists a disk's directory. It has this general form:

DIR [*file-name*] [/P] [/W]

If *file-name* is present, only files that match the file name will be displayed. Otherwise, the entire directory is listed. Wildcard characters are allowed in the file name. The /P option pauses the display every 23 lines. The /W option causes the directory to be displayed in four columns across the screen.

Example This command lists only files with the extension .BAT:

```
DIR *.BAT
```

DISKCOMP

The external DISKCOMP command is used to compare two diskettes for equality. The most common form of this command is

DISKCOMP *first-drive second-drive*

where *first-drive* and *second-drive* are drive specifiers.

Example This command compares a diskette in drive A to one in drive B:

```
DISKCOMP A: B:
```

DISKCOPY

The external DISKCOPY command is used to make a copy of a diskette. The most common form of this command is

DISKCOPY *source destination*

where *source* and *destination* are drive specifiers. DISKCOPY cannot be used to copy a fixed disk.

Example This command copies a diskette in drive A to one in drive B:

```
DISKCOPY A: B:
```

ECHO

The ECHO batch command is used to write messages to the screen and turn on or off the echoing of other batch commands. It takes this general form:

ECHO [on] [off] [*message*]

Example   This command prints the message "Backing up all files" to the screen:

```
ECHO Backing up all files
```

EDLIN

The external EDLIN command is used to create and maintain text files. It has this general form:

EDLIN *file-name*

where *file-name* is the file to be edited. EDLIN recognizes these commands:

Command	Meaning
A	Append lines from disk file
C	Copy lines
D	Delete lines
E	End edit and save file
I	Insert lines
L	List lines
M	Move lines
P	Display a page (23 lines)
Q	Quit without saving file
R	Replace text
S	Search text
T	Transfer lines (merges one file into another)
W	Write lines to file
line-num	Intra-line edit line *line-num*

For details, refer to Appendix A.

ERASE

The ERASE internal command erases files from a disk. It takes this general form:

ERASE *file-name*

where *file-name* is the name of the file to be erased. You can use wildcard characters in the file name to erase groups of files. DEL is another name for ERASE.

Example This command erases all files that have the extension .DAT from the disk in drive B:

```
DEL B:*.DAT
```

FASTOPEN

The external FASTOPEN command allows DOS to remember the location of files that are in deeply nested subdirectories, thus providing faster access to these files. The general form of the command is

FASTOPEN *drive-specifier*[=*num*]

where *num* determines the number of files DOS will remember. This number can be from 10 through 999. The default is 34. FASTOPEN is an installed command. That is, you can only execute it once each time you turn the computer on.

Example   This command causes DOS to remember the location of 34 files on the fixed disk:

```
FASTOPEN C:
```

FDISK

The external FDISK command is used to partition a fixed disk when it is first prepared for use. Refer to Appendix D for details.

FIND

The external FIND command searches for occurrences of a string in a list of files. FIND is a filter that sends its output to the standard output, which may be redirected. The general form of FIND is

FIND [/C] [/N] [/V] *"string"* *file-list*

where *string* is the string being searched for and *file-list* is the list of files to search. Notice that the options must precede the string.

The /C option causes FIND to display a count of the string's occurrences. The /N option causes the relative line number of each match to be displayed. The /V option causes FIND to display lines that do not contain the string.

Example   This command searches through the files REC1.DAT and REC2.DAT for the string "payroll":

```
FIND "payroll" REC1.DAT REC2.DAT
```

FOR

The FOR batch command is used to repeat a series of commands using different arguments. The FOR command takes this general form:

FOR %%*var* IN (*argument list*) DO *command*

where *var* is a single-letter variable that takes on the values of the arguments in *argument list*. The arguments in the list must be separated by spaces. The FOR command repeats *command* as many times as there are arguments. Each time the FOR command repeats, *var* is replaced by a new argument moving from left to right in the argument list.

Example This command prints the files TEXT1, TEXT2, and TEXT3:

```
FOR %%F IN (TEXT1 TEXT2 TEXT3) DO PRINT %%F
```

FORMAT

The external FORMAT command prepares a diskette for use. Its most common form is

FORMAT *drive-specifier* [/V]

The diskette to be formatted must be in the specified drive. The /V option causes FORMAT to prompt you for a volume label after a disk is formatted.

You must remember that formatting a disk destroys all preexisting data on that disk, so use the FORMAT command with care.

Example   This command formats the disk that is in drive A:

```
FORMAT A:
```

GOTO

The GOTO batch command directs DOS to execute the commands in a batch file nonsequentially. The general form of GOTO is

GOTO *label*

where *label* is a label that is defined elsewhere in the batch file. When the GOTO command is executed, it causes DOS to go to the specified label and begin executing commands from that point. Using GOTO you can cause execution to jump forward or backward in a batch file.

Example   This command causes execution to jump to the label DONE:

```
GOTO DONE
```

GRAFTABL

The external GRAFTABL command loads a character table that gives DOS extended foreign-language support. It requires a color/graphics adapter. Users of English, will not need this command.

GRAPHICS

The external GRAPHICS command lets you print graphics images on the printer using the print-screen function. The general form of the command is

GRAPHICS [*printer*] [/R] [/B] [/LCD]

where the name of *printer* is determined according to this list:

Printer type	Name
IBM Personal Graphics Printer	GRAPHICS
IBM Proprinter	GRAPHICS
IBM PC Convertible Printer	THERMAL
IBM Compact Printer	COMPACT
IBM Color Printer with black ribbon	COLOR1
IBM Color Printer with red, green, and blue ribbon	COLOR4
IBM Color Printer with cyan, magenta, and yellow ribbon	COLOR8

If no printer name is specified, the IBM Personal Graphics Printer is assumed. The Epson MX-70, MX-80, and MX-100 printers, which are commonly used with microcomputers, are also specified with the GRAPHICS printer name. By default, what is white on the screen prints black on the printer and what is black on the screen prints white. The /R option causes black to print as black, and white to print as white. Generally, the background color of the screen is not printed. However, if you have a color printer, you can print the background by specifying the /B option. Finally, specify the /LCD option for computers using the IBM PC Convertible Liquid Crystal Display.

Example   This command enables graphics images to be printed using the default GRAPHICS printer:

GRAPHICS

IF

The IF batch command takes this general form:

IF *condition command*

If the condition evaluates to true, the command that follows the condition is executed. Otherwise, DOS skips the rest of the line and moves on to the next line in the batch file, assuming there is another line. (Refer to Chapter 7 for details.)

JOIN

The external JOIN command joins one drive to the directory of another. Thus, files on the first drive may be accessed from the joined drive as if they were in a subdirectory. JOIN takes this general form:

JOIN *joining-drive joined-drive\directory* [/D]

The joining drive will appear to be in the specified directory of the joined drive. The /D option is used to disconnect a join.

Example This command would join the A drive to the C drive using the directory ADRIVE:

```
JOIN A: C:\ADRIVE
```

KEYB

The external KEYB command loads keyboard information for foreign-language support. Its most common form is

KEYB *keyboard-code, code-page*

where *keyboard-code* and *code-page* are determined using the following table:

Country	Keyboard-code	Code-page
Australia	US	437
Belgium	BE	437
Canada (English)	US	437
Canada (French)	CF	863
Denmark	DK	865
Finland	SU	437
France	FR	437
Germany	GR	437
Italy	IT	437

Country	Keyboard-code	Code-page
Latin American countries	LA	437
Netherlands	NL	437
Norway	NO	865
Portugal	PO	860
Spain	SP	437
Sweden	SV	437
Switzerland (French)	SF	437
Switzerland (German)	SG	437
United Kingdom	UK	437
United States	US	437

Users of English will not need this command.

Example   This command would configure the keyboard for use in Germany:

```
KEYB GR,437
```

LABEL

The external LABEL command creates or changes a disk's volume label. It has this general form:

LABEL [*drive-specifier*][*name*]

If no drive specifier is used, LABEL assumes the current disk. If you do not specify the volume name on the command line, LABEL prompts you for it. Disk volume labels may be up to 11 characters long.

Example   This command changes the volume label on the current disk to MYDISK:

```
LABEL MYDISK
```

LINK

The external LINK command is used only by programmers. (You may not have a LINK command in your version of DOS.)

MKDIR

The internal MKDIR (MD for short) command is used to create a subdirectory. Its general form is

MKDIR *path*

where *path* specifies the complete path name to the directory. The path name may not exceed 63 characters in length.

Example   This command creates a directory called \WP\FORMS:

```
MD \WP\FORMS
```

MODE

The external MODE command sets the way various devices operate. MODE is a very complex command with several different forms. (Refer to chapter 10 for details.)

MORE

The external MORE command allows you to page through a text file 23 lines at a time. It is a filter that reads standard input and writes to standard output. Its most common form is

MORE <*file-name*

where *file-name* is the file to be viewed.

You can also use MORE in conjunction with other commands, such as DIR, as a convenient way to page through displays that are longer than one screen.

Example This command would display the directory 23 lines at a time:

```
DIR | MORE
```

NLSFUNC

The external NLSFUNC command is used by DOS versions 3.30 or later to provide extended support for non-English-speaking users. You will most likely not need it. For information on this command refer to your DOS manual.

PATH

The internal PATH command defines a search path that DOS then uses to locate program files in directories other than the current one. The command takes this general form:

PATH *path[;path. . .;path]*

where *path* is the specified search path. You can define multiple search paths by separating each path with a semicolon. Spaces are not allowed in the path list.

Example   This command defines a path to the directory \WP\FORMS:

```
PATH \WP\FORMS
```

PAUSE

The PAUSE batch command temporarily stops a batch file's execution. It takes this general form:

PAUSE [*message*]

If a message is present, it will be displayed. PAUSE waits until a key is pressed, and then the batch file resumes execution.

PRINT

The external PRINT command prints text files on the printer. Its most common form is

PRINT *file-name file-name . . . file-name* [/T] [/C]

where *file-name* is the name of a file that you want to
print. The /T option cancels the PRINT command. The
/C option cancels printing of the file whose name
precedes the option.

Example   This   command   would   print   the   files
LETTER1 .WP and LETTER2.WP:

```
PRINT LETTER1.WP LETTER2.WP
```

PROMPT

The internal PROMPT command changes the DOS
prompt. It takes this general form:

PROMPT *prompt*

where *prompt* is the desired prompt. The prompt
string can contain one or more special format commands, which allow increased flexibility. The commands are shown here:

Command	Meaning
$$	Dollar sign
$b	¦ character
$d	System date
$e	Escape character
$g	> character
$h	Backspace
$l	< character
$n	Current drive letter

Command	Meaning
$p	Current directory path
$q	= character
$t	System time
$v	DOS version number
$_	Carriage return-linefeed sequence

Example This command creates one of the most popular prompts:

PROMPT pg

This prompt displays the current directory path followed by the > symbol.

RECOVER

The external RECOVER command attempts to recover damaged files. It has this general form:

RECOVER [*drive-specifier*][*file-name*]

If only the drive specifier is present, RECOVER attempts to recover all the files on a disk. Otherwise, only the specified file is recovered. When the entire disk is recovered, RECOVER creates file names following this convention: FILE*num*.REC, where *num* is a number from 1 through 9999.

Remember, not all files can be recovered. Further, recovered program files are generally unusable. It is best to use RECOVER only on text files, and then only as a last resort.

Example This command attempts to recover the file FORMLET.WP:

```
RECOVER FORMLET.WP
```

REM

The REM command is used to embed a remark in a batch file. It has this general form:

REM *remark*

The *remark* can be any string from 0 to 123 characters long. No matter what the remark contains, it is completely ignored by DOS.

Example This remark is ignored by DOS:

```
REM this is a sample batch file remark
```

RENAME

The internal RENAME (REN for short) command is used to change the name of a specified file. It takes this general form:

RENAME *old-name new-name*

where *old-name* and *new-name* are file names.

Example This command changes the name of a file originally called INV.DAT to INV.OLD:

```
RENAME INV.DAT INV.OLD
```

REPLACE

The external REPLACE command replaces files on the destination disk with those by the same name on the source disk. REPLACE takes this general form:

REPLACE *source destination* [/A] [/P] [/R] [/S] [/W]

If you specify the /S option, all files in all subdirectories are also examined and replaced. You use /A to add to a disk only files that are not currently on the destination disk. This prevents existing files from being overwritten. If you need to insert a different diskette before REPLACE begins, use the /W option and REPLACE won't start until you press a key. The /P option makes REPLACE ask you before it replaces a file.

Example This command replaces the files on drive A with those by the same name on drive B, and includes all subdirectories:

REPLACE B: A: /S

RESTORE

The external RESTORE command restores files to the fixed disk from diskettes created using BACKUP. It takes this general form:

RESTORE *backup fixed* [/A:*date*] [/B:*date*] [/E:*time*] [/L:*time*] [/P] [/S] where *backup* is a drive specifier defining the drive that holds the backup diskette, and *fixed* is a drive and path specifier for the fixed disk. The options are summarized here:

Option	Meaning
/A:*date*	Restore all files modified on or after the specified date
/B:*date*	Restore all files modified on or before the specified date
/E:*time*	Restore all files modified at or earlier than the specified time on a given date
/L:*time*	Restore all files modified at or later than the specified time on a given date
/M	Restore all files modified or deleted since the last backup
/N	Restore only files that do not exist on the fixed disk
/P	Prompt before restoring a file
/S	Restore all subdirectories

Example This command restores all files having the .DAT extension into the DATA directory, using drive A to read the backup diskettes:

```
RESTORE A: C:\DATA\*.DAT
```

RMDIR

The internal RMDIR (RD for short) command removes a subdirectory. It has this general form:

RMDIR *directory*

where *directory* is a complete path name to the desired directory. The specified directory must be empty. It is not possible to remove a directory that contains files.

Example This command removes the directory WP:

```
RMDIR \WP
```

SELECT

The external SELECT command is used to install DOS on a new disk. It allows you to define the country and keyboard codes. The command's general form is

SELECT *source target country-code keyboard-code*

where *source* is the drive specifier of the drive that holds the DOS disk and *target* is the drive specifier of the drive that holds the new disk. The country codes are listed under KEYB, earlier in this appendix, and the keyboard codes are shown here:

Country	Code
Arabic countries	785
Australia	061
Belgium	032
Canada (English)	001
Canada (French)	002
Denmark	045

Country	Code
Finland	358
France	033
Germany	049
Israel (Hebrew)	972
Italy	039
Netherlands	031
Norway	047
Portugal	351
South American countries	003
Spain	034
Sweden	046
Switzerland	041
United Kingdom	044
United States	001

CAUTION: SELECT must be used only on a new disk because it destroys any preexisting information.

Example   This command prepares the disk in drive B for use in the U.S. (the DOS disk is assumed to be in drive A):

```
SELECT A: B: 001 US
```

SET

The internal SET command puts a name and its value into DOS's environment. This command is used primarily by programmers and system integrators.

SHARE

The external SHARE command is used in system networks to prepare for file sharing and file locking. Refer to your network and DOS manuals for further information.

SHIFT

The SHIFT batch command shifts the command line arguments left one position to allow for more than ten arguments.

SORT

The external SORT command sorts text files on a line-by-line basis. It is a filter command, which reads standard input and writes to standard output. SORT takes this general form:

SORT [<*input*] [>*output*] [/R] [/+*num*]

where *input* and *output* are either file names, devices, or pipes. If input and output are not specified, SORT uses standard input and output. By default the file is sorted in ascending order (A-Z). The /R option causes the file to be sorted in reverse order. The /+*num* option causes sorting to begin with column number *num*.

Example   This command produces a sorted directory listing:

```
DIR | SORT
```

SUBST

The external command SUBST allows you to use a different drive specifier to access a drive and directory. That is, you can use SUBST to assign a drive specifier to a drive and directory and then refer to that drive and directory using the assigned drive specifier. In essence, the new drive specifier is like a nickname for the drive. SUBST takes this general form:

SUBST *nickname drive-specifier path*

where *nickname* is the new drive specifier for *drive-specifier* and *path* is the path to the desired directory.

To undo a substitution, use this form of the command:

SUBST *nickname* /D

Example   This command causes drive A to respond to both A: and E: as drive specifiers

```
SUBST E: A:\
```

SYS

The external SYS command copies the DOS system files to a disk. It has this general form:

SYS *drive-specifier*

where *drive-specifier* indicates the drive that will receive the system files. Note that SYS does not transfer COMMAND.COM, however. SYS must be able to read the system files off the current drive.

Example This command puts the system files on the disk in drive B:

SYS B:

TIME

The internal TIME command sets the system time. It takes this general form:

TIME [*hh:mm:ss*]

If you do not enter the time on the command line, you are prompted for it. TIME expects a number from 0 through 23 for the hours. That is, it operates on a military style, 24-hour clock. You do not need to specify the seconds.

Example This command sets the time to 12:00 noon:

TIME 12:00:00

TREE

The external TREE command prints a list of all directories on the specified disk. It has this general form:

TREE *drive-specifier* [/F]

where *drive-specifier* is the letter of the drive to be examined. If /F is used, the files in each directory are also displayed.

Example This command displays the directory structure for the disk in drive A:

```
TREE A:
```

TYPE

The internal TYPE command displays the contents of a file on the screen. It has this general form:

TYPE *file-name*

where *file-name* is the file to be displayed.

Example   This command displays the file TEST:

```
TYPE TEST
```

VER

The internal VER command displays the DOS version number. It takes no arguments.

VERIFY

The internal VERIFY command turns on or off verification of disk write operations. That is, when turned on, it confirms that data written to disk is completely accurate and that no errors have occurred. VERIFY takes this general form:

VERIFY [ON] [OFF]

where you specify either on or off.

Example   This command turns verification off:

```
VERIFY OFF
```

VOL

The internal VOL command displays the volume label of the specified disk. It has this general form:

VOL [*drive-specifier*]

where *drive-specifier* is the name of the drive whose volume label will be displayed. If no drive is specified, VOL displays the volume label of the current drive.

Example   This command displays the volume label of the current drive:

```
VOL
```

XCOPY

The external XCOPY command is a more powerful and flexible version of the COPY command. It takes this general form:

XCOPY *source target* [/A][/D][/E][/M][/P][/S][/V][/W]

where *source* and *target* are file or path names. The operation of XCOPY is largely determined by the options applied to it. The options are summarized here:

Option	Meaning
/A	Copy only files that have the archive attribute turned on (the state of the archive bit is not changed)
/D:*date*	Copy only files whose date is equal to or later than the one specified
/E	Create all subdirectories, even if they are empty
/M	Copy only files with the archive attribute turned on (the archive bit is turned off)
/P	Prompt before copying each file
/S	Copy files in subdirectories
/V	Verify each write operation
/W	Wait until a disk is inserted

Example This command copies all the files on a disk in drive A to a disk in drive B, including all the subdirectories:

```
XCOPY A: B:\ /S
```

Using DOS 4

►C◄

If you are using DOS version 4, you have the option of running DOS in two ways. You can use the command prompt, which is the method discussed in the main body of this book, or you can use the DOS Shell, which is a visually oriented interface. It is called a "Shell" because it encloses DOS and acts as a buffer between DOS and you, the user. This appendix provides an overview of the DOS Shell and its operation. For people who use DOS infrequently, the Shell may be easier to use than the command line because it provides menus from which you can select most of the common DOS commands. However, once you know your way around DOS, it is faster to execute commands from the command prompt than from the Shell. Whether you use the Shell or the command prompt is primarily a matter of personal taste.

The main body of this book discusses DOS from the point of view of the command prompt. Even if you intend to use the Shell, you should know how to run DOS from the command prompt because the vast majority of PCs do *not* use DOS 4 or its Shell. If you want to be able to run all versions of DOS, it is necessary to know how to run it from the command prompt. For this reason, you should work through the main body of this book using the command prompt before you finish this appendix. To activate the command prompt from within the Shell, press Shift and F9 at the same time.

NOTE: Even if your computer uses DOS 4, it is possible that the Shell will not be activated. DOS can be configured in such a way that the Shell is bypassed and the command prompt is automatically used. If this is the case on your system, you don't need to read this appendix.

THE DOS SHELL: AN OVERVIEW

The DOS Shell consists of three main parts:

- The Start Programs screen
- The file system
- The online, context-sensitive help system

When the Shell begins execution, you will see a screen like the one in Figure C-1. This is the *Start Programs*

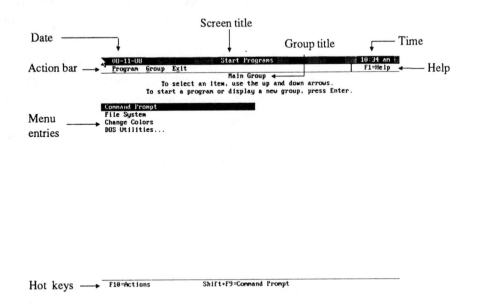

Date

Screen title

Group title

Time

Action bar

Help

```
┌──────────────────────────────────────────────────────────────────────┐
│ 00-11-00            Start Programs              10:34 an │
│ Program  Group  Exit                            F1=Help │
│                        Main Group                                       │
│        To select an item, use the up and down arrows.                   │
│        To start a program or display a new group, press Enter.          │
│                                                                         │
│ ▓Command Prompt▓▓▓▓▓▓▓▓▓▓▓                                               │
│  File System                                                            │
│  Change Colors                                                          │
│  DOS Utilities...                                                       │
```

Menu
entries

Hot keys

F10=Actions   Shift+F9=Command Prompt

FIGURE C-1.   The Start Programs screen

screen. As its name implies, the Start Programs screen
allows you to start the execution of a program.
However, you also use this screen to activate the file
system.

Let's take a closer look at the Start Programs
screen. At the top, three items are displayed. From left
to right they are the current system date, the title of
the screen, and the current system time.

The next line contains two items. On the left is the
action bar, which currently presents three options:
Program, Group, and Exit. Notice that the *P* in program, the *G* in Group, and the *x* in Exit are highlighted. These are the *hot keys* associated with each
option. We will talk more about them in a moment.

On the right side of the second line is a reminder that you can activate the online help system by pressing [F1].

The third line contains the *group title*, which in this case is Main Group. The instructions under the group title tell you how to select an item using the cursor keys.

The next few lines list the items that are in the main group by default. The selections are

- Command Prompt

- File System

- Change Colors

- DOS Utilities

It is possible to add items to the main group, so your display may show some additional options. Briefly, selecting Command Prompt activates the DOS command prompt. Choosing File System activates the file system, which is a menu-driven alternative to the command prompt that allows you to maintain your files. Change Colors allows you to change the colors of the Shell display. This option will only be present if you have a color display adapter. Finally, selecting DOS Utilities activates a menu of DOS commands from which you can choose.

The last line of the Start Programs screen contains two hot key reminders: First, it tells you that pressing [F10] activates the action bar, and second, that pressing [Shift] and [F9] at the same time activates the DOS command prompt.

MOVING THE HIGHLIGHT AND MAKING A SELECTION

The DOS Shell supports both the keyboard and the mouse as input devices. You can run the Shell using only the keyboard, but the mouse makes a handy addition. This section explores moving the highlight around the screen and making menu selections, first using the keyboard and then using the mouse.

Using the Keyboard

When the Start Programs screen is first displayed, the highlight is on the Command Prompt selection in the main group. To move the highlight to another selection, use the ⬆ or ⬇ key. Move the highlight down one line now, to the File System entry. (If it doesn't move, press ⟦Num lock⟧ once and try again.) Try pressing ⬇ several times. As you can see, the highlight continually cycles through the entries in the main group list.

To make a selection from a menu, position the highlight on the item you want to select and press ⟦Enter⟧. To try this, move the highlight to the DOS Utilities entry and press ⟦Enter⟧. After a few seconds, the group title will change to "DOS Utilities. . ." and a new list of options will be displayed. We will come back to these options later. For now, just press ⟦Esc⟧ to return to the main group.

To activate the action bar, press ⟦F10⟧. Try this now. As you can see, the Program option is highlighted. You can move the highlight using the ➡ and ⬅ keys. To select an option, press ⟦Enter⟧ when the highlight is over the desired item. To deactivate the action bar, press ⟦F10⟧ a second time. The ⟦F10⟧ key acts as a *toggle,* which switches back and forth between two states each time it is pressed.

Using the Mouse

Using the mouse to select a menu item or an action bar item is somewhat easier than using the keyboard. To move the highlight, move the mouse pointer to the item you want, and click the left button one time. The mouse pointer will either be a small arrow or a solid box depending on what video adapter your system uses. The DOS Shell does not use the right mouse button; however, you may have application programs that do use it.

To select an item, move the mouse pointer to the desired item and double click the left button. A *double click* is two presses in quick succession. You must be careful not to move the mouse between the two clicks. If the mouse is moved between the first and second click, no command will be activated. To try selecting an entry, position the mouse over DOS Utilities and double click. As you can see, this activates the DOS Utilities group. (It can take a couple of tries to get the hang of double clicking, so if you weren't successful the first time, try again.) Keep in mind that only items in the Start Programs menu (or one of its group menus) require a double click. As you will see in the next section, you can select from other types of menus with just a single click.

To cancel the DOS Utilities group, move the mouse pointer to the Esc = Cancel entry on the last line of the list and single click.

With the mouse, you do not have to press [F10] to activate the action bar. Instead, simply move the mouse pointer to the option you want and single click. Try this with the Program option. You will see a *pull-down menu* that presents additional options. (The action bar and its menus are discussed later.) Now, move the pointer to a blank space on the screen and single click. As you can see, the pull-down menu is removed from the screen. In general, until you have actually made a selection from a menu, you can change what you are doing by simply moving the mouse to some other part of the screen and single clicking.

Keep in mind that you can always mix keyboard and mouse commands. The DOS Shell doesn't care which method you use.

USING THE ONLINE HELP SYSTEM

The Shell's online help system is context sensitive—it provides information about whatever task you are presently doing. More specifically, it gives you information about whatever entry you have highlighted. Once the help system is activated you can also request information about other topics. Keep in mind that in general, the information displayed by the help system is intended to act as a reminder; it is no substitute for a good working knowledge of DOS.

To activate the help system, either press [F1] or move the mouse pointer to the message F1 = Help on the second line and click. For example, move the highlight to the DOS Utilities option, but don't select it.

Now, activate the help system. As you can see, a small window appears that contains information about the DOS Utilities option. At the top of the window is the name of the item you are receiving help about. To the far right of the window is the *scroll bar*, which allows you to move, or scroll, the text in the window up or down using the mouse. (If the Shell has been configured for text mode operation, up and down arrows will appear in place of the scroll bar.) We will look more closely at the operation of the scroll bar in a moment.

At the bottom of the window is a list of the hot keys that relate to the help system. You can activate an operation by pressing a hot key or by single clicking on its name in the list. Pressing F1 while a help window is already on screen displays information about the help system itself. Pressing F9 displays a list of all of the Shell's hot keys. Pressing F11 displays an index of help topics from which you can select to display information about a particular topic. To deactivate the help system, press Esc or click on the Esc = Cancel entry.

Go ahead and deactivate the help window now.

WINDOWS

In the preceding section, you investigated the help window. As you explore the Shell further, you will see several more windows, so it is important to know a few things about the way windows work. A *window* is a portion of the screen that is dedicated to one specific task. If you think of the screen as a desk, you can think of a window as a piece of paper on that desk. For example, activate the help window again, and notice that it overlays a portion of the screen. This is like laying one piece of paper over another. When you deactivate the window, whatever was on the screen previously is restored. This process of overlaying and restoring is common to all windows.

Although you can have many windows on the screen at the same time, only one window at a time can be active. For example, the file system uses several windows.

If the information a window contains exceeds the window's height, the window will include a scroll bar (or, if your system is configured for text operation, up and down arrows will be displayed). Scroll bars only work with the mouse, but all scroll bars work the same, regardless of the window they affect.

The components of the scroll bar are shown in Figure C-2. To move up one line, position the mouse pointer over the up arrow on the bar and single click. To move up one full window, click on the twin up arrows. A similar process moves down a line or a window. If you have a mouse, activate the help window and try using the scroll bar. Notice that the slider box moves up or down in the direction you are scrolling. Its position on the scroll bar indicates the position of the currently displayed text in relation to the total text. For example, when the slider box is in the middle of its range, the text displayed on the screen is halfway through the total text.

You can use the mouse to *drag* the slider box to a new position. To do this, position the mouse on the slider box, and then press and hold the left button.

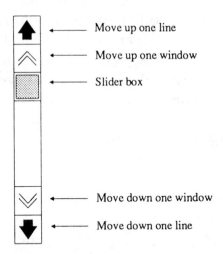

Move up one line

Move up one window

Slider box

Move down one window

Move down one line

FIGURE C-2.	The components of the scroll bar

Move the mouse, and an outline of the box will follow. When you release the left button, the box will be positioned at the new location, and the text on the screen will have moved by the same amount. Try this now, if you have not done so already.

As mentioned, in a text-only system, the scroll bar is replaced by up and down arrow symbols. To scroll the text using the mouse, click on the arrow that points in the direction in which you want the text to move. Each time you click, the text will move one line.

If you don't have a mouse, you can use the [↑] and [↓] keys to scroll the text one line at a time, or the [PgUp] and [PgDn] keys to scroll the text one full window. Deactivate the help window at this time.

USING THE FILE SYSTEM

Perhaps the most important part of the DOS 4 Shell is the file system. To activate the file system select the File System option from the main group menu on the Start Programs screen. If you are running DOS from a floppy, you will see a screen similar to Figure C-3. If you are running DOS from a fixed disk, the entries in the Directory Tree window and the file names in the file window will be different from those in the figure.

As you can see, the file system contains several windows. By default, the Directory Tree window is active. The active window is the focus of keyboard

```
 00-11-00                      File System                        4:09 pm
   File  Options  Arrange  Exit                                  F1=Help
   Ctrl+letter selects a drive.
   ▣A  ▣B  ▭C  ▭D

 A:\
         Directory Tree                              *.*

  ✓A:\                            ▣012345   .678         109    06-17-88
                                  ▣0E191012           17,138    08-09-88
                                  ▣0E291255            2,269    08-11-00
                                  ▣10061E4D            2,221    08-10-88
                                  ▣4201     .CPI       6,404    06-17-00
                                  ▣4208     .CPI         641    06-17-88
                                  ▣5202     .CPI         402    06-17-00
                                  ▣ANSI     .SYS       9,148    06-17-88
                                  ▣APPEND   .EXE      11,170    06-17-00
                                  ▣ASSIGN   .COM       5,785    06-17-88
                                  ▣ATTRIB   .EXE      10,247    06-17-00
                                  ▣AUTOEXEC .BAT          99    08-04-88
                                  ▣BASICA   .COM      36,205    06-17-00
                                  ▣CHKDSK   .COM      17,771    06-17-88
                                  ▣COMMAND  .COM      37,637    06-17-00
                                  ▣COMP     .COM       9,491    06-17-88
                                  ▣CONFIG   .SYS         114    08-04-88
                                  ▣COUNTRY  .SYS      12,838    06-17-88
                                  ▣DEBUG    .COM      21,606    06-17-00
                                  ▣DISKCOMP .COM       9,889    06-17-88
                                  ▣DISKCOPY .COM      10,420    06-17-00

  F10=Actions  Shift+F9=Command Prompt
```

FIGURE C-3.   The File System screen

input. To activate a different window using the keyboard, press [Tab]. Each time this key is pressed, a new window is activated in round-robin fashion, and the highlight moves to the active window. If you have a mouse, you can activate any window at any time by single clicking the mouse in the window.

As in the Start Programs screen, you can activate the online help system at any time by pressing [F1]. You can also activate the action bar by pressing [F10]. Although its selections differ from those offered in the Start Programs screen, its operation is the same.

When it is active, the drive identifier window highlights the currently logged-in drive. To select a different drive, use the [←] and [→] keys to move the highlight and press [Enter] to select the drive you want. If you have a mouse, you can simply single click on the drive you want to log in. When you switch drives, the information in the other windows is automatically updated to reflect this change.

The path window shows the current path name, but does not allow you to change it. The path changes automatically when you select a new directory or drive.

Scroll bars are provided for the Directory Tree and file name windows. You can use the mouse, the [↑] and [↓] keys, or the [PgUp] and [PgDn] keys to scroll the contents of these windows.

To select a directory using the keyboard, position the highlight on the directory you want and press [Enter]. To select a directory using the mouse, simply position the mouse pointer on the directory and single click. When you choose a new directory, the contents of that directory are displayed in the file name window. If your computer has a fixed disk that has been in use for a while, it will almost certainly contain a fairly complete directory structure. However, if you are running DOS from a floppy it may not have any subdirectories, so don't be surprised if none are listed.

To select a file using the keyboard, position the highlight on the file you want and press the Spacebar. To select a file using the mouse, position the mouse pointer on the file you want and single click.

To exit the file system and return to the Start Programs window, either select Exit on the action bar or press [F3].

NOTE: (for fixed disk users) If DOS was installed on your computer using the defaults suggested by IBM, you should see a directory called DOS in the Directory Tree window. If you move the highlight to that directory and press [Enter], the display in the directory listing area will be similar to that shown in the examples.

Assuming DOS has been installed on your computer in the normal way, the directory listing displayed in the file name window consists of files that come with DOS. The entry for each file contains four elements: First is the filename followed by the file extension. Next comes the length of the file in bytes. Finally, the file's creation date is shown.

If the Shell is running in graphics mode, a fifth element is included in the directory listing for each file: a small rectangular icon that appears at the start of each file name, to distinguish program files from other types of files. If the icon shows a computer screen, the file contains a program. If it shows a piece of paper with one corner turned down, the file does not contain a program. In text mode, no icons appear.

When a file is selected in graphics mode, its icon is highlighted. In text mode, a small triangle appears in front of the file name.

STARTING A PROGRAM

In this section you'll learn to execute a DOS external command or program using the file system. Activate the file system at this time. If you are running DOS from a floppy, make sure that a DOS diskette is in drive A, and log in to that drive. If you are using a fixed disk, log in to drive C and then select the DOS directory.

It is very easy to start a program using the file system. You simply highlight the program you want to start in the file name window, and then press (Enter), or using a mouse, simply double click on the program you want to execute. To see how this works, let's execute the CHKDSK external command.

If DOS has been installed following the instructions supplied by IBM, about two-thirds of the way down the file name window you will see the file CHKDSK.COM. This is the DOS program that reports on the status of your disk. To execute this file, position the highlight on its name and press (Enter). If you have a mouse, simply double click on CHKDSK.COM. The Open File window, shown in Figure C-4, appears,

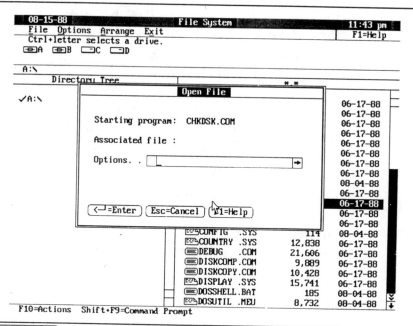

08-15-88	File System	11:43 pm

File Options Arrange Exit | F1=Help
Ctrl+letter selects a drive.
⌸A ⌸B ⌸C ⌸D

A:\

Directory Tree   *.*

✓A:\
```
                        ┌──────── Open File ────────┐
                        │                            │       06-17-88
                        │                            │       06-17-88
                        │  Starting program:  CHKDSK.COM     06-17-88
                        │                            │       06-17-88
                        │  Associated file :         │       06-17-88
                        │                            │       06-17-88
                        │  Options. .  [       ]  →  │       06-17-88
                        │                            │       06-17-88
                        │                            │       08-04-88
                        │                            │       06-17-88
                        │  [<─┘=Enter] [Esc=Cancel] [F1=Help]  06-17-88
                        │                            │       06-17-88
                        └────────────────────────────┘       06-17-88
            CONFIG   .SYS        114    08-04-88
            COUNTRY  .SYS     12,838    06-17-88
            DEBUG    .COM     21,606    06-17-88
            DISKCOMP.COM       9,889    06-17-88
            DISKCOPY.COM      10,428    06-17-88
            DISPLAY  .SYS     15,741    06-17-88
            DOSSHELL.BAT         185    08-04-88
            DOSUTIL .MEU       8,732    08-04-88
```

F10=Actions Shift+F9=Command Prompt

FIGURE C-4.   Executing an external DOS command from the file system

which tells you that DOS has opened the file CHKDSK.COM. Opening a file is different from selecting a file. When you select a file by pressing the Spacebar or by single clicking the mouse on the desired file, you tell the Shell that you are interested in this file and may want to do something with it; however, the file itself is not directly affected. On the other hand, when you open a file you're doing something with that file right now.

In the Open File window the cursor is positioned on the Options line. Some programs require that certain additional information be passed to them. For example, a word processing program file may need to know the name of the file you want to edit. You use the Options line to enter any such information. You don't have to provide any options for the CHKDSK command file, so press (Enter) now.

The screen will clear and DOS will access the disk drive. For some systems, CHKDSK may take a few seconds to finish execution. When it does, DOS tells you to press (Enter) to return to the file system. In general, whenever a program that you start from the file system finishes, you are prompted to press (Enter). The file system does not restart until you press (Enter) because you may need time to read information reported by a program before the screen is overwritten. Press (Enter) now to return to the file system.

A CLOSER LOOK AT THE FILE SYSTEM ACTION BAR

As you can see, the file system action bar has four options: File, Options, Arrange, and Exit. Each of these options displays a pull-down menu when it is selected. The following sections present an overview of each option.

The File Option

Most of the File options relate to a file you have selected in the file name window. So, to follow along, activate the file name window, move the highlight to the first file, which is called 012345.678, and press the

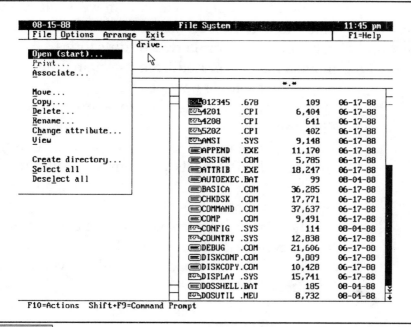

08-15-88	File System	11:45 pm

File | Options | Arrange | Exit   F1=Help

drive.

Open (start)...   ⌖
Print...
Associate...

Move...
Copy...   *.*
Delete...
Rename...   ▣₂012345 .678   109   06-17-88
Change attribute...   ▣₂4201   .CPI   6,404   06-17-88
View   ▣₂4208   .CPI   641   06-17-88
                       ▣₂5202   .CPI   402   06-17-88
Create directory...   ▣₂ANSI   .SYS   9,148   06-17-88
Select all   ▣APPEND   .EXE   11,170   06-17-88
Deselect all   ▣ASSIGN   .COM   5,785   06-17-88
                       ▣ATTRIB   .EXE   18,247   06-17-88
                       ▣AUTOEXEC.BAT   99   08-04-88
                       ▣BASICA   .COM   36,285   06-17-88
                       ▣CHKDSK   .COM   17,771   06-17-88
                       ▣COMMAND .COM   37,637   06-17-88
                       ▣COMP   .COM   9,491   06-17-88
                       ▣₂CONFIG .SYS   114   08-04-88
                       ▣₂COUNTRY .SYS   12,838   06-17-88
                       ▣DEBUG   .COM   21,606   06-17-88
                       ▣DISKCOMP.COM   9,809   06-17-88
                       ▣DISKCOPY.COM   10,428   06-17-88
                       ▣₂DISPLAY .SYS   15,741   06-17-88
                       ▣DOSSHELL.BAT   185   08-04-88
                       ▣₂DOSUTIL .MEU   8,732   08-04-88

F10=Actions   Shift+F9=Command Prompt

FIGURE C-5.   The File menu

Spacebar. This is a short text file that was created when DOS was installed on your system. (If you don't see this file, select the one called DOSSHELL.BAT.)

Select the File option now. Your screen will look similar to Figure C-5. The first option, Open, starts a program running. Selecting this option accomplishes the same thing as starting a program using the file name window. This option only applies to program files. You cannot run a nonprogram file with it.

If you have a printer, you can use the Print option to print the contents of a text file with it.

The Associate option links one file to another file.

The Move option lets you move a file from one place to another. In general, you can move a file between disks or between directories. When you move a file, it is erased from its original position after being copied to its new position.

The Copy option is like Move, except the original file is not erased.

The Delete option lets you remove, or erase, a file from a disk. It also lets you remove a subdirectory.

The Change attribute option allows you to change one or more of a file's attributes.

The View option lets you see the contents of a file. This is most useful with text files.

The Create directory option allows you to create a new subdirectory.

The Select all option selects all the files in the current directory.

The Deselect all option deselects all the files in the current directory.

Press [Esc] to remove the File menu from the screen.

The Options Entry

Select the Options entry at this time. The first option, Display options, is used to change the way files are displayed in the file name window.

The File options entry lets you change the way certain file operations take place.

The Show information option displays information about the current disk and directory.

Press [Esc] to cancel the Options menu.

The Arrange Option

Select the Arrange option. The first entry in the menu is Single file list. This option will not be active at this time because a single file list is displayed by default.

Selecting the Multiple file list option splits the screen horizontally and lets you display two separate directories.

Selecting the System file list option causes DOS to ignore the directory structure of the disk and display all files on the logged-in disk.

Press (Esc) to cancel the Arrange option.

The Exit Option

The Exit menu offers two options. The first terminates the file system and returns you to the Start Programs screen. The second simply returns you to the file system, and is the same as pressing (Esc).

MAKING A SELECTION FROM A PULL-DOWN MENU

The menus generated when you make a selection from the file system action bar are called pull-down menus because they appear to pull-down from the action bar. To make a selection from a pull-down menu, first highlight the item you want to select and then press (Enter). You can also select an option by positioning the mouse pointer on it and single clicking. Finally, you can simply press the highlighted letter in the item you want to select.

When a menu item cannot be activated it is shown in low-intensity gray if the Shell is running in graphics mode. In text mode, an inactive selection has an asterisk where its hot key would normally appear. A menu item is deactivated when there is no application for it in the current situation.

As you looked at the pull-down menus associated with the file system you probably noticed that some entries had three periods after the name and others did not. In general, an item is followed by three periods when selecting that item causes a prompt for additional information. Items that don't have periods after their names are activated as soon as you select them; no additional information is required.

USING THE SHELL

Let's leave the file system to explore more of the Shell's features. We will begin by discussing the way the Start Program window organizes information.

The Main Group Versus Subgroups

The Shell's Start Programs window uses a main group/subgroup organizational scheme. The main group can contain both programs and subgroups. For example, by default, the main group contains one subgroup called DOS Utilities and three programs: the Command Prompt, the File System, and Change Colors. In contrast, a subgroup can only contain programs.

The reasoning behind the main group/subgroup scheme is that related programs should have their own subgroup. For example, you might create a word processing subgroup to include the word processor, the spelling checker, and the thesaurus program. The Shell lets you manage and structure your applications by keeping related programs in separate subgroups.

NOTE: Don't confuse subgroups with subdirectories. The subgroup a program belongs to in the Start Programs window has no relation whatsoever to the directory the program occupies on the disk.

Adding a Program to the Main Group

You can add a program to a group so that you can execute it from the Start Programs window instead of using the file system. Not only is this convenient, saving you time and keystrokes, but it also helps ensure that the program always starts correctly.

Since all of DOS's external commands are programs, let's add CHKDSK to the main group. Activate the action bar and select the Program option. You will see a menu with the following entries:

Start
Add
Change
Delete
Copy

```
┌─────────────────────────────────────────────────────────────────┐
│ 08-22-88              Start Programs              6:59 pm          │
│ Program  Group  Exit                             F1=Help          │
│─────────────────────────────────────                             │
│                         Main Group                                │
│                                                                   │
│                                                                   │
│ Command Prompt                                                    │
│ File System      ┌────────── Add Program ──────────┐             │
│ Change Colors    │                                  │             │
│ DOS Utilities.. │ Required                          │             │
│                  │                                   │             │
│                  │ Title . . . . [           ]  →    │             │
│                  │                                   │             │
│                  │ Commands  . . [           ]  →    │             │
│                  │                                   │             │
│                  │ Optional                          │             │
│                  │                                   │             │
│                  │ Help text . . [           ]  →    │             │
│                  │                                   │             │
│                  │ Password  . . [        ]          │             │
│                  │                                   │             │
│                  │ (Esc=Cancel) (F1=Help) (F2=Save) │             │
│                  └───────────────────────────────────┘            │
│                                                                   │
│─────────────────────────────────────────────────────────────────│
│ F10=Actions              Shift+F9=Command Prompt                  │
└─────────────────────────────────────────────────────────────────┘
```

FIGURE C-6.   The Add Program window

Select the Add option. Your screen will look like
Figure C-6.

Each program has four fields of information associated with it. The first two must be filled in, because
they contain essential information. The second two
are optional.

The first piece of information you must enter is the
title of the program, which will then be displayed in
the window. For CHKDSK, type the title **Check the
disk**, and press (Enter). The second piece of information
you must provide is the command that you want to
execute. In its simplest form, the Commands line
contains only the program name. For now, this will do
fine, so enter **CHKDSK** on the Commands line.

If you wish, you can enter additional information about the program in the Help text field. This information can include up to 478 characters. As you enter text beyond the end of the window, the text will automatically scroll to the left. Type this text for the CHKDSK help information:

The CHKDSK program checks the disk drive for errors. It also reports the size of the disk, the size of memory, and the amount of each that is free.

When this text is displayed, the help system will automatically format it for you.

In the fourth field you can enter a program password if you like. If you do, each time you try to run the program, you will be prompted for the password. Leave the password field blank for now. We will come back to passwords a little later.

If you have entered anything incorrectly, you can go back to a field by pressing ⎡Tab⎤ the appropriate number of times.

Once you have entered all the information correctly, press ⎡F2⎤ to install the CHKDSK program into the main group. A moment later you will see the title "Check the disk" appear at the bottom of the list. Go ahead and execute the CHKDSK program. The screen will clear, the program will run, displaying its result on the screen, and then, without hesitation, the Shell will reactivate. You do not have to press a key to reactivate the Shell; however, this means you do not have time to read all the information on the screen. Also, notice that when the program began, you were not prompted for program parameters the way you are when you run a program from the file system. In fact, the CHKDSK program can take additional parameters. In the next section you will see how to add these and other features.

Before you go on, try this: Highlight the CHKDSK title, and then press ⏐F1⏐. The help text that you entered in the third field will appear.

Generally, you will not add programs to the main group, but rather to subgroups, so you can keep your programs organized. However, there will probably be a few programs you'll want to add to the main group. For example, if your most common task is using a spreadsheet, you will want to start that spreadsheet from the main group to save yourself the extra step of selecting a subgroup before you can select the program.

A FIRST LOOK AT PROGRAM STARTUP COMMANDS

As you saw in the previous section, when the CHKDSK program began execution it did not prompt you for parameters, and when it terminated, the Shell was immediately redisplayed, without allowing you enough time to read the output of the CHKDSK program. While this might not be a problem with some programs, it certainly would be with most. To correct these deficiencies, the Shell supports a large number of program startup commands, called PSCs for short. In this section we'll look at two of these commands.

NOTE: Program startup commands must be separated from each other with a special command separator: a pair of vertical bars. You generate these bars by pressing F4.

Adding a Prompt for Program Parameters

To make the Program Parameters window appear, you put a set of square brackets after the program's name on the Commands line of the Add Program window. The Commands line for CHKDSK should look like this.

```
CHKDSK  []
```

This line causes the default Program Parameters window to appear. Anything you enter in this window is automatically passed to the program.

To see how this works, you will need to change the Commands line for CHKDSK. First, position the highlight over CHKDSK's title. Next, activate the action bar and select Program. Select the Change option. This displays CHKDSK's information on the screen in a Change Program window. Use the Tab key to switch fields; press it one time to activate the Commands line. With the cursor on the Commands line, press the End key. Next, enter a space, and then enter [ ]. Your screen should look like Figure C-7.

NOTE: You do not use command separator (¦¦) between the name of the program and the square brackets.

Once you have changed the Commands line, press F2 to install the changes. Now, try the command. This time you are prompted for parameters. If no

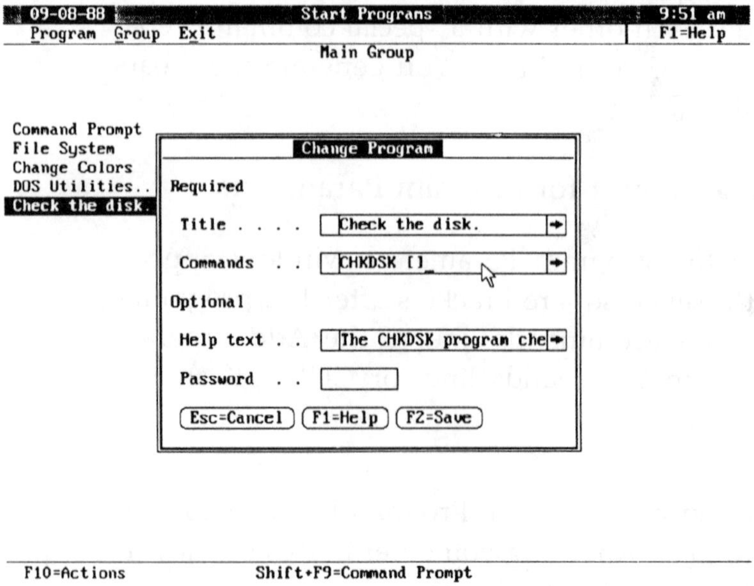
09-08-88
Start Programs
9:51 am
Program Group Exit
F1=Help
Main Group
Command Prompt
File System
Change Colors
DOS Utilities..
Check the disk.
Change Program
Required
Title . . . .
Check the disk.
Commands . .
CHKDSK [ ]
Optional
Help text . .
The CHKDSK program che
Password . .
Esc=Cancel
F1=Help
F2=Save
F10=Actions
Shift+F9=Command Prompt

FIGURE C-7. The Change Program window

additional parameters are specified, the CHKDSK command checks the currently logged-in drive. However, if you use a drive specifier as a parameter, CHKDSK checks the disk in the drive that you specify. Try this by specifying another drive in your system. (Remember, a drive specifier is the drive letter followed by a colon. For example, B: specifies the B drive.)

Pausing the Program

Although DOS now prompts you for parameters, the Shell still overwrites the screen before you can read all

```
 09-08-88               Start Programs              9:52 am
    Program  Group  Exit                           F1=Help
                          Main Group


 Command Prompt
 File System        ┌──────── Change Program ────────┐
 Change Colors      │ Required                       │
 DOS Utilities..    │                                │
 Check the disk.    │ Title . . . .  [Check the disk.  →│
                    │                                │
                    │ Commands  . .  [CHKDSK [] │ PAUSE_  →│
                    │ Optional                       │
                    │ Help text . .  [The CHKDSK program che→│
                    │                                │
                    │ Password  . .  [        ]      │
                    │ (Esc=Cancel) (F1=Help) (F2=Save)│
                    └────────────────────────────────┘




 F10=Actions              Shift+F9=Command Prompt
```

FIGURE C-8.   Adding the PAUSE command

the information displayed on it. To prevent this, you must use the PAUSE command in the Commands line of the program. The PAUSE command displays the line "Press any key to continue" when the program completes its execution.

To add the PAUSE command to the Commands line, activate the action bar and select Program. From the menu, select Change. Using the (Tab) key, advance to the Commands line. Press the (End) key. Next, enter one space, and then press (F4). Now, enter **PAUSE**. Your screen will look like Figure C-8. When you are through, press (F2) and try the CHKDSK command. Now, it displays the parameters prompt and also waits for a keypress before returning to the Shell.

```
 08-22-88                    Start Programs              7:03 pm
  Program  Group  Exit                                   F1=Help
                              Main Group
               ⤺
Command Prompt
File System        ┌──────────── Add Group ────────────┐
Change Colors      │                                    │
DOS Utilities..    │ Required                           │
Check the disk.    │                                    │
                   │   Title . . . .  [            →]    │
                   │                                    │
                   │   Filename  . .  [         ]       │
                   │                                    │
                   │ Optional                           │
                   │                                    │
                   │   Help text . .  [            →]    │
                   │                                    │
                   │   Password  . .  [         ]        │
                   │                                    │
                   │  (Esc=Cancel) (F1=Help) (F2=Save)  │
                   └────────────────────────────────────┘


  F10=Actions              Shift+F9=Command Prompt
```

FIGURE C-9.   The Add Group window

ADDING A GROUP

You can add a subgroup to the Main Group using the group option. To see how this works, select Group now. You will see a window similar to that in Figure C-9.

At the Title line enter **My Group**. This is the title that will be displayed on the screen. At the Filename prompt enter **MYGROUP**. This is the name of the file the Shell will use to store information about the group. Do not enter an extension, because the Shell automatically appends the extension .MEU.

If you like, you can add help text about the new group at the Help text line. The message can be up to 478 characters long.

You can control access to a group by entering a password. If you do this, users will be prompted for the password when they attempt to access the group. For now, leave the password field blank.

Once you have entered the information correctly, press F2 to install the group.

Adding a Program to a Subgroup

Adding a program to a subgroup is exactly like adding a program to the Main Group. First, select the subgroup that you want to add the program to; then activate the Program option. From the Program menu, select Add to add the program.

As an example, let's add one of DOS's external commands to the MYGROUP group. The command you will add is called MEM. It reports the amount of memory in the system, the amount of memory that is free, and the largest program that can fit in memory. As stated, MEM is an external command, so it must be on the currently logged-in disk.

Select MYGROUP. You'll see the message "Group is empty," because you have not yet added any programs to the group. Select the Program option and activate the Add entry. For the title type **Report system memory**. On the Commands line, enter

```
MEM ¦¦ PAUSE
```

The options available with the MEM command are primarily for programmers. For most purposes, the command does not require options, so in this case you didn't need to include the [ ], which would display the Program Parameters window. Try executing the MEM command now.

Copying Programs Between Groups

You can copy a program's entry from one group to another using the Copy command in the Program menu. The general method is as follows: First, highlight the program that you want to move inside its own group; then select the Copy option. Next, select the group that you want to copy the program into. Finally, press F2 to copy the program entry.

Let's try copying CHKDSK from the Main Group into MYGROUP. First, activate the Main Group and highlight the Check the disk entry. Then, activate the Program option and select Copy. Finally, select MYGROUP and press F2. As you can see, the information for the CHKDSK command is copied into MYGROUP.

Remember, the Copy operation does not erase the original entry for the program.

DELETING A PROGRAM FROM A GROUP

To delete a program from a group, first highlight the program you want to remove and then activate the Program option. Next, select the Delete option. You will see a safety check window that gives you one last chance to change your mind before the program is deleted.

Keep one fact firmly in mind: Removing a program's entry from a group does not remove that program from the disk.

Let's try removing the copy of the CHKDSK program from the Main Group. First, activate the Main Group and highlight the Check the disk entry. Next, activate the Program option and choose Delete. When the safety check window appears, choose to delete the program.

DELETING A GROUP

To remove a group you must use the Delete option on the Group menu. First, highlight the name of the group and then activate the Delete option.

CUSTOMIZING THE PROGRAM STARTUP WINDOW

Earlier, you were introduced to two program startup commands. However, the Shell supports a wide variety of program startup options. In this section you will learn to use three commands that let you control the content of the program startup window.

The program startup window has four sections: The top line is the window title; the next line is the instruction line; the third line is the prompt line; and the last line is the keys line. Of these four lines, you can control the content of the first three. Figure C-10 shows the default program startup window.

```
 08-22-88                     Start Programs                    7:07 pm
   Program  Group  Exit                                        F1=Help
                              My Group...


 Report System Memory
 Check the Disk



                        ┌───────────────────────────┐
                        │     Program Parameters     │
                        │                            │
                        │  Type the parameters, then press Enter. │
                        │                            │
                        │  Parameters . . [          ➡ │
                        │                            │
                        │  (<─┘=Enter) (Esc=Cancel) (F1=Help) │
                        └───────────────────────────┘



   F10=Actions  Esc=Cancel  Shift+F9=Command Prompt
```

FIGURE C-10.   The default program startup window

Before you begin changing the program startup window, you should understand the general format of the program startup commands.

Bracket Commands

Two types of program startup commands can appear on the Commands line. Commands that affect the appearance or operation of the program startup window must go inside the square brackets that cause the window to appear. These are commonly called *bracket commands.* Bracket commands do *not* need to be separated from each other by the command separator, the two vertical bars generated by pressing (F4). Most bracket commands begin with a slash (/).

The other type of command allowed on the Commands line goes outside the square brackets. An example is the PAUSE command. Commands of this type must be separated by vertical bars.

Specifying a Title

You can specify the title of the program startup window by using the /T command, which has this general form:

/T *"title - up to 40 characters"*

The title must be enclosed in double quotes and must not be more than 40 characters long.

To try specifying a new title, select MYGROUP, highlight the Check the disk entry, and then activate the Program option. From the Program menu, select Change. Using the (Tab) key, advance the cursor to the Commands line, and then move the cursor to the [ ] characters. If the Shell is not in insert mode, press the (Ins) key once. Now, enter this between the two brackets:

```
/T "Check the Disk"
```

The Commands line should look like this:

```
CHKDSK  [/T "Check the Disk"] || PAUSE
```

Remember, you won't be able to see the whole line at once. When you're sure the line is correct, press [F2] to install the change.

Try the CHKDSK command now, and you will see that the title of the program startup window has become "Check the Disk."

If an Error Occurs

If you accidentally enter something incorrectly on the Commands line, you will see an error message that briefly explains the problem when you try to run the program. For example, if you forgot the closing square bracket, you would see this error message:

```
Brackets missing in Program Startup Command.
```

If you receive an error message, simply look for the error and correct it. After a little experience you will have no trouble finding and correcting your errors.

Changing the Instruction Line

To change the instruction line, use the /I command, which has this general form:

/I *"instructions - up to 40 characters"*

The instructions must be enclosed in double quotes and must not exceed 40 characters.

To try changing the instruction line, add this to the Commands line for the CHKDSK program inside the square brackets and after the closing quote for the title:

```
/I "Enter the drive you want to check."
```

The Commands line should look like this:

```
CHKDSK  [/T "Check the Disk" /I "Enter the drive
you want to check."] ¦¦ PAUSE
```

Of course, there will be only one line, not two.

Install this change by pressing F2, and then try the command again. This time both the title and the instruction line will be different.

Changing the Prompt

To change the prompt that precedes the parameter entry area use the /P command, which takes this general form:

/P "prompt - up to 20 characters"

The prompt must be enclosed in double quotes and must not exceed 20 characters in length.

To try changing the prompt, add this to the CHKDSK Commands line inside the square brackets and after the closing quote for the instruction command:

/P "Drive specifier: "

The customized CHKDSK startup window

The Commands line will now look like this:

```
CHKDSK  [/T "Check the Disk" /I "Enter the drive
you want to check." /P "Drive specifier: "] ¦¦ PAUSE
```

Install the change by pressing ⟦F2⟧, and try the CHKDSK command. The program startup window will now look like Figure C-11.

Using a Default

The /D option lets you specify a default value to be shown in the Parameters section of the program startup window. The general form of this command is

/D *"default-string"*

This command must go inside the brackets. It can be up to 40 characters long.

For example, the following command would cause EDLIN to edit MYFILE.DAT by default:

```
EDLIN [/D "MYFILE.DAT"]
```

MORE PSC COMMANDS

There are several other PSC commands that you may need to use from time to time. They are discussed in this section.

Clearing the Entry Field

If you specify a default value for the Parameters line of the program startup window, you may also want to include the /R command. If this command is present, striking any key other than [Enter] causes the default string to be removed, so you don't have to erase it manually one character at a time. The /R command must go inside the brackets.

For example, this command line uses the /R command:

```
EDLIN [/D "MYFILE.DAT" /R]
```

Limiting the Length of an Entry

By default, an entry at the Parameters line can be up to 127 characters long. You can reduce this maximum by using the /L command, which has the general form

/L *"length"*

This command must go inside the brackets.

For example, the following command would limit the maximum length of an entry to 25 characters:

[/L "25"]

Requiring Existent Files

There are two PSC commands you can use to ensure that one or more files are present on a disk. The first is the /M "e" option. If this option is present in the program startup command, the program will only be executed if the file name you enter at the Parameters line exists on disk. The /M "e" command must go inside the brackets.

You can require that a specific file name be present on disk by using the /F command, which takes this general form:

/F *"file-name"*

This command must go inside the brackets. It prevents the program from executing unless the specified file name exists.

For example, this program startup command requires that EDLIN be present, and will only edit existing files:

```
EDLIN [/M "e"  /F "EDLIN.COM"]
```

Using Replaceable Parameters

You can use any batch file command except GOTO inside a program startup command. This means you can also use the parameters %0 through %9. These parameters take values based on what you enter at the Parameters prompt. A parameter can go either inside or outside the brackets. For example, this program startup command

```
EDLIN [%1] ¦¦ PRINT %1
```

causes the file you are editing to be printed after you are through editing it. (Remember, you generate the vertical bars by pressing [F4].)

You can use the value given to a parameter from the program preceding it by using the /C command, which has the general form

/C *"parameter"*

where *parameter* is the parameter you want.

REORDERING PROGRAMS WITHIN A GROUP

You can change the order of items in a group using the Reorder command in the Group window. The basic procedure is as follows: First, activate the group you want to reorder; then highlight the item whose position you want to change. Next, activate the Group option and select the Reorder option. Then, move the highlight to the position you want the item to occupy, and press [Enter]. The item will be moved and the list will reflect the new order. You might want to try this feature on your own.

USING A PASSWORD

You can restrict access to a program by giving it a password when you enter the program into a group. If you use a password, only people who know the password will be able to activate the program from the Shell. (The program can still be executed from the command line, however.)

You can use any characters you like for a password and the password may be up to eight characters long. Be sure to remember the password because you will need it to activate the Change option in the Program menu.

You can also control access to an entire group by giving the group a password when you define it.

WARNING: The password only controls access to a program if that program is executed from the Shell. Anyone who knows how to use the DOS command line prompt will still be able to run the program. Therefore, at best a password is a mild deterrent; it is not real protection. At worst, using a password provides a tip that you have a sensitive program on your computer. Frankly, a better security measure is to lock your computer when you are not using it.

THE SHELL'S EDITING KEYS

As you know, DOS supports several special keys that allow you to edit what is on the command line. Similarly, the Shell activates several special keys that can aid you when you are entering information such as program names or options. These keys are called *editing* keys. You have learned to use one of them— the Backspace key—already. In this section you will learn about several other editing keys.

For this section you will need to enter and modify information. One of the best places to practice is in the Set Date and Time window, because even if you accidentally activate an option with invalid information, no harm is done. Therefore, before continuing, select the DOS Utilities option from the Main Group and activate the Set Date and Time option.

The Home and End Keys

At the Set Date and Time parameters prompt, type the word **TEST**, but do not press the Enter key. Now, press the Home key. Note that the cursor jumps to the start of the field. Next, press the End key, and the cursor moves to the end of the word TEST. In general, whenever you are entering information in the Shell, pressing Home moves the cursor to the start of the field and pressing End moves it to the end of your entry.

The Arrow Keys

Once you have entered something in a field you can use the ⬅ and ➡ keys to move the cursor through that text. For example, if it is not already there, move the cursor to the end of TEST by pressing End. Now, press ⬅ three times. The cursor will be under the E. Press ➡ once, and the cursor will be under the S. As you can see, these operations have no effect on the text in the field; they simply reposition the cursor.

Insert Versus Overwrite Mode

The Shell supports two modes of input: insert and overwrite. By default, the Shell is in overwrite mode. In this mode, whatever is at the current cursor position is overwritten by any new character that you type. When the Shell is in insert mode, whatever is at the current cursor postion moves to the right when you add characters, so new entries do not overwrite existing text.

You can toggle between insert mode and overwrite mode by pressing the Ins key. The shape of the cursor tells you which mode you are in currently. In overwrite mode the cursor is a short horizontal bar similar to an underscore character. In insert mode, the cursor becomes a thin vertical bar in graphics mode or a small solid box in text mode.

To see the difference between the two modes, press End if necessary to advance the cursor to the end of the word TEST. Then, press ⬅ twice, so that the cursor is under the S. Make sure the Shell is in overwrite mode (the cursor should look like an underscore). Next, enter the characters **AK**. Your entry will now read TEAK.

Next, press the ⟨Ins⟩ key to activate the insert mode. Using ⟨←⟩, back the cursor up until it is on the *E* in TEAK; then type **W**. As you can see, EAK moves right and your entry now becomes TWEAK.

⟨Del⟩ Versus ⟨Backspace⟩

There are two ways to delete a single character in a field. First, pressing the ⟨Backspace⟩ key will cause the character immediately to the left of the cursor to be deleted and all text to the right of it to move over one place to fill the void. The second way to delete a character is to use the ⟨Del⟩ key. When you press this key, the character directly under the cursor is deleted and all text to the right of the deleted character is moved to the left to fill the void.

Starting Over

Assume that you have entered some information, decide that it is completely wrong, and want to start over. Instead of repeatedly striking the ⟨Backspace⟩ or ⟨Del⟩ key, you can simply press the ⟨F9⟩ key. Try this now. As you can see, the entire field is cleared and the cursor is positioned at the start of the line.

Installing DOS
on a Fixed Disk
►D◄

Generally, the fixed disk is already formatted and ready for use, so it is possible you will never need to use the information in this appendix. However, should your fixed disk fail and be replaced by a new one, you may need to prepare the new disk for use. Until a fixed disk is prepared and DOS is installed on it, it cannot be used. This appendix describes how to prepare a fixed disk and install DOS on it.

WARNING: The commands shown in this section will destroy any existing files on the fixed disk. Do not try these examples unless you are preparing a disk to be used for the first time.

PARTITIONING THE DISK

Before the fixed disk can be formatted, it must be partitioned. A *partition* is a portion of the fixed disk. It can be either part or all of the disk. It is possible to partition the fixed disk so that it can be used with two or more operating systems. The instructions in this appendix tell how to prepare a fixed disk for use with DOS alone, since this is the most common situation. If your system must support another operating system, such as UNIX, refer to the instructions in your DOS manual.

To partition the fixed disk, use the FDISK external command. Put a copy of the DOS diskette in drive A and start the computer. Once the DOS prompt is displayed enter the FDISK command. You will see the following display (the version number may vary):

```
IBM Personal Computer
Fixed Disk Setup Program Version 3.30
(C)Copyright IBM Corp. 1983,1987

FDISK Options

Current Fixed Disk Drive: 1

Choose one of the following:

     1.   Create DOS Partition
     2.   Change Active Partition
     3.   Delete DOS Partition
     4.   Display Partition Information
     5.   Select Next Fixed Disk Drive

Enter choice: [1]

Press ESC to return to DOS
```

Most of these options (and others that you will see shortly) are primarily for programmers or system integrators who are preparing a disk for a unique application. You will only need to use the first option. Since 1 is the default selection, simply press (Enter). You will see this display:

```
Create DOS Partition

Current Fixed Disk Drive: 1

     1. Create Primary DOS partition
     2. Create Extended DOS partition

Enter choice: [1]

Press ESC to return to FDISK Options
```

Again, you want the first selection, which is the default, so press (Enter) now.

What you see next depends on the state of the fixed disk. If, by chance, someone has already created a DOS partition, you will see the message

```
Primary DOS partition already exists.
```

If this message appears, just press (Esc) until you are back at the DOS prompt, and then skip to the section in this appendix called "Installing DOS Using SELECT."

If a partition does not exist, you will see this message:

```
Create Primary DOS Partition

Current Fixed Disk Drive: 1

Do you wish to use the maximum size
for a DOS partition and make the DOS
partition active (Y/N).............? [Y]

Press ESC to return to FDISK Options
```

Answer Yes, which is the default, by pressing Enter. (The only time you would not want to give DOS the largest possible partition is when two or more operating systems are going to occupy the same disk—a very rare situation.)

The largest partition that DOS can create and use is 32 megabytes. Since many fixed disks are larger than this, it is possible to create a second DOS partition, which is accessed as a separate drive. This process will be discussed shortly.

After pressing Enter, you will see this message:

```
System will now restart

Insert DOS diskette in drive A:
Press any key when ready . . .
```

Press a key.

If you will not be creating a second DOS partition, skip ahead to the section called "Installing DOS Using SELECT" at this time.

CREATING A SECOND DOS PARTITION

After the system has restarted, execute FDISK once again and select option 1 from the first options menu. You will again see this display:

```
Create DOS Partition

Current Fixed Disk Drive: 1

    1. Create Primary DOS partition
    2. Create Extended DOS partition

Enter choice: [1]
```

```
Press ESC to return to FDISK Options
```

This time select option 2. You will see prompts similar to those you encountered when you created the first partition. Answer them just as you did before. DOS will treat the second partition as drive D.

INSTALLING DOS USING SELECT

The easiest way to install DOS on the fixed disk is by using the SELECT command. (If your version of DOS does not include SELECT, skip to the next section.)

TABLE D-1.   The DOS Country Codes

Country	Code
Arabic countries	785
Australia	061
Belgium	032
Canada (English)	001
Canada (French)	002
Denmark	045
Finland	358
France	033
Germany	049
Israel (Hebrew)	972
Italy	039
Netherlands	031
Norway	047
Portugal	351
South American countries	003
Spain	034
Sweden	046
Switzerland	041
United Kingdom	044
United States	001

SELECT is used to load DOS on a disk. It also allows you to configure DOS for foreign-language operation. SELECT takes this general form:

SELECT *source target country keyboard*

where *source* is the drive that contains the DOS system and *target* is the drive that will receive DOS. *Country* is one of the country codes defined in Table D-1 and *keyboard* is one of the keyboard codes shown in Table D-2. Keep in mind that DOS will still only respond to English and will display all messages in English. However, languages that use non-English characters, will now have these available on the keyboard and on the screen.

To create the standard, U.S. version of DOS, enter this command (make sure that the DOS disk is in drive A):

```
SELECT A C: 001 US
```

You will see this warning:

```
SELECT is used to install DOS the first
time.  SELECT erases everything on the
specified target and then installs DOS.
Do you want to continue (Y/N)?
```

Answer Yes. You will now see another, stronger warning:

```
WARNING,  ALL DATA ON NON-REMOVABLE DISK
DRIVE C: WILL BE LOST!
Proceed with Format (Y/N)?
```

TABLE D-2.	The DOS Keyboard Codes
Country	**Keyboard code**
Australia	US
Belgium	BE
Canada (English)	US
Canada (French)	CF
Denmark	DK
Finland	SU
France	FR
Germany	GR
Italy	IT
Latin American countries	LA
Netherlands	NL
Norway	NO
Portugal	PO
Spain	SP
Sweden	SV
Switzerland (French)	SF
Switzerland (German)	SG
United Kingdom	UK
United States	US

Again, answer Yes. The formatting process will take several minutes. When the formatting is complete you will see this message:

```
Format complete
System transferred

Volume label (11 characters, ENTER for none)?
```

Enter a volume label of your choice. SELECT then copies DOS onto the hard disk.

At this point, remove the DOS disk from drive A and press Ctrl - Alt - Del simultaneously to restart the computer. If you have performed all these steps correctly, DOS will now load from drive C.

INSTALLING DOS USING FORMAT

If your version of DOS does not have the SELECT command, you must use the FORMAT command to install DOS on the hard disk.

Put your DOS work disk in drive A and enter this command:

```
FORMAT C: /V /S
```

The /S option causes the DOS system files to be transferred and /V tells FORMAT to request a volume label. The formatting will take several minutes. When it is done, you will see this message:

```
Format complete
System transferred

Volume label (11 characters, ENTER for none)?
```

Enter a volume label of your choice.

Remember that the /S option only transfers DOS's hidden system files, not its external commands. To copy these commands to the fixed disk, enter the following command:

```
COPY A:*.* C:
```

Now, remove the DOS disk from drive A and press Ctrl - Alt - Del simultaneously to restart the computer. If you have performed each step correctly, DOS will now load from drive C.

Answers

►E◄

1. The parts that all computers have in common are the system unit, the monitor, and the keyboard.

2. The two types of disk drives are floppy disk drives and fixed disk drives. A floppy disk uses a flexible magnetic medium, encased in plastic, to store information, and it can be removed from the disk drive.

The magnetic medium of a fixed disk is rigid and may not be removed from the drive. Also, a fixed disk can store much more information than a floppy disk.

3. No, smoking around your diskettes is not a good idea because the smoke may damage the magnetic medium.

4. A *byte* is the smallest unit of memory.

2 SKILLS CHECK

1. A diskette is used in a floppy disk drive. It is removable. A fixed disk uses a nonremovable rigid disk.

2. The major parts of your computer are the keyboard, the monitor, and the system unit. You may also have a printer, a modem, a mouse, or other devices.

2 MASTERY SKILLS CHECK

1. To start DOS from a fixed disk, simply turn on the computer. To start DOS from a floppy, insert the DOS diskette in drive A and then turn on the computer.

2. To give DOS a command, type the command at the DOS prompt and press [Enter].

3. To view the directory, use the DIR command.

4. To make a backup copy, use the DISKCOPY command.

5. You can restart DOS by pressing [Ctrl], [Alt], and [Del] at the same time.

SKILLS CHECK

$$3$$

1. DIR lists the contents of the directory.

2. You can use the [Backspace] key to correct a typing error prior to pressing [Enter].

3. You must use these formats to enter the date and time:

mm-dd-yy
hours:minutes:seconds

If you enter the information incorrectly, DOS repeats the prompt until you provide a correctly formatted response.

4. You might restart DOS for either of these reasons:

- You have accidentally issued a command and you aren't sure of its consequences, so you restart DOS to cancel the command.

- A bug causes a program to crash, and you must restart DOS to restart the computer.

3.1

EXERCISES

1. The valid names are a, b, and g. Name c is invalid because the filename portion is too long. Name d is invalid because the extension is too long. Name e is invalid because the + character cannot be used in a file name. Name f is invalid because the [and] characters cannot be part of a file name.

2. DOS reserves the .COM and .EXE extensions for program files.

3. The three basic types of files are text, program, and data files.

4. The DIR command lists a file's name, its length, and the date and time of its creation.

3.2

EXERCISES

2. The pause option is specified as /P, not \P.

3.3

EXERCISES

1. `DIR MORE.COM`

2. `DIR D*.COM`

3. DIR *.

4. The * matches any sequence of characters. The ? matches any single character.

EXERCISES

3.4

2. The internal commands are c and f. The others are external.

3. The DOS diskette must be available for you to use an external command because most external commands do not remain resident in memory; they must be loaded from disk each time they are exucuted.

EXERCISES

3.5

1. C:

2. C:CHKDSK

3. DIR C:

| 3 |

MASTERY SKILLS CHECK

1. The disk directory contains the names of the files on a disk and certain other information about each file. The directory tells DOS where a specific file is located on the disk.

2. The two parts of a file name are the filename and the extension. The filename can be up to eight characters long and the extension can be up to three characters in long. The following characters cannot be used in a file name:

. " / \ [ ] : ¦ < > + = ; ,

3. `DIR /P`

4. The wildcard characters are * and ?. They are used to reference groups of files. The * matches any sequence of characters in a file name, and the ? matches any single character.

5. `DIR *.COM`

6. An internal command is resident in memory and is instantly accessible. An external command resides on the DOS disk and must be loaded into memory each time it is used.

7. To change the current drive, simply specify the letter of the new disk drive followed by a colon. To execute a command that is on a different disk drive, precede the command with a drive specifier.

SKILLS CHECK

1. DIR /W

2. CLS

3. DIR *.DAT

4. A drive specifier is a drive letter followed by a colon. It specifies which drive is being referred to. This command would list the directory of drive C:

   DIR C:

5. False. With very few exceptions, external commands are loaded each time they are used. They do not remain memory resident.

6. The CHKDSK command reports the status of your disk.

EXERCISES

1. FORMAT B:

2. Formatting a diskette that already contains information causes that information to be lost.

3. To transfer the system during formatting, use the /S option with the FORMAT command.

5. A *track* is a narrow circle around one side of a disk. A *sector* is the smallest unit of disk space that DOS can access and is usually 512 bytes long. A *cylinder* is the pair of tracks that correspond to each other on opposite sides of a disk.

6. Formatting a diskette establishes its tracks and sectors and initializes the directory.

4.2   EXERCISES

1. `COPY FIND.EXE C:`

This command would copy FIND.EXE to drive B:

`COPY FIND.EXE B:`

2. Two files with the same name cannot exist in the same directory. If you tried to enter this command, DOS would issue the following error message:

`File cannot be copied onto itself`

3. `COPY FIND.EXE MYFIND.EXE`

EXERCISES

4.3

1. `COPY A: DISK*.COM B:`

2. DOS automatically uses the single diskette drive in the system as both A and B, alternating between the two and prompting you to insert the appropriate diskette as necessary.

3. `COPY A:*.* B:`

or

`COPY A:????????.??? B:`

EXERCISES

4.4

1. Abort causes DOS to cancel the command. Retry causes DOS to try the command again.

EXERCISES

4.5

1. `ERASE B:MIKE.WP`

2. `ERASE *.PIF`

3. `RENAME CHKDSK.COM DISKCHK.COM`

4. RENAME *.COM *.SAV

5. The DOS synonym for ERASE is DEL. The synonym for RENAME is REN.

4.6   EXERCISES

1. To generate a control-key combination, press and hold the Ctrl key while you press the second key in the combination.

2. You can pause output to the screen by pressing either the Pause key or the Ctrl -S key combination.

4   MASTERY SKILLS CHECK

1. FORMAT B:

2. Formatting a disk sets up the tracks and sectors that DOS uses and initializes the directory.

3. *Tracks* are concentric narrow bands around the disk that are comprised of several sectors. A *sector* is the smallest unit of disk space DOS can access.

4. COPY A:BACKUP.COM B:

5. `COPY A:R*.COM C:`

6. To erase a file, you use the ERASE command. Its general form is

   ERASE *file-name*

7. `RENAME HARRY.DAT JERRY.INF`

8. Abort cancels the command. Retry causes DOS to try the command again.

9. You pause the display by pressing either the Pause key or Ctrl-S.

10. To cancel a command, press either Ctrl-Break or Ctrl-C. A command cannot be canceled once it has passed its "point of no return"—the point at which it actually begins its operation.

INTEGRATING SKILLS CHECK

4

1. A file name cannot contain the square bracket characters.

2. To pause a directory listing, you can specify the /P DIR option, which causes output to pause every 23 lines. You can also use the Pause key or the Ctrl-S keystroke commands to pause a listing.

3. No. The COPY command does not apply any defaults.

5 | SKILLS CHECK

NOTE: Some of the questions in Chapter 5 have two or more correct solutions. If your answer differs from the one shown here but accomplishes the same result, consider it correct.

1. COPY A:PRINT.COM B:

2. FORMAT B: /S

3. RENAME

4. ERASE *.DAT

5. To cancel a command you press either `Ctrl`-`C` or `Ctrl`-`Break`. You cannot cancel a command once it has begun to alter the contents of the disk.

6. To print the contents of the screen, press `Shift`-`PrtSc`.

EXERCISES

1. `PRINT LET1 LET2 LET3`

2. `PRINT LET2/C`

3. The /T PRINT option cancels printing of all files remaining in the print queue.

4. PRINT is unique for two main reasons: First, it partially installs itself in memory, unlike other external commands. Second, it runs in the background, so you can do other things with the computer while it is running.

EXERCISES

1. `COMP A:CHKDSK.COM B:CHKDSK.COM`

2. `DISKCOMP A: B:`

EXERCISES

1. `F2` Y `F2` Y `F1` `Ins` 2 `F3` `Backspace`

2. `F2` Y `F1` * B: Then, press `Del` repeatedly to reach the end of the line.

3. Simply press [F3] to repeat the last command.

4. Pressing [F4] deletes all characters from the current position up to, but not including, the specified character.

5. Pressing [Esc] cancels the current line and restarts the editing process.

| 5.6 | **EXERCISES** |

1. LABEL ACCOUNTING

2. No. You cannot use [or] in a volume label.

3. VOL displays the current volume label. LABEL lets you change the volume label.

4. The /V option causes FORMAT to request a volume label as part of the formatting process.

| 5 | **MASTERY SKILLS CHECK** |

1. TYPE displays the contents of a text file.

   TYPE MYTEXT

2. PRINT MYTEXT

3. The /T option cancels the printing of all files currently in the print queue.

4. Pressing F3 displays the previous command.

5. F2 B C F3

6. The DATE and TIME commands display the system date and time.

7. A volume label is the name that you assign to a disk. You label a disk using either LABEL or FORMAT /V.

8. `LABEL WORDPROC`

9. `COMP FILE1 FILE2`

10. `DISKCOMP A: B:`

INTEGRATING SKILLS CHECK

1. Assuming you executed this command using your DOS work disk, a file called MORE.COM would already be on the disk and you cannot have two files with the same name in the same directory. To remedy this problem, you would have to rename the file using some other name. If you executed this command from another disk, the file MYTEXT

would not be in the directory, and you would have to copy the file to the disk before you could rename it.

2. COPY ABC∗.X∗ B:

3. No. You cannot use COPY to copy a volume label.

4. Yes. DISKCOPY makes an exact copy of the disk, including the volume label.

5. If you press PrtSc while you are printing a file, DOS ignores the print screen request.

SKILLS CHECK

1. TYPE

2. PRINT FORMLET.WP

3. COMP compares two disk files of the same length for equality. DISKCOMP compares two diskettes that have the same storage capacity for equality.

4. Pressing F1 at the DOS prompt displays the next character from the previous command, assuming the command has another character.

5. VOL displays a disk's volume label.

6. `LABEL MYDISK`

EXERCISES

6.1

2. A parent directory encloses its subdirectory.

3. The root directory has no parent directory. Also, it is the only directory that is guaranteed to be on any formatted disk.

4. To create a subdirectory use the MD, or MKDIR, command. To change the current directory, use CD, or CHDIR.

5. `CD`

EXERCISES

6.2

2. A path name describes the route DOS must take to find a directory.

3. `COPY \ACCTING\AR\MYFILE \SPSHT`

4. `TYPE \ACCTING\AR\MYFILE`

5. `CD ..`

6. CD \

6.3 | EXERCISES

2. TREE C:

6.4 | EXERCISES

1. COPY \WP\LARRY\MYFILE \ACCTING\GL

2. \SPSHT\CHKDSK

3. The number of files a subdirectory can hold is limited only by available disk space.

6.5 | EXERCISES

1. A subdirectory cannot be removed if it contains files or directories other than the . and .. directories or if it is the current directory.

2. RD \ACCTING\AR

3. `RD \ACCTING\AR`
   `RD \ACCTING\AP`
   `RD \ACCTING\GL`
   `RD \ACCTING`

MASTERY SKILLS CHECK

6

1. A subdirectory is a directory within a directory.

2. Tree-structured directories allow any directory to contain one or more subdirectories in parent-child relationships. Further, the child directories are more specialized than their parent. When the structure of such a directory is diagrammed, it resembles the root system of a tree.

3. `MD MYDIR`

4. CD

5. `\WP\COMP`

6. `COPY \WP\LARRY\MYFILE \ACCTING\GL`

7. `RD \SPSHT`

8. `TREE`
   `CHKDSK /V`

INTEGRATING SKILLS CHECK

1. TYPE \WP\LARRY\MYFILE

2. COMP \WP\JANET\MYFILE \ACCTING\AR\MYFILE

3. DOS links the file name with the path name, so two files that have the same name but reside in different directories are logically separate.

4. ERASE \WP\LARRY\MYFILE

SKILLS CHECK

1. A path name is essentially a route to a subdirectory.

2. CD \ACCTING\GL

3. To create a subdirectory, you use the MD (or MKDIR) command.

4. To remove a subdirectory, you use the RD (or RMDIR) command. You cannot remove the root directory. Also, you cannot remove a directory if it contains any files or subdirectories.

5. CD \WP\JANET

6. A path name can be up to 63 characters long.

EXERCISES

7.1

1. A batch file must have the .BAT extension.

2.
```
CHKDSK
TREE
COPY R*.* B:
```

3.
```
COPY ACCOUNTS.DAT A:
COPY PAYROLL.INF A:
COPY FORMLET.TXT A:
```

EXERCISES

7.2

1. The batch file parameters are called %0 through %9.

2. %0 contains the name of the batch file.

3.
```
TYPE %1
PRINT %1
```

4.
```
DIR %1:
DISKCOPY %1: %2:
DISKCOPY %1: %2:
DIR %2:
```

7.3 | EXERCISES

1. The command ECHO OFF prevents batch file commands from being displayed.

2. The PAUSE command displays this message:

   ```
   Strike a key when ready . . .
   ```

   Then, it waits for the user to press a key.

3. `ECHO Backing up files`

4. To embed a comment in a batch file, use the REM command.

5.
   ```
   :AGAIN
   ECHO To stop, press Ctrl-C or Ctrl-Break
   CHKDSK
   GOTO AGAIN
   ```

6. The @ prevents the command it precedes from being displayed.

7.4 | EXERCISES

1. `IF EXIST A:SORT.EXE COPY A:SORT.EXE B:`

2. This general form of the IF command compares two strings:

IF *string1* = = *string2 command*

3. `IF ERRORLEVEL 3 ECHO Error occurred.`

EXERCISES

1. `FOR %%F IN (SORT.EXE PRINT.COM) DO IF EXIST %%F ECHO On disk`

2. The SHIFT command moves the contents of the replaceable parameters left one position. If there are more than ten command line arguments, a new argument is placed in %9. Thus, SHIFT allows access to more than ten command line arguments.

3. During the execution of a batch file, the CALL command executes another batch file and then resumes execution of the original file.

EXERCISES

1.
```
TIME
DATE
ECHO Prepare to back up files
PAUSE
COPY A:*.* B:
```

MASTERY SKILLS CHECK

1. A batch file is a list of one or more DOS commands that has the extension .BAT. When you enter the name of a batch file at the DOS prompt, DOS automatically executes the commands that are listed in the file.

2.
```
CLS
CHKDSK
DIR
PAUSE
```

3. It would prevent batch file commands from being displayed as they were executed.

4. The REM command lets you embed comments in a batch file.

5. The replaceable parameters are %0 through %9.

```
ECHO %1 %2
```

6.
```
FOR %%F IN (%1 %2 %3 %4) IF EXIST B:%%F ECHO %%F exists
```

7. The GOTO command causes execution of a batch file to jump to a specified label.
   The ECHO command in the following file would never be executed.

```
GOTO JUMP
ECHO This will never be printed
:JUMP
```

8. If it exists in the root directory of the DOS disk, AUTOEXEC.BAT is automatically executed when DOS starts.

9. The CALL command executes one batch file from within another batch file.

10. The SHIFT command moves the contents of the replaceable parameters left one position.

INTEGRATING SKILLS CHECK

7

1.
```
TIME
DATE
ECHO Insert directories disk
PAUSE
```

2.
```
IF NOT EXIST *.%2 RENAME *.%1 *.%2
```

3.
```
IF NOT EXIST %1:*.* GOTO OK
ECHO Files exist on target disk.
ECHO To cancel press Ctrl-C or Ctrl-Break
:OK
FORMAT %1:
```

4.
```
ECHO OFF
:AGAIN
IF %1 == END GOTO DONE
ECHO %1
COPY A:%1 B:
SHIFT
GOTO AGAIN
:DONE
```

8   SKILLS CHECK

1. FORMAT B: /S

2. The AUTOEXEC.BAT file is a batch file that is automatically executed when DOS starts. It must be located in the root directory of the DOS disk or in the root directory of the fixed disk, if one exists.

3. The command searches for a file called MYFIL-E.DAT. If MYFILE.DAT does not exist, the batch file displays the message "File not found."

4.
```
ECHO OFF
IF %1 == Jon ECHO Jon's instructions
IF %1 == Rachel ECHO Rachel's instructions
IF %1 == Sherry ECHO Sherry's instructions
```

5. MD MYDIR

6. A disk volume label is the name of a disk.

8.1   EXERCISES

1. The > operator creates a new file and redirects output to that file. Any preexisting file by the same name is destroyed. The >> operator appends output to the specified file if it exists, and the contents of any preexisting file are preserved.

2. `CHKDSK > CHKDSK.OUT`

3. `FILE1.DAT`
`FILE2.DAT`
`N`

EXERCISES

8.2

1. `CHKDSK /V > PRN`

2. It simply echoes what you type at the keyboard on the screen. To stop this command, press ⌨Ctrl⌨-⌨Z⌨.

3. DOS refers to the first serial port as COM1 or AUX.

EXERCISES

8.3

1. The MORE command displays a text file one screen at a time.

2. Yes, the command is valid. It would match any line that had a space in it.

3. `FIND /N "and the" MYTEXT`

8.4 EXERCISES

1. `SORT < INVTRY.DAT`

2. To sort a file in reverse order, you use the /R option.

3. `SORT OUTDIR /+24`

8.5 EXERCISES

1. A pipe routes the output of one command into the input of another.

2. `TREE ¦ MORE`

3. `CHKDSK /V ¦ SORT`

8 MASTERY SKILLS CHECK

1. Standard input and output are psuedo devices that route data to actual, physical devices. The keyboard and the screen are the default devices linked to standard input and output.

2. `TREE > TREE.OUT`

3. The > operator creates a new file and redirects output to that file. Any preexisting file by the same name is destroyed. The >> operator appends output to the specified file, and the contents of any preexisting file are preserved.

4. DOS's three filter commands are MORE, FIND, and SORT.

5. `SORT < PHONE.DAT > PHONE.SRT`

6. `FIND "On your behalf" FORMLET`

7. The MORE command displays a text file one screen at a time.

8. A pipe routes the output of one command into the input of another. This command would display only the amount of free disk space:

`CHKDSK ¦ FIND "available"`

INTEGRATING SKILLS CHECK

8

1. `TIME`
`DATE`
`CHKDSK >> CHKDSK.LOG`

2. `FOR %%X IN (%1 %2 %3) DO FIND "%%X" MYTEXT`

3. Technically, the command is not wrong in the strictest sense. However, it is not meaningful because FIND is designed to operate only on text files, not on program files.

4. `TREE > PRN`

5. The printer, denoted by PRN, cannot be used as an input device.

9 SKILLS CHECK

1. The RD command deletes a subdirectory.

2. `DIR > PRN`

3. `SORT /R <OVERDUE.TXT >OVERDUE.SRT`

4. In the first line, the label AGAIN must be preceded by a colon.

5. The IF batch file command can check the existence of a file, the equality of two strings, or value of the error variable.

6. There is no difference. ERASE and DEL are just two different names for the same command.

7. The COPY command would copy only the files in the current directory, while the DISKCOPY command would copy the entire disk. Even if no subdirectories existed, DISKCOPY would make an exact copy of the original disk while COPY would copy the same information but would not place it in exactly the same location on the target disk that it occupies on the original disk.

EXERCISES

9.2

1. `COPY MYDATA.DAT BACKUP.DAT /V`

2. `COPY MARY*.WP MARY.OUT`

3. `COPY FILE1.WP+FILE3.WP+FILE2.WP FILE.OUT`

EXERCISES

9.3

1. `ATTRIB *.*`

2. Yes. A read-only file can be copied.

3. `ATTRIB -R *.COM /S`

9.4 | EXERCISES

1. XCOPY A:\ACCTING B: /S /E

2. XCOPY A: B: /V

3. One reason you might copy files based on their creation date is to make it easier and less time-consuming to back up new files. This way, older files that have already been backed up are not copied again.

   The following command would copy files that begin with R and have the .EXE extension if they were created on or after January 20, 1990:

   XCOPY A:R*.EXE B: /D:01-20-90

4. XCOPY A: B: /S /M

5. The /P option causes XCOPY to prompt you before it copies each file.

9.5 | EXERCISES

1. REPLACE A:*.* C:

2. REPLACE A:*.* C: /A

3. The /P option causes REPLACE to prompt you before replacing a file.

4. The /R option replaces read-only files.

EXERCISES

9.6

2. RECOVER INFO.DAT

3. RECOVER \WP\LARRY\MYFILE

EXERCISES

9.7

1. The GRAPHICS command is needed to correctly print graphics screen images to the printer using DOS.

EXERCISES

9.8

1. You must copy COMMAND.COM to the disk.

2. If the target diskette already contains files and was not formatted using the /B option, you cannot install the DOS system files on it.

MASTERY SKILLS CHECK

9

1. VERIFY ON

2. `COPY TEXT1+TEXT2 MORETEXT`

3. The /V option causes COPY to verify the accuracy of the copy.

4. `ATTRIB -A SAMPLE.DAT`

5. `XCOPY A: B: /E`

6. `XCOPY A: B: /D:02/28/90`

7. `REPLACE A:*.* B: /A`

8. RECOVER recovers the information stored in the good sectors of a file that has had some of its sectors damaged.

9. GRAPHICS

10. This command installs the DOS system files on the disk in drive B.

INTEGRATING SKILLS CHECK

9

1. `ATTRIB *.* ¦ FIND " R "`

2. DISKCOPY

3. `IF NOT EXIST B:MYFILE COPY A:MYFILE B:`

4. To remove a subdirectory, you must first erase any files and subdirectories that it contains. Only a completely empty directory can be deleted.

SKILLS CHECK

10

1. `ATTRIB *.*`

2. `DIR ¦ SORT`

3. The /E option to XCOPY causes directories that are empty on the source disk to be created on the target disk.

4. SYS

5. The > and >> operators cause standard output to be written to a disk file or to a device other than the screen. The > operator overwrites any preexisting files, while the >> operator appends new output to the end of a preexisting file.

6. REPLACE A:*.* B: /A

7. RECOVER

8. CLS

9. VERIFY ON causes DOS to double-check the outcome of a write operation. VERIFY OFF stops the double-checking process.

10.1 | EXERCISES

1. PROMPT BL

2. PROMPT Drive $N:

3. PROMPT

EXERCISES

10.2

1. `MODE CO80`

2. `MODE COM1:19200, N, 8, 1`

3. `MODE LPT1:132,6`

EXERCISES

10.3

1. `PATH A:\SPSHT`

2. No. You can only execute CHKDSK from drive A. To make the PATH command work correctly, regardless of the current drive, you could add a drive specifier to the path, as shown here:

`PATH A:\ACCTING\GL`

3. `PATH ;`

EXERCISES

10.4

1. `APPEND A:\ACCTING\GL`

2. APPEND A:\ACCTING\GL;A:\ACCTING\AR;A:\ACCTING\AP

3. APPEND ;

| 10.5 | EXERCISES |

1. SET MYDIR=C:\MYFILES\WORK

| 10.6 | EXERCISES |

1. The CONFIG.SYS file contains configuration commands that DOS must process when it first begins running.

2. BUFFERS = 15

3. BREAK ON causes DOS to check more frequently for a [Ctrl]-[Break] keypress.

4. Yes. BREAK is both a configuration command and a command line command.

5. False. Both files are processed.

6. LASTDRIVE = C

EXERCISES

10.7

1. A device driver is an installable program that controls a device.

2. A virtual disk is a simulation of a disk drive that uses memory to store information.

3. `DEVICE = VDISK.SYS 128 128 32`

4. `DEVICE = ANSI.SYS`

MASTERY SKILLS CHECK

10

1. `PROMPT [$P]`

2. `$T`

3. `MODE CO40`

4. `MODE COM1:1200, N, 8, 2`

5. `MODE LPT1:132,8`

6. The PATH command lets you enter one or more paths that DOS will search for an executable file if that file is not found in the current directory.

7. `PATH \MIKE\WORK\SPSHT`

8. APPEND is the same as PATH except it works with both nonexecutable files and executable files. (To work with executable files, specify the /E option.)

9. The FILES command determines how many files DOS can have open at once. It should be placed in the CONFIG.SYS file.

10. To create the specified virtual disk, you would add this command to the CONFIG.SYS file:

`DEVICE = VDISK.SYS 384 256 48`

10 INTEGRATING SKILLS CHECK

```
1. ECHO OFF
   IF %2 == NORM GOTO NORMAL
   IF %2 == CONDENSED GOTO CONDENSED
   GOTO ERROR
   :NORMAL
   MODE LPT1:80,6
   PRINT %1
   GOTO DONE
   :CONDENSED
   MODE LPT1:132,8
   PRINT %1
   GOTO DONE
   :ERROR
```

```
ECHO You must use either NORM or CONDENSED
:DONE
```

2. `PATH \APS;\DOS`
   `APPEND \WP`

SKILLS CHECK

1. `DEVICE = VDISK.SYS 128 128 32`

You would have to put this command in the CONFIG.SYS file.

2. `DIR ¦ SORT > PRN`

3. The PATH command tells DOS what path to follow to find an executable file when that file is not found in the current directory.

4. `RECOVER MYDATA.DAT`

5. `ATTRIB +R TREE.COM`

6. `COPY FILE1+FILE2 OUTFILE`

7. You can create as many subdirectories as you like on a disk, as long as free disk space is available.

8. PROMPT LT$G--$G

EXERCISES

11.1

1. BACKUP C:\WP\BOB*.* A:

2. BACKUP C:*.* A: /D:01-10-91/S

3. /M

4. /L

5. In general, you must use BACKUP to back up your fixed disk because a fixed disk contains too much information to be copied to a single floppy. BACKUP automatically uses multiple floppy disks to store information, and is more reliable than a manual backup procedure.

6. You must number each diskette, starting with 1.

EXERCISES

11.2

1. You cannot restore a file using COPY because the BACKUP command stores information using a compressed format, which only RESTORE can read.

2. `RESTORE A: C:\INVTRY\BACKORD\INFO.DAT`

3. The /M option causes RESTORE to restore only files that have been modified since the last backup.

4. `RESTORE A: C:\*.* /S /A:10-20-90 /L:14:00`

5. `RESTORE A: C:\*.* /S /B:10-20-90 /E:14:00`

EXERCISES

11.4

2. `FASTOPEN D:=45`

MASTERY SKILLS CHECK

11

1. You should periodically retire backup diskettes to prevent an error from corrupting every copy of an important file.

2. `DISKCOPY`

3. `BACKUP`

4. `BACKUP C:\*.* A: /S`

5. RESTORE

6. BACKUP C:*.* A: /M/S

7. RESTORE A: C:*.* /S /A:07-20-90

8. FASTOPEN allows DOS faster access to files in deeply nested subdirectories.

11 | INTEGRATING SKILLS CHECK

1. FIND "INFO.DAT" MYLOG

2. To have DOS verify the success of each disk write operation, you must issue this command before beginning backup or restore operations:

VERIFY ON

▶Index◀

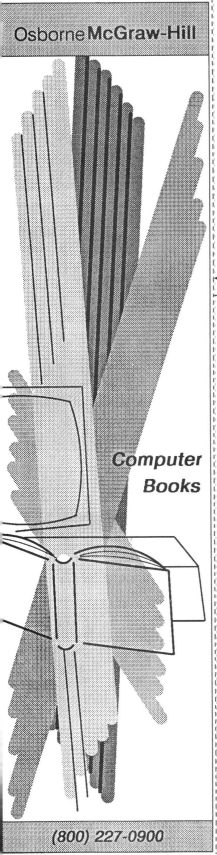

Osborne McGraw-Hill

Computer Books

(800) 227-0900

Bookmarker Design — Lance Ravella

Tear off for Bookmark

▼
You're important to us...

We'd like to know what you're interested in, what kinds of books you're looking for, and what you thought about this book in particular.

Please fill out the attached card and mail it in. We'll do our best to keep you informed about Osborne's newest books and special offers.

▶ *YES, Send Me a FREE Color Catalog of all Osborne computer books*
To Receive Catalog, Fill in Last 4 Digits of ISBN Number from Back of Book (see below bar code) 0-07-881 _ _ _ – _

Name: _____ Title: _____

Company: _____

Address: _____

City: _____ State: _____ Zip: _____

I'M PARTICULARLY INTERESTED IN THE FOLLOWING *(Check all that apply)*

I use this software
- ☐ WordPerfect
- ☐ Microsoft Word
- ☐ WordStar
- ☐ Lotus 1-2-3
- ☐ Quattro
- ☐ Others _____

I use this operating system
- ☐ DOS
- ☐ Windows
- ☐ UNIX
- ☐ Macintosh
- ☐ Others _____

I rate this book:
- ☐ Excellent ☐ Good ☐ Poor

I program in
- ☐ C or C++
- ☐ Pascal
- ☐ BASIC
- ☐ Others _____

I chose this book because
- ☐ Recognized author's name
- ☐ Osborne/McGraw-Hill's reputation
- ☐ Read book review
- ☐ Read Osborne catalog
- ☐ Saw advertisement in store
- ☐ Found/recommended in library
- ☐ Required textbook
- ☐ Price
- ☐ Other _____

Comments _____

Topics I would like to see covered in future books by Osborne/McGraw-Hill include:

_____

IMPORTANT REMINDER
To get your FREE catalog, write in the last 4 digits of the ISBN number printed on the back cover (see below bar code) 0-07-881 _ _ _ – _

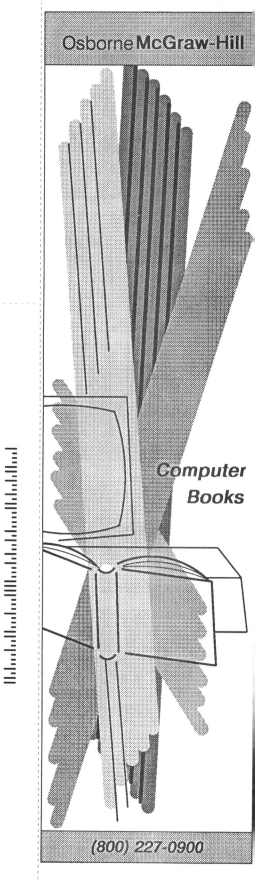
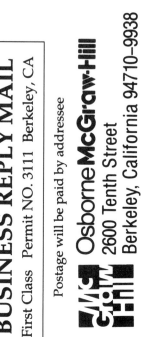